California

FEUDS

Vengeance, Vendettas
& Violence on
the Old West Coast

by
William B. Secrest

Sanger, California

Printed in the United States of America
Published by Quill Driver Books/Word Dancer Press, Inc.
1831 Industrial Way #101
Sanger, California 93657
559-876-2170 • 1-800-497-4909 • FAX 559-876-2180
QuillDriverBooks.com

Quill Driver Books' titles may be purchased in quantity at special
discounts for educational, fund-raising, business, or promotional use.
Please contact Special Markets, Quill Driver Books/Word Dancer Press,
Inc. at the above address or at 1-800-497-4909.

Quill Driver Books/Word Dancer Press, Inc. project cadre:
Doris Hall, Susan Klassen, John David Marion, Stephen Blake Mettee,

First Printing

To order another copy of this book, please call
1-800-497-4909

Library of Congress Cataloging-in-Publication Data

Secrest, William B., 1930-
  California feuds : vengeance, vendettas & violence on the Old West coast / by
William B. Secrest.
    p. cm.
  ISBN 1-884995-42-X
  1. Vendetta--California--History--19th century. I. Title.

HV6452.C29S425 2004
303.6'2--dc22

                          2004014145

Dedicated to

JOHN BOESSENECKER

*Eminent historian—always helpful
and generous friend.*

Table *of* Contents

Introduction

"A tumultuous assault: a violent engagement or action." This is Webster's Dictionary definition of the archaic word "affray." Add the adjective "deadly" to "affray" and the term takes on an even more serious, homicidal meaning. And, "deadly affrays" was often the term used to define the deadly gunfights, knife fights and street brawls in feuding nineteenth century California.

Personal and family feuds are an integral part of history. Down through the ages, like the warring nations they mirror, people of a certain temperament could not control either their emotions, or the circumstances that can lead to disaster. Often, public opinion and pride have driven otherwise rational people into situations that could only end in bloody encounters and death. Given the progressive history of mankind, however, this state of mind was not only a natural occurrence, but was probably socially inevitable.

From the beginning of time, man has been a territorial creature. Continuing through the nineteenth century, this has been an important and necessary aspect of the human condition. We can be reasonably certain that, at some point, groups of cavemen banded together to protect their caves and other turf from mutual enemies, be it man, beast, or nature. Down through the years, where there was little or no law, it was necessary that each man look out for himself and his group.

As civilization progressed and city-states began to emerge, there was continual trouble as larger states sought to impose either religious or political control over smaller neighbors. Whatever law existed, extended only so far as those who believed in it. By medieval times, a spin-off of clashes between armies involved personal combats where two individuals resolved differences with the lance or sword. God was thought to have guided the arm of the winner in such contests. Those who could fight, did so. Others had little recourse but to move on.

The more famous feuds of Italy and Corsica were probably diminutive when compared to the Serb-Croat blood vendettas originating in Yugoslavia and Albania in the fifteenth century. Among the primitive predecessors of such documents as the American Bill of Rights was the Kanun of Lek Dukagjin, a code handed down from generation to generation. It decreed that there were four major offenses to personal honor: calling a man a liar before other men; insulting his wife; disarming him; and violating his hospitality.

In this particular region of Europe, it is related that during the mid-nineteenth century a vendetta originated in a dispute over four rifle cartridges. The result was 1,281 houses burned down and the death of 132 men. These ancient blood feuds have resulted in the cultural animosities that ravage the Kosovo area, even today.

The New World was peopled by those who were fleeing the wars, vendettas and political and religious turmoil of their ancient homelands. The old ways, however, died hard. While the formal duel had been popular for centuries, in America other forms of combat evolved. The duel, evolving with the aristocracy of Europe, was not comprehendible to the lower classes and the family blood feuds of Europe found a resurgence on the frontiers of the former English colonies in America.

But even before the first settlers arrived on American shores, there were blood feuds among the Mohawk, Seneca, Oneida, Cayuga and Onandaga Indians of the Northeast prior to the formation of the Iroquois Confederation. Nor was this an isolated situation. Treaty conflicts and removal to Indian Territory wreaked havoc among the Cherokee during the 1840s. Among the Ross and Ridge factions, men were stabbed and beaten to death as their horrified families watched. Ambushes were common and all the brutalities of the white man's feuding was practised and refined.

Traditionally, it was in isolated, American mountain communities, with limited, or ineffective, law and courts, that the early family feuds developed. The famous Hatfield-McCoy feud in West Virginia and Kentucky comes to mind, a quarrel originating from Civil War loyalties and a dispute over ownership of a hog. But there were many other such conflicts. In 1891, the Sims-McMillan feud turned Choctaw County, Alabama, into a slaughterhouse of bullet-riddled bodies, lynchings, and burned houses. Kentucky seems to have been a hotbed of feuds, with the Martin-Tolliver and Underwood-Holbrook feuds erupting in the late 1870s. The French-Eversole war in Kentucky was said to have resulted in some seventy-four deaths between 1887 and 1894.

The cause of all this savagery and mayhem was usually political, territorial, or commercial in origin, although conflicts could often be traced to personal disputes. In researching early feuds, however, it is frequently difficult to discover exactly how and when the trouble began. Even years afterwards, participants seldom wanted to talk of the feud for fear of stirring up old troubles. Too, feud origins of a mercantile or political nature were often so convoluted and disputed that even the participants did not know the whole story, or knew only their own version of the troubles.

As might be suspected, in the American West, the feud mentality was as prevalent as in the rest of the country. The origins, however, might be different. Here, cattlemen, sheepherders, and farmers were often the antagonists as in the notorious Graham-Tewsbury feud, of the mid-1880s, which made the Tonto Basin area of Arizona a virtual coroner's paradise. The Earp-Clanton feud in and around Tombstone was both political and personal in nature and followed all the terrible rules of ambush and murder, involving two factions that would not back down. It was the same with the relentless and bloody power struggle we now know as the Lincoln County War in Billy the Kid's frontier New Mexico.

Early California was not exempt, and deadly feuds began in the earliest days of the great Gold Rush. Southerners, hot-blooded and possessing a dueling history and temperament, were in the vanguard of the Gold Rush, but they had no corner on the duelling business. In the South, as well as other frontier portions of the country, family and property were primary concerns in these early days of the nation. And there was personal honor. Many men would protect and defend these precious entities to the death and would expect their families to do the same.

It did not matter whether a feud originated over gold, cattle, mercantile matters, land, a broken promise or politics. Nor did the thought of widows and orphans enter into the equation. To some, personal honor was all important. It was a matter of courage, and the opinion of outsiders was frequently more important than that of family. Whether one initiated the feud, sought revenge, or some kind of personal justice was immaterial. The family name must not be sullied.

It seldom mattered what tactics were used in these feuds. The harming of women and children was to be avoided, but they sometimes got in the way. There were no rules, and ambushes, lynchings, house burnings and treachery were resorted to by both sides.

As tragic and bloody as many feuds were, it is hard not to smile at the antics of some, such as the deYoung brothers in their sometimes less than ethical efforts at building their puny little tabloid into one of the country's great newspapers.

And, in old California, feuds were as savage and feud origins were often every bit as incomprehensible as in other parts of the country. So read on about yet another facet of early California history of which you were perhaps unaware; a time of uncompromising feudists, gunfights, murders and a legal system frequently too weak or too aligned with one side or the other to cope impartially with deadly situations and emotions.

And of a time when some men's pride meant more than the lives and well-being of their own wives and children.

Acknowledgements

I am indebted to many people and institutions for help in researching these tales of frontier California. My good friend John Boessenecker generously shared his files, his photographic collection, and his knowledge of our state's pioneer days. His own tales of early feuds in his *Badge and Buckshot* and *Gold Dust & Gunsmoke* are premier efforts at illustrating this particularly obscure facet of nineteenth century California history.

Others have helped in great and small ways: Lee Edwards, who provided information on the Kern County escapades of the Walker and Burton brothers. Lee is always there when you need him. Bob Powers was another wonderful historian who could always be depended upon to help. Sadly, Bob passed away recently, and his widow, Marge, graciously assisted with my last request. Vera Gibson, Kern County Clerk; Eugene Burmeister; Mrs. Minna Shuler of the Kern County Library; and Ardis Walker were also helpful. C. Russell Georgeson provided a copy of the Ernest Klette autobiography, for which I am very grateful.

I want to thank Virginia Peterson and Beverly Everest of the Trinity County Historical Society at Weaverville, as well as Erica Nordmeier and her associates at the Bancroft Library, Berkeley. Many thanks to Robert J. Lee, a longtime northern California historian whose wonderful collection of old photographs has enhanced many publications over the years. William L. Klette, of Carson City, Nevada, was very helpful in supplying photographs long sought by the author.

Elisabeth E. Jones, of Austin, Texas, shared her material on Jesse

Graham with the author and was very helpful. Many years ago, the late, Madera County historian, Nathan Sweet introduced me to the Graham story and other early history.

The late Judy Hazelton Hill not only agreed to several interviews, but provided much material on the Hazelton and Church families, as well as some valuable family photographs. My thanks also to Robert B. Johnston of Salinas, Lori Garcia of Santa Clara, and Phil Reader of Santa Cruz.

And, a special thanks to a special lady. Corrinne Buttram has done research for years among the Mono and Chukchansie Indians of Madera County. She has helped and inspired countless local Indians and others with their genealogy and property history research over the years and her input concerning the Bethel-Indian feud was invaluable and very much appreciated.

My wonderful wife and son have helped me in many ways, besides just always being there when needed.

I must not forget to mention my indebtedness to the various libraries without which California writers and historians could not function. Many interlibrary loans and rare books were utilized at the Fresno County Main Library's California History and Genealogy Room, efficiently operated by Ray Silvia and his staff. Other libraries utilized were The Henry Madden Library at the California State University, Fresno, The Bakersfield Public Library, The Monterey Public Library, The Bancroft Library at the University of California, Berkeley, and the California State Library and the California State Archives, both at Sacramento.

Some of the generous people mentioned above have passed on since I began my research many years ago. To them, and to all those who have helped over the years, thanks again. You are all a constant reminder of how impoverished we are without friends, and how wealthy we are with them.

William B. Secrest

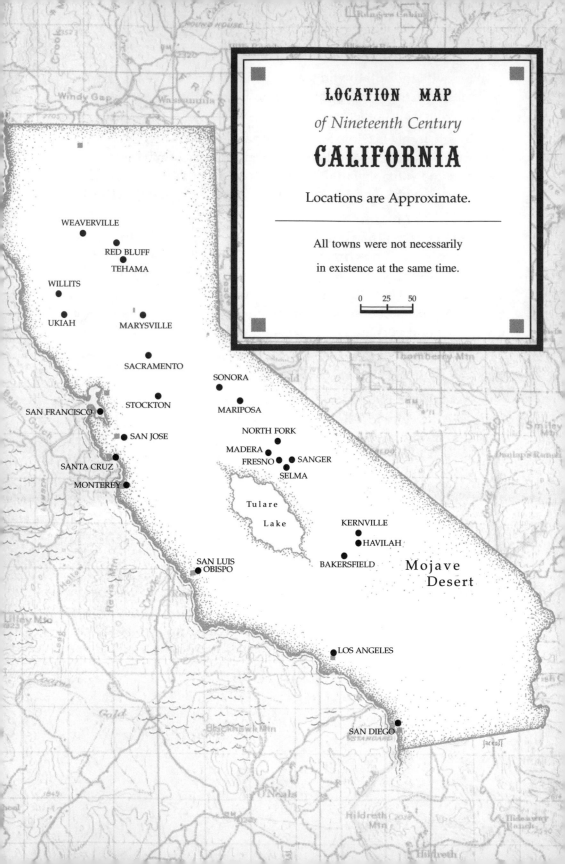

LOCATION MAP

of Nineteenth Century

CALIFORNIA

Locations are Approximate.

All towns were not necessarily
in existence at the same time.

0   25   50

WEAVERVILLE

RED BLUFF
TEHAMA

WILLITS

UKIAH   MARYSVILLE

SACRAMENTO

SONORA

STOCKTON   MARIPOSA

SAN FRANCISCO   NORTH FORK

MADERA
SAN JOSE   FRESNO   SANGER
SELMA
SANTA CRUZ
MONTEREY

Tulare

Lake

KERNVILLE

HAVILAH

SAN LUIS   BAKERSFIELD   Mojave
OBISPO   Desert

LOS ANGELES

SAN DIEGO

Chapter 1

Curse of the Sanchez Treasure

The Roach ~ Belcher Feud

It had been a long trip across the San Joaquin Valley under a sky overcast with black and rolling clouds. A bitter cold chilled the air this December day in 1852. The riders rode at a steady pace, nursing the strength of their horses. Intermittent and severe rains had made roads quagmires and rivers nearly impassable as the riders entered the first low hills of the Coast Range. Newspapers reported that stagecoaches had stopped running between San Francisco and San Jose.

Jose Maria Sanchez was forty-eight years old and the aches from these long rides didn't go away so easily any more. Sanchez and his vaqueros were returning from delivering a herd of beef cattle to the mining country. The packs on their mules were heavy with gold and they were all eager to get home. It was Christmas day when they arrived at John Gilroy's Rancho San Ysidro, just north of the Pajaro River and some twenty miles south of San Jose. It was pouring rain, but the end of the journey was in sight.

Sanchez was one of the wealthiest of the Monterey County ranchers. He owned the 16,000-acre Rancho Llano del Tequisquite, as well as various other properties totaling some 44,000 acres. The ranchero had several business enterprises, also, besides large herds of cattle, sheep, hogs and horses. He built his bride a two-story ranch house on high ground, above the Pajaro River from which he supervised his empire.

While so many of the Hispanic landowners in California watched as their lands were usurped by foreign-ers during the great Gold Rush, Sanchez

The early California vaqueros were among the best in the world. *California State Library.*

saw the times as a marvelous opportunity. Cattle, which had here-tofore been sold for their hides, tallow and horns at a few dollars a head, now could be sold to the foreigners at $70 or $80 each at Stock-ton, Sacramento, and other large cities. Horses, too, had previously been a glut on the market, selling for between $5 and $10. Now, the Sanchez vaqueros were routinely driving large herds of horses north to be sold at prices as high as $200 each. A skilled businessman, Sanchez was referred to locally as "El Judio," the Jew, as a compli-ment to his business acumen.

John Gilroy invited Sanchez and his men into his rough home to warm themselves at his fireplace. The Scotch ranch man was an uncle by marriage to Sanchez' wife, Encarnacion. The two ranch men exchanged news of the day, as the travelers tried to rub the chill from their weary bones. When Gilroy suggested they stay over-night, Sanchez shook his head. His men might stay, but Chona (his wife's nickname) and their five children were waiting for him. It was Christmas day and home was only fifteen miles away. When he shook hands with Gilroy and disappeared into the scattered oak trees leading to the Pajaro River, it was the last time Gilroy would see him.

The following day, when the Sanchez vaqueros rode up to the ranch house, Chona was surprised to see that her husband was not with them. After a careful search of the route between San Ysidro and the Sanchez home, it was concluded he had drowned trying to cross the river. The rancher's body and the gold he was carrying were never found.

Senora Sanchez was startled at the news. Only twenty-eight years old, she had been raised as a typical Spanish girl of the time, taught only the arts of housekeeping and the wiles of womanhood. She was illiterate and would not be able to manage her late husband's affairs in the new American state of California. Although beautiful, Chona was helpless and knew she must marry again as soon as possible if she hoped to protect herself and her children.

The face of the widow Encarnacion Sanchez reflects the pain and misery that would follow her through life. An old newspaper print from a daguerreotype. *John Boessenecker collection.*

Everyone in the nearby village of San Juan knew the situation. It was almost exactly a year ago that Chona had taken her five children and left her husband, filing for divorce in February 1852. She was afraid of Sanchez. Like so many of the California rancheros, he had become addicted to drinking and gambling over the years and often beat her. There had been no recourse for women under Mexican law, but now that California was a state of the Union, women could divorce cruel husbands. When he promised to mend his ways, Encarnacion returned to her husband, but the relationship was probably not the same. In any case, now, he was gone.

The late Sanchez had discussed with his wife how some of their friends had lost property to unscrupulous American settlers and their lawyers. Rustlers would soon be stealing her cattle herds, while squatters would be settling on her lands. Chona knew she must act quickly.

Possessing a $300,000 estate (about $9 million in today's money), the beautiful widow quickly surveyed the local prospects. She settled on Thomas B. Godden, a young Boston lawyer who had recently arrived in San Juan. Just over a month after Sanchez' death she and Godden were married, and her new husband promptly secured the

Contemporary engraving of the *Jenny Lind* tragedy. *California State Library.*

appointment of a guardian for the estate. Chona felt safe again, but it was a false security.

More adept at gambling than practicing law, Godden couldn't wait to get his hands on the Sanchez money. His choice of estate administrator had been one of his gambling pals, Samuel C. Head, and the two men promptly began pilfering the estate's assets. In early April of 1853, Godden made two promissory notes for nearly $3,500. He then took a herd of cattle to San Francisco, pocketing all the money himself, probably to pay gambling debts. Sam Head also helped himself. He sold over $60,000 worth of ranch stock, without any accounting, and paid out over $20,000 in fraudulent creditor's claims.

When Godden found a government note in a desk at the Sanchez Rancho, he planned a trip to San Francisco to see what he could get for it. The note concerned horses and equipment commandeered from Sanchez by Major John C. Fremont during the late Mexican War. Godden planned to catch the Bay steamboat *Jenny Lind* at Alviso, put in his claim at San Francisco, then test his luck at the gambling tables on the trip back.

It was some sixty miles, via San Jose, to the embarcadero at Alviso at the southern tip of San Francisco Bay. The ride was beautiful, and on the morning of April 11, 1853, Godden walked up the gangplank of the *Jenny Lind*, as it built up steam to get underway. A small, three-year-old sternwheeler, the boat soon cast off from the wharf carrying one hundred and twenty-five passengers. Godden strolled the deck and talked with acquaintances until the dinner bell rang, signalling the noon meal.

The fifteen- by twenty-foot dining room was filled up by 12:15, when suddenly a shudder ran through the boat. Instantaneously, an explosion blew out the wall separating the dining passengers from the boiler room. Bits of timber and metal fragments cut through the cabin like a scythe, mowing down everything in their path. Clouds of scalding steam burst through the room at the same time, and the screaming passengers made the carnage seem like a scene out of Dante's Inferno. Victims staggered about, as unharmed passengers rushed into the demolished room to aid survivors.

A fireman on the craft had been standing in front of the boiler door which had flown open and ripped a chunk out of his skull, exposing the brain. When a passenger tried to help him, he was waved away. "No," he groaned, "I'm a dead man, go help the others."

Amid the scattered corpses, the wounded were helped and carried to the outer deck where they were laid out. A man swam ashore to alert the authorities and a dispatch was sent to San Francisco, giving the terrible news. Immediately upon hearing of the tragedy, Captain Johnson, of the river steamer *Kate Kearny*, gathered medical supplies and a group of physicians and by nine o'clock that evening was on his way south. An hour later, the *Kate Kearny* met the steamer *Union*, which had picked up the survivors and was taking them to San Francisco. The doctors and supplies were transferred to the *Union*, which then proceeded on to the city. A reporter from the San Francisco *Herald* described the heartbreaking scene:

> It was not without many a shudder that we made our way through those groups of dead and dying that lay stiff and cold or in silent agony along the entire length of the deck, so that at each step the gaze would meet either the glazed eye of death or the disfigured countenance of some tortured wretch, whose glance would be upturned to ours with a painful and piteous expression... The peculiar odor of scalded flesh told such a tale of suffering as made one faint and sick at heart.

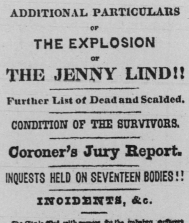

San Francisco *Herald*, April 13, 1853. *Author's collection.*

5

The reporter gathered the names of twenty-nine dead or injured, several having died during the trip up the bay. Thomas Godden, listed as being badly scalded, and several others were taken to Jones' Hotel in San Francisco, where they were cared for. Some twenty men, women, and children were dead or dying, those killed instantly being the most fortunate. Godden died the next day and the body was shipped to San Juan for burial.

Exactly when Chona received the news is not known, but it must have been a terrible blow. Not only did she lose her second husband within a few months of Sanchez' disappearance, but Godden had died such a painful and disfiguring death. Indications are she stayed in her room for some time, grieving, but also trying to determine her next move. She needed another protector for herself and her children. Nothing had changed.

As it became increasingly obvious that Sam Head was pilfering the estate, he prepared to sell some forty barrels of beans from the Sanchez warehouse. In emptying the barrels, Head discovered some $30,000 in gold dust hidden by Sanchez in one of the barrels. He made off with this also, just prior to his being dismissed as administrator by the district court on June 27, 1853. He was ordered to repay all the money, but it had vanished and all his bondsmen turned out to be worthless gamblers, like Head himself.

Monterey, in the 1850s, was livened up considerably by the Roach-Belcher feud.
John Boessenecker collection.

The sheriff of Monterey County at this time was one William Roach, a native of Ireland. Roach emigrated to America in 1830 and engaged in

David Jacks, a prominent Monterey businessman, was one of Roach's bondsmen. *Author's collection.*

steamboating on the Mississippi River. He was in the East in 1847 when Stevenson's New York Regiment of Volunteers was being formed and he jumped at the chance to sign up and sail to the far west during the Mexican War. When Sergeant Roach was mustered out in California, the great Gold Rush was underway and he promptly rushed to the mines. The big Irishman returned to Monterey with enough gold to engage in ranching and become the local political boss.

When California gained statehood in September 1850, Monterey was one of its original counties. There were only 1,872 residents in the county at the time and the seacoast village of Monterey became the county seat. Despite the recent war, local Californians and the Americans got along surprisingly well and at the first state election William Roach was elected sheriff.

Popular, and with many friends, Roach was also greedy and anxious to make his fortune in California. There is little doubt that while sheriff he was taking bribes and packing juries, although the charges were refuted by those who knew him. He was looking around for some really big money when fate dropped a prize plum in his lap.

Shortly after the death of her second husband, the widow Sanchez y Godden had succumbed to the romantic blandishments of a young physician who had taken up residence in San Juan. Dr. Henry L. Sanford managed to ingratiate himself with the family in some way, tradition suggesting it was by tending some of the Sanchez children during an illness. The physician and the comely widow were married just two months after Godden's death.

Dr. Sanford immediately involved himself in the business of the estate, as his new wife wished him to do. As a physician, he had met many of the important people of Monterey, one of whom was Lewis T. Belcher. Born about 1825 in Orange County, New York, Belcher had traveled west and arrived in California in 1847. He finagled a contract out of the local army post to furnish beef to the troops and in this way became friendly with William Roach and others of the New York Volunteer contingent.

Although having had no formal schooling, Belcher was a hustler, land speculator, and rancher with an acute business sense. In time he parlayed his army contract into goods and land grants, becoming a wealthy man. His property included two ranchos in the Carmel Valley and portions of other grants near Monterey and in the Salinas Valley. Besides portions of yet other properties, Belcher owned town lots in San Francisco, Monterey, Sonora, and Stockton. Described in the press as "a stout, well-built, handsome man," Belcher was known as the "Big Eagle of Monterey" and was very popular both on the coast and in San Jose, where he lived with a wife and young daughter.

In consulting with Belcher, Dr. Sanford asked whom he might recommend as a new guardian of the Sanchez estate. Belcher suggested Sheriff Roach for the job, as he thought the influence of the officer would insure protection from any more theft. Sanford and his wife readily agreed.

When Judge Josiah Merritt appointed Roach to his new position, the sheriff immediately resigned his office and took possession of the gold making up the estate. Belcher and one David Jacks acted as his bondsmen. The treasure was taken to Roach's home where it was concealed, probably buried, somewhere on his property.

As the year 1854 progressed, Dr. Sanford and his wife assumed the children's inheritance was in safe hands and they went about their lives. When they received few reports from Roach and began to hear rumors of the ex-sheriff's various expenditures, Sanford became concerned. Confronting Roach and asking for an accounting, Dr. Sanford was given evasive answers and finally told to mind his own business. Becoming alarmed, the doctor decided an accounting of Roach's actions and expenditures must be made and he filed suit to have him removed as guardian of the estate. When Judge Merritt denied the suit, both Belcher and David Jacks resigned as sureties and three others were appointed. By now Sanford was certain the judge had been bribed by Roach and they sought other means of redress. Merritt thought it was time for a vacation in the East, but his lack of probity was attested to by a later article in the Stockton *San Joaquin Republican* of March 14, 1855:

> Josiah Merritt, who was charged by a late number of the *Los Angeles Star* with sundry crimes and misdemeanors, has arrived from the East. He was formerly Probate Judge of Monterey county.

Belcher determined to obtain the return of the Sanchez estate, or what was left of it. He hired David S. Terry, a Stockton lawyer, who immediately charged Roach with stealing $84,654 worth of gold dust. He also sued the three new sureties and asked the court to remove Roach as guardian of the estate. A change of venue to San Joaquin County was now made on the basis that Merritt had been taking bribes from Roach. Stockton Judge Charles M. Creanor had Roach arrested and placed in the Stockton jail in June 1854, for refusing to obey a court injunction to hand over the Sanchez estate moneys. The ex-sheriff finally relented, however. Accompanied by an officer, he was allowed to return to Monterey to obtain the gold in his charge. Once on his home turf again, Roach made his escape and went into hiding among friends.

David S. Terry was a brilliant, but volatile attorney, who played a part in the feud. *California State Library.*

In late February 1855, Belcher received news that Roach had left for Mexico to avoid any accounting of the estate in his charge. Furious at the thought of Roach escaping, Belcher sent Bill Byrnes on an urgent mission.

After being the recipient of many threats from Roach partisans, Belcher had hired Bill Byrnes and several others as bodyguards. Byrnes was just the man for the job. Born in Maine about 1824, he had served in the Mexican War, hunted Apaches in the Southwest, joined the Gold Rush in

California, and fought Indians during the El Dorado County Indian trouble. More recently, he had been one of Harry Love's California Rangers who had tracked down and killed the legendary Mexican bandit Joaquin Murrieta.

William Wallace Byrnes was one of the more colorful characters involved in the Roach-Belcher feud. *Author's collection.*

Belcher instructed Byrnes and his men to follow Roach south as fast as they could and capture him at any cost. He must be taken alive since only he knew where the treasure was hidden. By riding furiously and taking shortcuts, Byrnes and his posse caught up with Roach at the coastal village of San Buenaventura, between Santa Barbara and Los Angeles. The fugitive was spotted in the old mission building and Byrnes detailed several of his men to keep him under surveillance while he went after a warrant and Santa Barbara Sheriff Russell Heath.

But Roach had already been spotted by others. San Joaquin

The mission village of San Buenaventura as it appeared in 1873. Roach was captured in the mission itself, at far left. *Author's collection.*

County Sheriff Taylor had offered a $500 reward for the escaped prisoner and stationed two deputies in Santa Barbara to watch all travelers. Early on the morning of March 15, 1855, the ten-year-old son of Stockton deputy sheriff VanRiper had awakened early and gone out to play. When two men rode by, the boy instantly recognized Roach from descriptions he had heard given to his father. Sheriff Heath was notified and was already headed south when Byrnes intercepted him.

At the San Buenaventura mission, Roach was reading a newspaper when arrested by Sheriff Heath, Byrnes and his men. Though armed, he made no resistance, but was later caught trying to destroy an $8,000 note made out to himself. Although he protested vigorously, the fugitive was quickly on his way back to Stockton. The *San Joaquin Republican*, March 28, 1855, reported:

> William Roach. - Our indefatigable sheriff arrived in Stockton yesterday morning on the steamer, *Urilda*, having in charge the above named individual, who is now lodged in jail.

Back in the Stockton courtroom, Roach refused to testify on advice of his counsel, attorney Pacificus Ord. Judge Creanor found Roach guilty of embezzlement and ordered him held in jail until the money was refunded. Creanor also castigated Judge Merritt for his fraudulent actions in the case and issued an injunction prohibiting him from trying any case in which Roach was involved. At this time, Belcher was appointed guardian of the estate, the guardianship to take effect immediately. Roach would not talk and settled down for a long stay in jail.

Sheriff Russell Heath.
Author's collection.

Residents of Monterey, meanwhile, were becoming concerned about the steadily escalating situation. Belcher had been shot at several times, and one of his men had received a minor wound, while Dr. Sanford had several angry confrontations with Jerry McMahon, Roach's brother-in-law. On the afternoon of March 15, 1855, Dr. Sanford, his wife, and brother-in-law, H. Atwood, arrived in Monterey to attend court. They took rooms at the Washington Ho-

Monterey's first hotel and liveliest place of entertainment, the Washington Hotel, where three of the Roach-Belcher feud deaths took place. *Monterey Public Library.*

tel, a large structure encompassing rooms, restaurant, and saloon at the corner of Pearl and Washington streets. Although Sanford tried to avoid any contact with McMahon, the two met in the hotel bar and a violent argument took place. When McMahon "assailed Sanford with the most opprobrious language," the doctor drew his pistol and in the scuffle a shot was fired into the ceiling. Saying he was unarmed, McMahon was ushered from the room by friends. What happened next was reported by a correspondent of the *San Jose Telegraph*, March 22, 1855:

> ...The parties were separated, and several hours afterwards, while Sanford was at his hotel smoking, McMahon entered, and exclaiming, "Sanford, God damn you, where are you now," and shot him through the heart. Sanford immediately drew his pistol, and shot McMahon through the heart. They both died in a few minutes...

The two men managed to stagger to the saloon's doorway, McMahon firing another shot into Sanford before both men collapsed and died. The unarmed Atwood rushed upstairs to his room and locked his door. McMahon partisans were right on his heels and pounded on his door demanding that he "come out shooting." Terrified, outnumbered and feeling he had no chance, Atwood put his pistol in his mouth and pulled the trigger. As shocked crowds gathered and discussed the incident, a promptly convened coroner's jury examined witnesses and the two bodies were carried off by the families. There would be no easy solution to the troubles now, and Mrs. Sanford was a widow for the third time.

Meanwhile, in the Stockton jail, Roach was desperate to gain his freedom. He proposed drawing a map for lawyer Terry that would show where the money was hidden, in exchange for his immediate release from jail. Terry agreed, but as soon as the map was in his hands, he informed Roach that he would only be released after the funds had been retrieved.

Article in the *San Jose Telegraph*, March 22, 1855, describing the Sanford-McMahon shooting. *Author's collection.*

Terry and Belcher rode off toward Monterey immediately. The map detailed where the treasure had been hidden in the adobe foundation of Roach's brother-in-law, Jerry McMahon's, home. The fum-

Monterey, shown here in the 1850s, was a battleground for a pack of scoundrels trying to rob a woman and her children of their inheritance. *Monterey Public Library.*

THE SENTINEL.

Monterey, Saturday, Nov. 17, 1855

Horrible Murder.

Our community was thrown into an intense state of excitement, on Saturday last, by the report that Isaac B. Wall and Thomas Williamson had been murdered and that their bodies lay exposed by the road side. The rumors proved true, and one of the most fiendish and diabolical murders has been committed in our midst, in the open broad day light, that we believe to be unparalelled in the annals of crime in California.

The particulars of this horrid affair, as near as we can learn are substantially as follows:

Isaac B. Wall Collector of the Port of Monterey, and Thomas Williamson, ex-

Notice of the Wall and Williamson murders appearing in the *Monterey Sentinel*, November 17, 1855. *Author's collection.*

ing Roach called jailor Franklin Foote over to his cell. The two had become friends over the past few months and now Roach pleaded with Foote to release him, so they could beat Terry to Monterey and share the treasure. The jailor finally unlocked his cell and the two men were soon riding hard for Monterey over trails not familiar to lawyer Terry.

Terry and Belcher nearly demolished the McMahon home looking for the gold, but they found nothing. Roach had either beaten them there, or had lied about the location. Ex-sheriff Roach and Foote quickly went into hiding when they heard that Belcher had given orders to kill Roach on sight. After Belcher won a court case relative to some notes taken from Roach following his capture at San Buenaventura, he later narrowly escaped ambushes on several occasions.

Lewis Belcher stayed true to the Sanchez cause and hounded the Roach bondsmen for a settlement of the $84,654 the Stockton court had ordered Roach to pay. When it became clear Roach's sureties were going to stall and drag their feet forever, Belcher petitioned the court to allow him to compromise the amounts. "By compromising with the sureties," noted the *Monterey Sentinel* on October 6, 1855, "a little will be saved, but the children, it is believed, will lose, [due to] Roach, at least $50,000." In the end, Belcher was able to recover only some $9,000.

The same issue of the *Sentinel* reported that Anastacio Garcia had returned to town. Born in Monterey about 1825, Garcia was described as a "man of uncommon personal attractions—large and finely proportioned, with regular features, dark eyes and a profusion of curly hair—the very beau ideal of a brigand." For all his personal appearance, Garcia was bad to the bone. He had once told his wife that he had committed fourteen murders, the worst being the killing of a small boy whom he had inveigled into stealing a church poor box.

During a Monterey dance hall fandango in 1854, Garcia, Tiburcio Vasquez, and several others initiated a rowdy brawl, during which a local constable named William Hardmount was killed. Hardmount had also been a popular member of Stevenson's Regiment. One of Garcia's troublemakers, Jose Heiguerra, was seized and lynched the next morning. Garcia and Vasquez quickly fled the area.

Isaac Wall. The jury is still out on his status as a feud victim. *Courtesy The Bancroft Library.*

In early October 1855, Garcia returned to Monterey and surrendered to the local authorities. The fugitive had no doubt discovered that none of the witnesses against him were still in the area. "The prosecution," reported the *Monterey Sentinel*, "not being able to find any testimony against Garcia, the proceeding was dismissed, and he is now at liberty."

The presence of the returned fugitive was quickly felt. Roach had recently hired a new lawyer, young Isaac B. Wall, former speaker of the state assembly and a recent appointee to the post of Collector of the Port of Monterey. Together with his friend Thomas Williamson, an ex-constable, Wall left on November 9, 1855, for a trip south. Wall was headed for San Luis Obispo, while Williamson was going to visit the newly discovered placer mines at Santa Ynez. The men were on horseback, Wall having a loaded pack animal, also. Despite their announced destinations, it was suspected locally that the two were taking money to the fugitive Roach.

Making about twenty-five miles on the first day, the two slept that night at the Malarin rancho in the Salinas Valley.

Thomas Williamson's grave in the Monterey Catholic Cemetery. *Author's collection.*

They were up at seven o'clock the following morning and proceeded on their journey. About nine o'clock, shots were heard some miles to the south. A short time later, Wall's horse came galloping into the Gonzales rancho wounded in the flank. Williamson's mount arrived a short time later, both animals riderless, but still bridled and saddled. The bodies of the two men were found later in a ravine. Both had been shot in the head and dragged by lariats off the road and into the ravine. Their belongings had been scattered about, indicating a search had been made. Money belts carried by each man were not found. "The villains," commented the *Monterey Sentinel,* "evidently had taken alarm and fled before they had accomplished their hellish business." It was concluded that the two travelers had been murdered by men whom they knew.

At that time the coastal roads were terribly dangerous. Individual highwaymen and gangs of cutthroats pounced on any unsuspecting traveler unprepared for trouble. Wall and Williamson knew this and were both well armed. It was supposed some acquaintance, or a group, hailed them and rode with them for a while. Then, saying they were turning off the road, they dropped back and shot the two unsuspecting travelers in the head.

There were whispers that Lewis Belcher was behind the terrible deed. Based on testimony by Monterey County undersheriff Joaquin de la Torre, however, a coroner's inquiry concluded that Anastacio Garcia was involved in the deaths. A servant of Wall's had been seen talking to Garcia prior to his master's departure, and Garcia left town shortly after the two victims. Too, Garcia attended a rodeo at Malarin's rancho the day that Wall and Williamson stayed there. Sheriff John Keating and his

The Crane house, in San Juan, is still in use. Encarnacion lived here for many years and died here in 1894. *Author's collection.*

16

undersheriff put together a posse, consisting of themselves, lighthouse keeper Charles Layton, A. C. Beckwith, James B. Wall, brother of the murdered man, and a Mexican named Soria. Armed with a warrant for Garcia's arrest, the determined men left at three o'clock in the morning for Garcia's adobe home at El Tucho, some twelve miles from Monterey. The *Sentinel* detailed the action that followed:

> The house was surrounded, and on De la Torre entering, he received a shot from Garcia, right through the heart, and fell back dead on the ground. A number of shots were immediately afterwards fired from the inside and Mr. Charles Layton and A. C. Beckwith [were] severely wounded. Anastacio ran out of the house immediately afterwards, it is said in company with one or two others, and plunged into the thicket near by to the house, and immediately on the river banks. This thicket can hide a hundred men, and it would be as easy to find them, or capture them, as a needle in a haystack. It is said that the wife of Anastacio fired the pistol which wounded Beckwith [and] she also received a dangerous wound in the breast.

The shoot-out had been a deadly one, with Garcia using his wife as a shield before fleeing into the thicket. With the first news of the fight, reinforcements rushed to the scene and about one o'clock that afternoon, two other men were wounded when they discovered Garcia in the thickets. Although a hundred men, both Americans and Californians, searched the area for several days, Garcia was not captured. "Facilities for escape," reported the *Sentinel*, "renders a capture next to an impossibility from the very nature of the country to the south of Monterey. A fugitive from justice may secrete himself for years and yet watch all the movements of his pursuers." And Anastacio Garcia knew the country well. A reward of $3,000 was now offered for the killers of Wall and Williamson.

De la Torre's death was widely mourned, and when Layton died from his wounds, the two fatalities, when added to that of the wounded, made the toll terrible, indeed. There were those who thought the posse had acted too impulsively, however. "If a little more coolness and judgement had been shown," noted the *Sentinel*, "(Garcia) would, it is more likely, either have delivered himself up, or been taken unawares. Too much bravery amounts to rashness..."

Garcia stayed in the area until he was sure his wife was out of danger. Before leaving for Southern California, however, he may have lingered for one more job.

The Big Eagle of Monterey, Lewis Belcher, had made bitter enemies during his crusade to recover the Sanchez estate, and as he rode through the countryside supervising his ranch operations, Byrnes and his men were always in attendance. But his enemies were patient.

On the afternoon of June 18,1856, Lewis Belcher and Bill Byrnes rode into Monterey to take care of some business. That evening they strolled over to the Washington Hotel. It was late and the bar was almost empty, due to some exciting games in the adjoining billiard room. The two men talked at the bar with a friend, and then Belcher sent Byrnes out on an errand. Shortly before ten o'clock, Belcher was still chatting at the bar when an explosion of gunfire erupted from the hallway and the Big Eagle staggered and fell.

Bleeding badly from a stomach wound, Belcher was carried to his room and a physician was summoned. He died in great pain the next afternoon, but was clearheaded to the end. He accused Roach, Aaron Lyons, John Robertson, Franklin Foote, and Anastacio Garcia, all bitter enemies, of the shooting. "They did not give me a chance," muttered the dying Belcher, "but shot me down like a dog. They were afraid to meet me face to face. My poor wife and child. God knows how they will fare in this country so full of lawyers and laws and such bad justice." And, according to at least one contemporary observer, Judge Edward McGowan, Belcher's family did receive very little of his vast estate when the lawyers were finished.

George W. Crane and Encarnacion were reportedly married in April 1855. George is holding daughter Virginia, while Chona cradles Lydia in her arms. *Author's collection.*

Few doubted that William

Roach was behind the Belcher murder, but Roach and Foote were still in hiding and could not be located. Aaron Lyons had been one of Stevenson's Volunteers and had come to California with Roach. He had been elected sheriff when Roach had resigned and both he and Robertson, the rancher, were arrested and examined on the charge. "It is proper to say here," opined a Monterey newspaper correspondent, "that both Mr. Lyons and Mr. Robertson proved clearly by a number of witnesses, that they were at the Shades Tavern, five hundred yards off, at the time of the occurrence, and the citizens of the town acquit them of an act so base and foul."

The wild card of this hand seemed to be Anastacio Garcia, a wanted man himself at this time. Roach is thought to have contacted Garcia and put him on his payroll. If true, Garcia soon began stalking his victim and finally caught him without his bodyguards at the Washington Hotel. Whether it was Garcia, or some other assassin, the identity of Belcher's killer was never discovered.

Several months after Belcher's death, Encarnacion, the Widow Sanford, married again. George W. Crane, a lawyer and former state legislator, had arrived in California in 1844. Handsome and popular, Crane quite naturally succumbed to the wiles of the much-married widow and the two settled down in San Juan. Although Crane kept up the pressure on recovering the Sanchez estate, he made little progress.

Mrs. Garcia was watched after her recuperation. When she booked passage on a coastal steamer for San Pedro, near Los Angeles, she was shadowed by a Monterey school teacher named Tom Clay. A nephew of the noted statesman Henry Clay, Tom had been employed to follow Mrs. Garcia, and he became acquainted with her during the voyage. At San Pedro she asked him to obtain for her a buggy and team, indicating her ultimate destination was San Juan Capistrano. Clay sent word to the sheriff's office in Los Angeles and Undersheriff W. H. Peterson, together with a three-man posse, was quickly on the road.

Amazingly, about thirteen miles from town, Peterson and his men saw three vaqueros riding toward them. Recognizing Garcia from a description, Peterson rode up to the group and was surprised when Garcia readily admitted his name. Asked for any weapons, the outlaw produced two six shooters and a sixteen-inch knife. Garcia was returned to Monterey on the steamer *Goliah* and housed in the local jail.

Just after Garcia's capture, a curious sidelight of the Wall and Williamson deaths came to light. A letter, published in the *Santa Cruz Daily Sentinel* on November 8, 1856, reports some revealing information relating to the murders:

> We have been kindly permitted to extract the following from a private citizen of this place, written under date of the 3rd instant:

> On yesterday we heard of a camp of Spaniards in the willows a little below the Tom Blanco Crossing, on the south side of the river, so we made up a company of men and went to arrest them. They resisted and several shots were fired on both sides. There were two Spaniards—one was shot dead, and the other gave himself up. The one killed is said to have been concerned in the murder of Wall and Williamson. They were notorious rascals. The one killed had shot a man in Monterey, and they both intended to leave for parts unknown as soon as they could learn what Anastacio Garcia, who was brought from below last week, had to say. These fellows had stolen a saddle from us a few days before. The one taken had stolen Smith's mule last spring. So we took them out to the side of the road, laid one down, and hung one up; left the dead to take care of themselves, and have heard nothing from them since.

Did these two men assist Garcia in the Wall and Williamson murders? Because of the hasty action of the vigilantes, we'll never know.

Back on his home turf, Garcia found himself in serious trouble. The San Francisco *Daily Evening Bulletin* listed a series of indictments that indicated his chances of not being convicted in the Monterey court were slim to nothing:

> The late Grand Jury, in session at Monterey, have found five distinct bills of indictment for murder against the notorious Anastacio Garcia. Garcia is now in jail at Monterey. One of the indictments is for the murder of Isaac B. Wall; another, for the murder of Thomas Williamson; another for the murder of Joaquin de la Torre; another for the murder of Charles Layton; and another for the murder of an Indian... He will be in extremely good luck to get clear of all these charges.

Various elements now came together to solve the Garcia question. Elements of the recent Juan Flores gang were reported to have

Monterey's jail, where Anastacio Garcia was lynched. It was the end of a vicious career of robbery and murder. *California State Library.*

fled to the San Jose area, after many of the gang had been killed or hung in Los Angeles for the killing of Sheriff Barton and several deputies. Garcia was said to have been associated with the gang and a rescue attempt was rumored to be imminent. There were also rumors that the jailed killer had called some of Belcher's friends to his cell. Mincing no words, Garcia threatened to expose the Wall and Williamson murders if he were not released from jail, one way or another. And released he was, but not in the way he expected.

Either Belcher's friends were afraid the outlaw would talk, or local vigilantes were concerned that he might be rescued by members of the Flores gang. Whoever the culprits were, the Santa Cruz *Pacific Sentinel* reported Garcia's "release" on February 28, 1857:

> Anastacio Garcia, who has been for several months confined at Monterey... was found on Tuesday morning, hung by the neck in the jail. As we have heard the story, it is this: On that morning some citizens of Monterey, upon going to the jail, found the Sheriff and Jailor inside with their hands and feet tied, and the prisoner, Garcia, suspended by the neck to a beam, with a heavy log tied to his feet. Life was entirely extinct.

With the death of Garcia, the infamous feud was thought to have sputtered and gone out. But there was still a loose end... a final addendum to the tale.

William Roach had been able to come out of hiding after Lewis Belcher's murder. Only then had he dared to resume his life. He purchased a farm in Santa Cruz County, three miles from Watsonville, and he and his wife, Annie, began rebuilding their lives. Just how much of the Sanchez funds he had been able to hold onto is not known, but he was never prosecuted. Inquiries into the case provided too little evidence for an indictment. It is known that the five Sanchez children eventually received something over $10,000 each and some property as their share of the estate. There is little doubt that Roach had stolen a large amount and made many loans to his friends. But that was all in the past now.

A saloon near Watsonville. Roach had his last drink in such a place before being assasinated. *Author's collection.*

On the afternoon of September 3, 1866, Roach rode into Watsonville to vote. After casting his ballot, he headed for his favorite saloon and joined the crowd in drinking and talking politics. About eleven o'clock that night he bid his friends goodby and, mounting his horse, galloped off into the darkness.

The next morning Roach's horse was found near a well on the Whiskey Hill road. A search of the area produced a body at the bottom of the well which, when brought to the surface, proved to be the battered corpse of the missing ranch man. A coroner's jury concluded the death was accidental, and the wounds and bruises on the body were indicative of his falling into the well, although nothing was said of his being intoxicated at the time. Later, it was remembered that he had rope burns around his ankles and various bruises on his face, suggesting he had been roped and dragged to the well.

The *Pajaro Times*, quite critical of the inquest, questioned whether an autopsy might have established if Roach had been strangled, or died of drowning. It was not critical of the man, however:

> The remains of Mr. Roach were interred Wednesday afternoon in the Catholic burial ground. The funeral was the largest ever witnessed in this section of country, people from the extreme ends of Monterey and Santa Cruz counties attending. The ceremonies were imposing, and few were the eyes that remained dry as the noble form of the good, the generous and brave, passed forever from our sight.

For everyone who thought the death was accidental, it was inevitable there were others who conjured up connections to the old feud. It was the final payback. The old score was finally settled, it was said. There were other stories also. Roach talked too much while drinking. There were those who were afraid he would link them to the old feud killings and they did away with him to protect themselves. Others claimed Roach had argued with a Mexican a few days before his death, and the Mexican had threatened to kill him. But always Roach's death was linked to the bloody feud.

What is probably the true story of what happened surfaced some forty years later. Farm workers of the Pajaro Valley were primarily Indians and Mexicans who sometimes could not save enough money to buy food through the winter. Threshing bosses would stake these workers to sacks of potatoes and beans to feed their families, but Roach always refused to issue this aid. Further, he was a bully who would push his way into a crowd of Mexicans at a saloon bar, shouting for them to "get out of the way and let a white man get up to the bar." His arrogance and intolerance led to the formation of a group of workers who determined to kill him.

Six Indians and Mexicans laid in wait for Roach that election evening. As he rode by their hiding place, they swarmed over the drunken man, pulling him from his horse and pummeling him with stones. Looping a lariat around the unconscious man's ankles, they drug him to the well and heaved him into the black hole. The killers then faded into the hills and stayed out of sight for some time.

For those who believe in other types of justice, a notice in the *Santa Cruz Sentinel*, September 30, 1865, is tragic, indeed:

> Sorrowful Record - Under the appropriate head will be seen the death of three little children, sons of Mr. William Roach, an old pioneer, residing near Watsonville. We also learn that a little daughter died this week, with the same fateful disease, diphtheria, and that another, and now the only child, is sick and not expected to recover. We sincerely console the heartbroken parents...

Luckily, the last mentioned child did survive.

Encarnacion Crane, the much-married widow, lost her latest husband to a smallpox epidemic in San Juan during 1868. She married once more, but when this husband was killed in a hunting incident she settled down to a quiet life at her home in San Juan. She died there in 1894, mourned by her children and neighbors as a kindly person who did not deserve the many tragedies that beset her life.

In retrospect, one early chronicler of the Sanchez treasure saga perhaps correctly observed that few people really benefitted from the Sanchez estate, "except the ancient fraternity of constables, scribes and lawyers."

To which might have, with a little more thought, appropriately been added "gamblers."

UNPUBLISHED MATERIALS

1850 U.S. Census, Monterey County, California

1860 U.S. Census, Santa Cruz County, California, Pajaro Township

1857 Monterey County jail register, prisoner no. 313, Anastacio Garcia

BOOKS

Bancroft, Hubert Howe. *The Works of Hubert Howe Bancroft,* History of California. San Francisco: The History Company, Publishers, 1886.

Chapter 1
NOTES

Boessenecker, John. *Gold Dust & Gunsmoke*, New York: JohnWiley & Sons, Inc., 1999.

Elliot & Moore (publishers). *History of Monterey County, California*. San Francisco, 1881.

Fink, Augtusta. *Monterey County.* Fresno: Valley Publishers, 1978.

Harrell, Nita. *The Sanchez Treasure.* San Juan Bautista: San Juan Bautista Historical Publisher, 1975.

Johnston, Robert B. *Old Monterey County.* Monterey: Monterey Savings and Loan Association, 1970.

MacMullen, Jerry. *Paddlewheel Days in California.* Stanford: Stanford University Press, 1944.

Mylar, Isaac L. *Early Days at the Mission San Juan Bautista.* Fresno: Valley Publishers, 1970.

Pierce, Marjorie. *East of the Gabilans.* Fresno: Valley Publishers, 1977.

NEWSPAPERS

Monterey Sentinel, November 17, 24, 1855; March 15, 1856

Pajaro Times, September 8, 1866

San Francisco *Daily Alta California*, April 12, 13, 1853

San Francisco *Call & Post*, August 23, 1919

San Francisco *Daily Evening Bulletin*, November 1856

San Francisco *Herald*, April 12, 13, 14, 1853

San Jose Pioneer, May 15, 1880

San Jose Telegraph, March 22, 1855

San Jose *Weekly Tribune*, March 20, 1855

Santa Cruz *Pacific Sentinel*, June 28, 1856

Santa Cruz Daily Sentinel, September 30, 1865; September 8, 1866

Santa Cruz Surf, December 31, 1901

Santa Cruz *Times*, May 11, 1867

Stockton *San Joaquin Republican*, August 2, 1851; March 24, 28, 1855

Watsonville Pajaronian, January 2, 1879

OTHER SOURCES

Curtis, Mabel Rowe. "Sequel to the Roach Case," Pajaro Valley Historical Association, no date.

O'Donnell, Mayo Hayes. "Peninsula Diary," a 1951 series of columns pertaining to the Sanchez treasure and resulting feud, appeared in the Monterey *Peninsula Herald*.

Parker, Paul P. "The Roach Belcher Feud," *California Historical Society Quarterly*, March 1950.

Chapter 2

Long, Long Trail to Santa Cruz

The Graham - Bennett Feud

As he watched the scenery racing by his train window, Jesse Graham stretched out in his seat. He smiled at the changes he had seen in the Valley. It was April of 1888, and trains were unheard of in this country when he had arrived in California nearly forty years previously. It was always beautiful here in the spring. In the clear air, the oak-clustered foothills and mighty Sierra Nevada mountains were inspiring in their snow-capped majesty.

Graham's attorney, Russ Ward, engaged in conversation with another passenger while Sheriff Jim Meade was thumbing through a newspaper. Tipping his hat over his eyes, Jesse tried to relax. He had gotten up early and the monotonous clacking of the train wheels seemed to induce a drowsiness in the old settler. He knew he should be worried. In his conversations with Ward, both men felt there was a good chance for an acquittal, but still the fact remained that he was on his way to Santa Cruz to be tried for murder.

As the coach rumbled across the San Joaquin Valley, Graham thought back to those faraway days of his youth. He smiled at the thought of the fresh-smelling redwood forests surrounding his father's rancho above Santa Cruz. He could still recall the puzzled look on Isaac Graham's face when he had ridden onto the Zayante Rancho and seen his father's face for the first time in twenty years.

Jesse dozed in his seat as the train chugged across the prairie heading for Lathrop, then San Jose.

Born in Virginia in 1800, Isaac Graham moved with his family to Kentucky in 1803. Young Isaac never learned to read and write and left home at an early age. He eventually settled in Tennessee where he married a Miss Jones in 1823. The couple had four children, Isaac Wayne being born the year after the marriage, then followed by Jesse Jones Graham and two sisters. But home and family quickly palled on Isaac Graham. In late 1829, he joined a trapping expedition heading west from Fort Smith, Arkansas.

The next few years were filled with the adventurous life of a free trapper. Young Graham hunted and fought Indians from the Canadian River north to the Platte Valley country with his companions, George Nidever, the Sublette brothers, Kit Carson and other legendary figures. He attended the great trapper rendezvous on Green River in July of 1833 and may have come to California with Joseph Walker's party later that year.

In California Graham continued to trap and hunt on the coast, but in 1836 he leased some property from the grantee of the Rancho Natividad and constructed a whiskey still. Located some twenty-five miles east of Monterey, Graham's groggery became noted as a hangout for deserting sailors, American trappers and general loafers of the area. Graham was characterized by men who knew him at the time as being generous and friendly, as well as noisy and troublesome.

Stage road from San Jose over the mountains north of Santa Cruz. *Vischer's Pictorial of California.*

But there was trouble in paradise. The raw, thinly-populated California territory was a long way from the Mexican capital and 1836 was a year of political instability south of the border. Within sixteen months four California governors came and went. Nicolas Gutierrez, the last of the group, was deposed by a politico named Juan Bautista who had recruited Graham and some fifty Americans to help him in his revolution. It was a bloodless coup, but when Graham and his men were not rewarded as promised by the new government, an estrangement developed. Governor Alvarado, with events in Texas as a straw in the wind, cast a jaundiced eye on Graham and his roughneck American friends.

Suspected of plotting to over-throw the government, Graham and some forty odd other foreigners were rounded up in the dead of night in April of 1840. Guilty or not, the foreigners were brutally treated, and after a brief hearing were shipped off in chains to Mexico. The captives received good treatment in

The famous mountain man and early California pioneer, Isaac Graham. *California State Library.*

their Mexican prison, thanks to the British consul. There was considerable furor over the situation and after some fifteen months the captives were returned to California.

The "Graham Affair" became a celebrated incident, and Graham promptly initiated suit for damages and lost property. Winning a hefty settlement from Mexico, Isaac, with several partners, invested in a rancho across the bay, some eight miles north of Santa Cruz.

Graham's new home was located on Zayante Creek where he operated the first water-powered sawmill in California. He also ran cattle and built another distillery. Cranky, irascible and loud-mouthed, Graham was the subject of constant accusations of theft, assault, and trouble-making. He participated in the Micheltorena campaign in 1844–45 and in September of 1846 was the plaintiff in the first jury trial in California.

Graham refused to play any part in the American acquisition of California. He was bitter over the recent death of a friend and the continued failure to acquire title to his Zayante property. Recluse and malcontent that he was, the old mountain man still had enough charm to woo and win twenty-one-year-old Tillatha Catherine Bennett. The depth of her feelings for old Graham are not known, but probably anything was preferable to her squabbling parents, overbearing mother, and a house full of children.

Vardamon and Mary Bennett, Catherine's parents, brought their eight children west with the Hastings party in 1842. Mary was hard-working, but insisted on having her own way in everything. She wore down her husband and they separated later, Mary and her children taking up residence just north of Graham's property where they established a sawmill. Isaac and Catherine Bennett were married on September 26, 1845. Unfortunately, the ceremony was of questionable validity since only Catholic clergy could perform marriages in Mexican California.

Outraged when she received news of her daughter's marriage, Mary Bennett complained to Thomas Larkin, the American consul at Monterey. She insisted the couple be separated immediately, and Larkin instructed the Santa Cruz justice of the peace to break up the union. Jose Antonio Balcoff, the hapless justice, was all but thrown off the Zayante Rancho. "Graham said they were well married," he wrote to Larkin, "and that he would not separate from

Tillatha Catherine Bennett was the original cause of the feud. Author's collection.

the side of Bennett, that he would lose a thousand lives before he would give her up." Larkin got the message and nothing further was done.

Mary Bennett was furious. A large woman, weighing over 200 pounds, she was as tough as rawhide. She had finally separated from Vardamon when he opened a saloon in San Francisco and she was not about to have a daughter linked to the whiskey-swilling likes of old Graham. When Matilda Jane Graham was born in early July 1846, Grandma Bennett tried to behave herself. She vowed that Graham had not heard the last of this, however. One way or another, she would have her way yet. Amanda, the Grahams' second daughter, arrived in 1849.

On September 15, 1849, a party of Texans arrived in Southern California and stopped at the Isaac Williams ranch near Los Angeles. The travelers rested and bought supplies while they questioned their host about the new country. Williams had lived in California since 1832 and had been a member of the Bean trapping expedition of 1830. Two of the Texans were Mexican War veterans named Reuben Chandler and Jesse Jones Graham. In talking with Williams, young Graham was delighted to learn that Williams had trapped with his father many years before. He was even more surprised to hear that his father was alive and living in California.

The family hadn't heard from the father for nearly twenty years and had assumed he had long ago been killed by Indians or perished crossing some lonely desert. Chandler was anxious to go to the mines, but Jesse was soon riding up the coast, along the old mission trail to Santa Cruz.

The reunion between father and son must have been dramatic. Although disturbed to find his father remarried, Jesse was assured that word had arrived that his mother had died in Texas. Jesse's young stepmother treated him with reserve and he soon found out why. The Graham-Bennett marriage was already on shaky legal ground and when Jesse divulged that his father's first wife was very much alive, the Bennetts had even more reason to be disturbed. Jesse's sudden appearance also meant he was heir to the Graham estate in California—a claim that would take precedence over the two Graham daughters who were now deemed to be illegitimate. Mary Bennett and her sons, Mansel, Jackson, Winston, and Dennis, were not happy with the turn of events. Soon ugly remarks and accusations were being exchanged.

Jesse and his father traveled to San Jose on a horse-buying trip in March 1850. The callousness of the elder Graham was well illustrated when the father and son departed immediately after Catherine had delivered a stillborn baby. A Bennett sister was left with his distraught wife, while Graham and Jesse headed over the mountains for San Jose.

When the Grahams returned on April 3, it was to an empty house. Noche, an Indian servant girl, told Graham that his wife had taken their children and fled after breaking into a chest of Graham's gold. Noche had identified Mary Bennett and her daughter, who had been staying with Catherine, as aiding in her flight.

Finding some $7,000 missing, along with his children, Graham was enraged. He directed his son to fire off the loads in his shotgun, then reload it, but when Jesse went out into the yard and discharged the weapon, it exploded, burning his face and hands. The two Grahams were furious, convinced they were victims of an assassination plot. Questioning Noche further, the Grahams were told Dennis Bennett had loaded the weapon, stuffing the barrel with rocks in an obvious attempt to kill either father or son. Old Graham promptly rode over to the Bennett sawmill and accused Mary and her sons of engineering his wife's flight and attempting to murder him and his son. The Bennetts

Mary Bennett was the chief instigator of the feud between her family and the Grahams. *Courtesy Conrado Family Archives.*

Scene on Isaac Graham's Zayante Rancho, in the redwood-forested mountains north of Santa Cruz. *Vischer's* Pictorial of California.

vigorously denied knowing anything of Catherine's actions or whereabouts. Graham talked to everyone in the area, then put detectives on his wife's trail.

Jesse naturally took his father's side. He also called on the Bennetts demanding to know where Catherine was. In the resulting shouting match, he threatened violence if they refused to cooperate.

The threats worried Mary Bennett. With her son Jackson, she appeared before the Santa Cruz alcalde on April 22 and obtained a restraining order to prevent Jesse from carrying out his threats. Jesse was noticeably upset when he appeared before the alcalde and was required to give bonds to assure he would not carry out his threats against the Bennetts. He spent the afternoon with friends in a Santa Cruz saloon, then mounted his horse and headed back toward the redwood groves of his Zayante home.

As he rode along the trail this late afternoon, Jesse suddenly saw Mary and Jackson Bennett in the distance. Jack was on a mule, while Mary rode a horse. There seemed no way to avoid a meeting and Graham exchanged greetings and rode alongside the mother and son. Several men, who were building a fence nearby, heard several shots and looked up from their work. They saw Jackson Bennett's clothes were on fire and watched his mule run off. Mary Bennett jumped to the ground and hid behind her animal, but as the horse reared, Graham emptied the other barrel of his shotgun at her. The shot hit the woman in the hip and legs, but she stayed on her feet. As Jackson Bennett made his way back to his mother, Jesse spurred his horse up the trail. Both Bennetts received minor wounds, and headed back towards Santa Cruz.

A short time later, Jesse appeared at the Bennett home. Several people were in the yard and he asked to see Dennis Bennett. "My brother came out," Samantha Bennett later recalled, "and asked Jesse to get off his horse and passed the time of day ... Dennis was speaking of the new horse Graham had, and while examining it, got away slightly from the other men. Jesse Graham then shot him. He did not put the gun to his shoulder, he only raised it a little..."

As Dennis sprawled dying on the ground, Jesse spurred his horse up the road towards the Graham ranch. After discussing the events with his father, it was decided to hide him on the property and see what developed. The Bennetts had many friends in the area, while Graham had many enemies. A $3,000 reward was posted for the fugitive, but Jesse could not be found.

After six months of hiding, Jesse bade his father goodby and headed east over the Coast Range and across the San Joaquin Valley. He knew his Texas friend, Chandler, was in Mariposa County and he was able to locate him on his mining claim. Recounting the events leading up to his flight from the coast, Jesse no doubt was assured by Chandler that he would be safe in the mining country.

In the early days of 1848 and 49, mining had concentrated in the northern portion of the gold country. The few prospectors who had drifted into the Mariposa area had been scared off by hostile Indians. By the spring of 1849, however, larger groups of well-armed prospectors were finding rich diggings in the Mariposa hills.

Miner Enos Christman wrote that when he first came to Mariposa in March of 1850, there were so many miners in the area that claims were impossible to find. If this was the case, Jesse probably worked for shares with his friend, the two of them being able to turn out a greater volume of work as partners.

Although late in the year, the weather was still pleasant and there had been little rain. Mining was still in full progress, but other matters concerned the miners more than the weather. Chandler told Jesse of the constant rumors of Indian trouble. Just the previous month a trader named Savage had taken a delegation of local Indians to San Francisco to impress them with the numbers of white men and the futility of war.

Despite peacemaking attempts, war was immenent. The Indians were being pushed off their land, while the native women were being raped and stolen. The Indian food supplies and villages were in the foothill country where the gold was and they were being steadily driven higher up into the mountains. When trouble did come, it was swift and deadly.

An Indian rancheria in Mariposa County, about 1859. From a salt print by Carleton Watkins.
Courtesy the Bancroft Library.

On December 17, Savage's trading post on the Fresno River was attacked, three of his clerks killed, and the place looted. Rumors of other attacks were everywhere and miners left their isolated claims to join larger groups. An armed party under county Sheriff Jim Burney attacked the Indians in a mountain rancheria, but made a poor showing. Later the sheriff appealed to the government for aid. When a group of thirteen settlers in the Four Creeks country, to the

John Boling was briefly Jesse's company commander in the Mariposa Battalion. *Author's collection.*

south, were massacred, Governor McDougal authorized three companies of militia to be formed in February of 1851.

Jesse and Reuben Chandler promptly enlisted. They were members of John Boling's company and were mustered into service at the mining camp of Agua Fria. After electing officers the men celebrated at Dutch Frank's saloon, then set up camp several miles below town. Jim Savage was elected commander of the battalion and Jesse helped elect his friend Chandler first lieutenant of Boling's company.

The battalion began drilling and gathering supplies for the upcoming campaign. Graham watched with interest as Major Savage reconnoitered with his Indian scouts. James D. Savage had lived locally with the Indians since 1848 and had become quite wealthy operating several trading posts. He was a colorful figure and, by marrying daughters of various local Indian chiefs, had acquired great influence among the Indians in the area. But the hostilities had changed all that.

Jack Hays, the famous Texas Ranger, joined the Gold Rush to California and became sheriff of San Francisco. *California State Library.*

On March 3, Colonel Jack Hays visited the militia camp. The famous Texas Ranger was now sheriff of San Francisco County and was looking for Jesse with an eye towards the $3,000 reward. Hays was so popular that the cheering of other Texans in camp alerted his quarry and Graham thought it prudent to slip out of camp with a hunting party. By the time he returned, Hays was gone, but Jesse was worried. If Hays could find him, others would surely show up also. Meanwhile, a group of federal Indian commissioners, a representative of the governor, and a detachment of United States Infantry had arrived at the battalion camp.

On the same day Jesse returned from his hunt, an evening dance

Captain Erasmus D. Keyes commanded the U.S. troops in Mariposa County when Jesse was arrested. *National Archives.*

was held. There were few women in the area and the men mostly danced with each other, drank and had a good time. In the midst of the festivities, San Francisco police captain William Lambert made his appearance. The lawman had already consulted with Major Savage and Captain Erasmus D. Keyes, commander of the U.S. troops present. Captain Boling at first denied Graham was a member of his company, but finally admitted to his presence.

Jesse was accosted at the dance, where Lambert read a warrant and placed him under arrest. Giving Graham's pistol to Captain Keyes, the officer then called on the volunteers to cooperate with him. Jesse's many friends had no intention of giving him up, however, as noted by a correspondent of the *Stockton Times* who was present:

> Instead of this, however, a large number of them procured their rifles and pistols and pointing them at the heads of Captain Keyes and Lambert, threatened to blow their brains out if they did not release Graham. Capt. Keyes addressed them, urging them to support the laws of their state, and while he was trying to induce them to perform their duty, Captain Lambert, calling upon Mr. Templeton to aid him, got Graham some distance on the way to the camp of the regulars, but the Volunteers, breaking from Capt. Keyes, followed them and took Graham by force, setting him at liberty...

Accompanied by several friends, Jesse fled into the surrounding wilderness where he spent the night. After talking the matter over, however, it was decided his best course was to surrender. In several diary entries, a member of the battalion noted the situation:

> ...Jesse Graham has given or about to give himself up to the authorities ... A subscription has been got up for the purpose of employing counsel to defend Graham ... The largest amount subscribed was $100 by Major Savage... .

The following day Jesse surrendered. Andy Firebaugh took his place in Boling's company, while Jesse was escorted back to Santa Cruz by Reuben Chandler and a small detachment of volunteers. The fugitive's friends were determined to keep him from the clutches of San Francisco lawmen, and the Bennetts, before he could obtain a fair trial.

In Santa Cruz, no local officials or magistrates could be located. It suddenly dawned on the volunteers that as a result of California recently attaining statehood, local governments were in a state of disorder. Jesse and his friends were satisfied: He had tried to turn himself in and found no takers. After a brief visit with his father, Jesse disappeared. The following month an indictment for murder was brought against him by the Santa Cruz Grand Jury, but by that time Jesse was aboard a ship bound for Mazatlan and Texas.

Jesse fought with Terry's Rangers at the advent of the Civil War and later served in General Hood's brigade. He took part in many engagements and was wounded several times. When he returned to California after the war, he visited briefly in Santa Cruz, where he

Jesse Jones Graham, as he appeared in the mid-1880s just prior to his trial. Photo by E. R. Higgins. *Elisabeth Jones' collection.*

heard his father had died in 1863. Later he settled on the Merced River, moving in the early 1870s to Fresno County, where he farmed and made many friends.

In April 1883, Jesse received a letter from his half-sister Matilda, who lived in Santa Cruz. Now Mrs. David Rice, she had kept in touch with Jesse over the years and warned him that the Bennetts intended to have him arrested for the murder of Dennis, over thirty years earlier. Jackson Bennett had died in Central America in the

A San Joaquin Valley farm of the 1880s. *Author's collection.*

early 1850s, while Mary Bennett had died in late 1868. Others in the family were behind the suit, but just who is not clear.

Jesse was startled at the news, but he must have smiled when informed that the Bennetts might reconsider their intentions for a cash settlement. "Not a cent for tribute," was his wry comment, "but millions for defense."

On April 22, Fresno County sheriff O. J. Meade rode over to Graham's farm. The two men were good friends and the lawman assured him as he handed him the warrant that he could take several days to settle his affairs before making the trip to Santa Cruz.

"You know, Jim, them Bennetts are mean cusses. Any objection to my taking my pistol along, just to avoid any surprises?" asked Graham. Meade smiled. No, there would be no objections. Graham had always been a law-abiding citizen in Fresno County and, after hearing a recital of the Graham-Bennett troubles, Meade saw no reason not to allow his friend some self-protection.

After two days, Graham presented himself to the sheriff in Fresno. A reporter for the *Daily Evening Expositor* promptly cornered the old man and obtained a long story of his early troubles. "Jesse J. Graham," noted the article, "is a large, hale, well preserved man, sixty-three years old, with a genial and intelligent countenance. He has the reputation of being a good citizen, but a courageous and resolute man, and when attacked is devoid of fear. There is a chapter in this story that he declines to speak of, and which will fully explain the purpose of this

State Senator A. J. Meany, a former Merced County sheriff, was an important character witness for Jesse. *Author's collection.*

movement at this late date. He announces himself as ready to abide the result, whatever it may be."

Early on the morning of the 26th, Sheriff Meade and Graham left on the owl train for Santa Cruz. In Merced they picked up attorney Russ Ward and continued their journey.

At Santa Cruz, Jesse met Matilda at the Pacific Ocean House. The following day he was jailed. His Superior Court arraignment took place on April 30, and Ward tried unsuccessfully to have the indictment dropped on various technicalities.

A trial date of June 11 was set by Judge Ferdinand J. McCann and, when bail was refused, Jesse took up residence in the local county jail. The Santa Cruz *Daily Sentinel* commented:

> The proceedings in the trial of Graham will be watched with interest all over the state, and add an important chapter to criminal history. When the trial takes place the witnesses will have to turn back the pages of memory for many a year, and again tell the story that thrilled Santa Cruz County in the days of long ago... .
>
> In the meantime justice stands blindfolded, with scales in her hand, awaiting to hear both sides.

William J. Howard served with Jesse in the Mariposa County Indian troubles. *California State Library.*

When the trial commenced, several days were taken up in the selection of a jury, and Ward and his associates were careful to screen out any jurors with an anti-Confederate bias. On the morning of June 13, the prosecution opened its case, calling the three sisters of Dennis Bennett to the stand. Although only ten years of age at the time, Mrs. Samantha Hicks told a straightforward story of how Jesse had ridden up to the Bennett cabin and began talking to Dennis. "Jesse Graham then shot him," she testified. "He did not put the gun to his shoulder, he only raised it a little. Graham looked for a few moments at Dennis lying on the ground and rode away..." Her sisters verified the recital of events, although they were not eyewitnesses.

Called next was seventy-year-old mill worker Lansing Haight. He and several other men had been working at the Bennett mill at the time of the shooting and corroborated Mrs. Hicks' testimony. A member of the original coroner's

A Santa Cruz street scene about the time of the Jesse Graham trial. The city was already a popular resort area. *Author's collection.*

jury swore that Jesse had made threats against the Bennett family.

O. K. Stampley next took the stand. He and a crew of men were building a fence along the road when the incident occurred. Stampley had turned from his work when a shot had been fired:

> ...The mule on which Jackson Bennett was riding ran away and Jackson was trying to get off it, as it had become scared at the shot which had struck Jackson and set his clothes afire. Mrs. Bennett also slid off her horse and hid behind it. Graham pointed his gun and the horse reared back, exposing the woman. Graham fired, inflicting a serious wound, and immediately rode off.... Jackson... fired at the fleeing Graham....

An array of prosecution witnesses bolstered the premise that a vicious and cold-blooded murder had taken place. Indeed, it was difficult to imagine that any set of circumstances could justify Jesse shooting the unarmed Dennis Bennett or the shoot-out on the road with Jack and his mother. When the prosecution rested its case, many in that hot and crowded courtroom were nodding their heads in agreement.

But Russ Ward had prepared his defense well. As he stood up and faced the jury, he chose his words carefully, well aware that a life hung in the balance. He stressed Jesse's unblemished record as a hard-working citizen of the San Joaquin Valley. A parade of character witnesses validated Ward's oratory.

Reuben Chandler quickly refuted the prosecution's insistence that Jesse had been a fugitive from justice all those years since the Bennett troubles. Jesse had worked for Chandler after the Civil War and had always been known by his real name. Indeed, directories and official

county records had always listed him as "Jesse J. Graham." Chandler testified that he had accompanied Jesse to Santa Cruz when he tried to turn himself in, but that he had not been able to do so due to the unsettled condition of affairs when California had become a state.

The Santa Cruz courthouse as it appeared at the time of the Jesse Graham trial. *Author's collection.*

William J. Howard testified to Jesse's qualities as a friend and citizen. They had served together in the Mariposa Indian troubles and Howard had since become a widely respected rancher, deputy sheriff, and district attorney. State Senator A. J. Meany, a former Merced County sheriff, lauded Jesse as a solid citizen, as did the Fresno County sheriff and other officials.

After a procession of character witnesses, Ward put Jesse himself on the stand. The attorney had already laid the groundwork for his case. The Bennetts had plotted to do away with both Isaac Graham and his son. Jesse was seen by the Bennetts as an interloper who stood between Graham's two young daughters and their legitimate inheritance. Mary Bennett had instigated the plot against the Grahams, helping her daughter to break into Graham's cash box while he was away, then sending Catherine and the two children off to Hawaii, then Oregon.

When Jesse and his father returned to find Catherine and the children gone, there had been another incident that lent validity to charges of a family feud. Jesse remembered the incident well. He had taken his double-barreled shotgun out to fire it off, then reload it. The trigger had clicked twice, but on the third try the weapon had exploded at the breach. Jesse had been badly burned and discovered the barrel had been tamped full of rocks and sand. Stunned, Jesse asked Noche, the Indian servant, who had last used his shotgun: It was Dennis Bennett.

On the stand, Jesse was his own best witness. In a calm, matter-of-fact manner he told of being put under bond by the Santa Cruz alcalde. Afterwards he headed back towards home and met Mary Bennett and her son on the trail:

> The old lady spoke to Jackson in a strange language, some kind of Indian, and stopped her horse. Jackson reined his mule to the left and away from Graham, but as he did so he fired at Graham, cutting his coat sleeve at the elbow. Graham then shot him and turning again to the old lady.... saw that she was on the ground with a six-shooter in her hand. He pointed his gun at her and fired it off...

As he rode away, Jesse looked back and saw the Bennetts talking, but he knew he was in serious trouble. He went home first, trying to decide what to do, then rode over to see Dennis Bennett. The meeting began amicably enough, but quickly developed into an argument over the whereabouts of Catherine and the stolen money:

> I leaned forward on my horse and told him that I wanted to know about my stepmother and the children ... He said he didn't know and didn't care and then grasped the gun and tried to wrest it from me...

In the struggle for the weapon, there was a sudden explosion and young Bennett slumped to the ground. Dennis was larger and stronger than Graham and his motive then and now seemed quite clear to Graham. Far from being cold blooded murder, it was self-defense.

When Jesse's half-sister testified to the conspiracy also, there was another shift in courtroom sentiment. A letter, written in 1854 by Catherine Bennett, was presented to support the contention that a blood feud had existed. Catherine claimed in the letter that al-

The Graham Case.

The following telegram to this paper was received yesterday afternoon, and indicates that while there has been considerable of a change in the jury since Tuesday night, a verdict has not been reached. The telegram reads:

"Graham jury still locked up. It is rumored that they stand eleven for acquittal and one for conviction."

The citizens of Monterey county would seriously object to paying the bills incident to a retrial of the Graham case. The murder, if it was a murder, was committed thirty odd years ago when such things were of almost daily occurrence, and in all probability Bennett deserved all the punishment he received from Graham. The witnesses who went from here say they were not only put to considerable trouble to collect their fees and mileage and that the citizens fairly howled when the bills were paid. We don't blame them, for we believe the whole case was an attempt to blackmail Graham in the start, and failing in this, the Bennett family saddled the case onto the county to get revenge and not justice.

An article in the *Fresno Morning Republican*, June 28, 1888, indicates the fluctuating daily drama of Jesse's Santa Cruz trial. *Author's collection.*

though she had good reason to leave Isaac Graham, her mother had been the instigator of the affair and had even at one point suggested she poison her husband. Mary Bennett had gotten most of the money and was determined that Catherine's children should be Graham's heirs, and not Jesse. Catherine, now Mrs. Daniel McCusker, insisted the letter was a forgery, but it was admitted into evidence.

Finally, it was over. On June 25, court was convened for the summations of the case. Russ Ward reviewed all the evidence and asked why the case had been revived after all these years when Jesse's presence had always been known to the Bennetts. "In the name of mercy," Ward demanded in an emotional tone, "in the name of justice, let this old man go free!"

After a parade of lawyers from both sides had their say, the case was finally given to the jury. That night the trial was discussed on street corners, in homes and in saloons all over California. In Santa Cruz, feelings seemed to have crystallized in favor of the defense. When the jury asked for some documents, it was rumored the members stood nine for acquittal and three for conviction. The general feeling was that they would either disagree or acquit the defendant.

On the morning of June 27, 1888, the jury announced it was deadlocked, with "no probability for an agreement." After polling the jurors, the judge sent them back again, but late that night they again reported that no agreement could be reached. The jury stood ten for acquittal and two for conviction.

Ward immediately applied for bail and asked for a new trial. Jesse took advantage of the recess to catch the train for home. In the "Locals" column on July 10, the Fresno *Daily Evening Expositor* reported, "Jesse Graham was on our streets today greeting old friends."

Editorials in Jesse's defense appeared in the press, while petitions for his release were being circulated. "The law need not stretch out its iron hand for a victim in this case," noted the *Santa Cruz Sentinel*. "It can afford to be merciful towards the defendant and allow him to live the few short years allotted to him in peace." And there was always the practical side to the trial. It had nearly bankrupted the county!

Judge McCann put off fixing the date for a new trial for ten days. On September 8, 1888, however, the indictment against Graham was dismissed and Jesse was free.

Before he left the coast, Jesse spent a week with his half-sister Matilda at her home in Capitola. As he stepped aboard the train leaving for Fresno, the old frontiersman smiled at the sister who had stood by him against her own mother and grandmother. Even at this late date, the terrible feud was still taking its toll.

Over the years, Jesse owned various parcels of land in Fresno County which he farmed with indifferent success. He lost some property in 1892 over an unpaid debt, perhaps connected to the expenses of his trial. He is thought to have lived with the children of his half-brother, Hassel Jewell, for a time, but as he became more and more infirm he probably did not want to burden them. Sometime in the mid-1890s, he moved to Washington state to live with a relative, and died there about 1897.

As history, the feud itself took a back seat to the long-delayed trial of Jesse Graham. Nevertheless, the proceedings are still a little-known incident of California's pioneer days, and one of the more remarkable and bizarre legal cases in California's history.

DOCUMENTS

Elizabeth E. Jones, Mexican War Pension of Jesse Jones Graham, National Archives

Elizabeth E. Jones, various pension application forms for increase in pension, National Archives

Elizabeth E. Jones, U.S. Pension Agency, notice of termination at Jesse's death, National Archives

Elizabeth E. Jones, letters to the author, October, 25, 1995; January 8, May 29, 1996; July 27, 2001

Chapter 2
NOTES

Santa Cruz County Clerk, letters to the author re Graham trial, August 20, 1962

Nathan Sweet, letter and research notes to the author, January 7, 1972

BOOKS

Bancroft, Hubert Howe. *The Works of Hubert Howe Bancroft*, Volume XIX, History of California, Vol. II. 1801–1824. San Francisco: The History Company, Publishers, 1886.

Craig, Donald Monro (ed.). *Letters from California, 1846-1847, William Robert Garner.* Berkeley, Los Angeles, London: University of California Press, 1970.

Crampton, C. Gregory (ed.). *The Mariposa Indian War*, 1850-1851: The Diaries of Robert Eccleston... Salt Lake City: University of Utah Press, 1957.

Hammond, George Peter (ed.). *The Larkin Papers.* Berkeley: University of California Press, 1951–64.

Nunis, Doyce. *The Trials of Isaac Graham*. Los Angeles: Dawson's Book Store, 1967.

NEWSPAPERS

Fresno *Daily Evening Expositor*, April 24, July 10, 1888

Fresno *Morning Republican*, June 10, 14, 15, 19, 28, 1888

Fresno *Weekly Expositor*, April 25, May 2, June 20, 1888

San Francisco *Pacific Daily News*, April 27, May 16, November 26, 1850

San Francisco *Examinber*, June 15, 16, 1888

Santa Cruz Daily Sentinel, April 27, 29, May 1, 4, June 12, 24 - 28, 1888

Stockton Times, March 15, 1851

OTHER SOURCES

Early, Mabel Dorn, "Biographical Narrative of the Bennett Family," *The Pony Express*, September, November 1950.

Secrest, William B., "Trail to Santa Cruz," *Real West*, March 1988.

Chapter 3

Between the Cow and the Plow

The Hazelton - Church Feud

George Stevens' classic film, *Shane*, portrayed a particular moment in American history when homesteaders and their families began the process of settling and civilizing our Western frontier. Fortunately, the acting and breathtaking scenery in the film overwhelmed a hokey plot which could have been lifted from a 1940s B Western movie. Still, it was a film to be enjoyed on many levels. Watching grizzled cattlemen lecture homesteaders about fighting Indians and settling the country, we sat back and nodded knowingly. Now that it was safe, farmers were coming in to take over the open range. We could identify with both sides in the conflict, but when the cattlemen brought in the menacing hired killer, as played by Jack Palance, they quickly assumed the role of villains.

Although heavily dramatized, and sometimes overacted, the film told a true-to-life story of the epic struggle between open range cattlemen and the settlers and sheep men throughout the Trans-Mississippi West. Frequently, these struggles erupted into full-blown range wars, such as the tragic Tonto Basin War in Arizona, Wyoming's Johnson County War, and New Mexico's bloody Lincoln County War. Thankfully, most California feuds were of a less murderous nature, but they were no less disturbing to those involved. Rash, initial conduct was mellowed by contact, compromise, and time, and the West was eventually amicably shared by all sides.

Moses Joshua Church was caught unawares by the attitude of the cattlemen who opposed his farming plans. *Fresno City and County Historical Society.*

Born in Chatauqua County, New York, in 1818, Moses Church early learned the blacksmith trade and worked in Pennsylvania, Alabama, and Georgia. After his marriage to Sarah Whittington, Church continued in iron work, later moving to Indiana. He took his wife and three children to California in 1852, and since there was a great need for iron tools and machinery in the new land, he again took up metal work. It was while helping in the construction of a mining ditch near Diamond Springs that he noticed how some of the diverted water was being used to irrigate various local gardens.

The great San Joaquin Valley of California was at that time primarily a vast desert, roamed by countless herds of elk, deer, and wild horses. The possibility of growing crops by bringing in water must have occurred to Church at this time. But he had a family to feed. In 1854, he moved to Napa County where he again concentrated on the iron business.

On the opposite side of New York state, William Hazelton was born on September 7, 1824, in Albany County. As a young man, Hazelton clerked in a store, but the frontier beckoned. The country was new and growing and he yearned for adventure. He joined the army in 1845 and was

Mariposa in 1859, as it appeared a few years after Hazelton's gambling days there. *California State Library.*

48

stationed in Florida with the Second Dragoons. It was probably during this period that young Hazelton's origins earned him the nickname, "Yank." He had just been discharged when the war with Mexico erupted, and he headed for Texas as a teamster with the army commissary department. He served throughout the war, later returning briefly to New York.

When news of the gold discovery in California electrified the world, it was all the excuse young Hazelton needed to head west again. He spent the winter of 1849 in San Diego, after the long journey across the southern plains route to California. In the spring he headed north for the mining country and worked a claim in Mariposa County. Although he managed to eke out a living as a miner, when times got tough, Yank dealt faro in the Mariposa saloons and gambling halls. Miners and prospectors were everywhere, paying claims were becoming scarce, and it wasn't difficult to see that the mining days were limited. Becoming weary of the hectic life in a mining camp, Yank looked around for a more dependable line of work.

A daguerreotype, apparently made during Yank Hazelton's gambling days, shows him to be a dashing frontiersman ready to go where fortune directed him. *Hazelton family collection.*

Remembering the rich foothill country he had passed through on his way north, in 1853 Hazelton settled on a quarter section of government land some sixty miles to the south. He built a cabin on the Kings River, in what was still Mariposa County. The stock business seemed to be particularly lucrative, with the great influx of immigrants coming into the state. Horses and cattle were worth little in Mexican California, but now prices had increased dramatically. Yank and a friend named William Patterson became partners, but both men also gambled in an attempt to keep food on the table.

Among the first to settle in the area, the two pals found themselves in an isolated foothill area with scattered neighbors and many Indians. The land was rich and promising, and a newly established village called Scottsburg suggested at least a hint of civilization. Founded at the Campbell brothers ferry on the Kings River, the village eventually hosted a grist mill, a few shops, a hotel of sorts, and the inevitable restaurant and saloon, owned by William Scott, the village's namesake.

Yank had known Scott in Mariposa. Having led an adventurous life, Scott's body was described by a friend as being covered with "more wound scars—bullets, knife and arrow—than any human being he had ever known or heard of." The surrounding settlers were engaged in stock raising and agriculture, both to feed their animals and themselves.

One afternoon in Scott's saloon, Hazelton and Patterson sat in on a monte game and began a winning streak that continued into the night. The next morning the tired, but exhilarated, friends left the game with some $20,000 between them. Now they had a stake, and the men swore off gambling.

Mexican vaqueros roamed the plains capturing wild horses, but

An ad for a Scottsburg hotel that appeared in the short-lived *Fresno Times*, February 4, 1865. *Author's collection.*

Centerville about 1900, as it appeared long after its boisterous heydays in the 1870s. *Fresno City and County Historical Society.*

Hazelton and Patterson wanted to start out with blooded stock. Recalling the large California ranches of the Los Angeles area, Hazelton brought twenty brood mares up from Southern California and their venture was launched.

Yank next headed for Mexico where he bought a herd of longhorn steers. He hired several vaqueros for the trip north, but since they were strangers he worried about his safety. He later told his family he slept at night with one eye open for fear his herders might kill him. He was greatly relieved when he was back on the Kings River and could relax.

About this time, Patterson sold out his interest and moved on. Over the years as neighbors left the area, Hazelton bought up their land and soon he was the largest rancher in the area.

Moses Church had encountered only sporadic and limited success after moving to Napa County. From his blacksmithing and iron work, he had gone into sheep raising, but this, too, proved unprofitable when drought made pasturage unavailable. In the summer of 1868, Napa acquaintance A. Y. Easterby suggested he move south and get into agriculture. Easterby owned large tracts of land in the San Joaquin Valley and offered the sheep man a partnership in a farm venture.

Church liked the idea. Moving his family and sheep to the Millerton area on the San Joaquin River, he put in a wheat crop, but the light rainfall that winter proved disastrous on the arid plains. The two men determined that irrigation was the only way to farm successfully. In 1866, Anderson Akers and S. S. Hyde had constructed a canal from the Kings River at a point below the Hazelton ranch. They sold their ditch to the Centerville Canal and Irrigation Company, which sold water to various farms in the area. Another canal operation was under construction by one J. B. Sweem. Since Easterby had other properties in the Kings River area, Church decided to set up his farming operation there after an 1870 survey showed that these canals could successfully be extended to his farm.

Church set about his new project. Besides his new farming operation, he tended his sheep, bought the Sweem ditch and began the task of extending it to the Easterby properties. When the extended ditch intersected the Centerville Canal, Easterby bought that ditch also and continued the extension. No irrigation effort of any substance had been attempted in California up to that point, and the venture began to attract wide interest. There was no doubt in anyone's mind that if farming could be taken out of the hands of nature and a water supply guaranteed, there was a bright agricultural future in the great San Joaquin Valley.

Although the country was still sparsely settled, there had been great changes since Yank Hazelton had established his ranch in the early 1850s. The new counties of Tulare, Merced and Fresno had been carved out of Mariposa County by 1856, breaking up the huge mother county substantially. Scottsburg had suffered severely during the floods of 1861–62 and had been moved down river to higher ground where it was soon superceded by the village of Centerville. Millerton, the county seat, was the only other village of any size in new Fresno County, but a railroad was under development down the valley and new towns were being established. In lieu of this steady growth and promise, the irrigation work of Church and Easterby became all the more important. Writing in the Millerton *Expositor* in March of 1871, a local resident gave some indication of the interest being given Church's work:

> I took a little jaunt over to Pumpkin River, alias Kings River, yesterday, and I must say I was agreeably surprised to see the flourishing condition of that part of our county... Mr. M. J. Church, who is the individual owner of the Sweem ditch, has turned the whole of the water in the canal of the Fresno Canal and Irrigation Company, which is sufficient to meet the present demand for water. Mr. Church offers quite an inducement to settlers. He proposes to furnish all water that can be used on one quarter section of land for the period of fifty years for the sum of $250, and an assessment per annum for keeping up repairs of $16. Just think of it! All the water that can be used for fifty years at such a low figure.

The country was still so new and unsettled that it probably never dawned on Church and Easterby that anyone could possibly object to their venture. After all, this was progress, and progress was what civilization was all about. Some one hundred men were employed in digging the ditch and the workers were spending their pay in the Centerville saloons and stores. Even a local stockman, who admitted to working against the project at first, had come around. Writing in the *Expositor* that same month, he commented favorably on both Church and his ditch project:

> ... I have got to be able to respect any earnest worker, although not working my way. Having been out with our rodeo of horses the other day, it was hailed by our thirsty crowd, horses and men, as second only to a good horn of Len Farrar's coaxing juice. Our cattle too, appeared to enjoy the boon and were as much at home as if a sand-fly never existed. There is one thing about it, the cattle men do not fret over the progress of the ditch— such years as this it is just the thing. I would say to ditch men and settlers, go ahead, don't be alarmed over cattle men; we don't want monopoly; this is a big country—big enough for years to come for all hands and big enough anyhow.

When her husband brought her some oranges from Los Angeles, Mary Jane Hazelton saved the seeds and planted some orange trees. *Hazelton family collection.*

But if this one particular rancher wasn't concerned about the ditch, he was speaking only for himself. Others watched Church's progress with a jaundiced eye. Yank Hazelton heard reports of the ditch and discussed it frequently with his foreman, his cowboys and neighboring ranchers. Hazelton was a power in the county, now. He could not see why the valley had to develop so fast. This was open range—his range. He had been here when there were only Indians and wild animals roaming these dry plains. But if he thought like the typical cattleman, Yank knew the value of irrigation. In 1860, he and several others had built a small ditch in the foothills to water some of their own property. That was different. Now Church had brought in his damned sheep and began construction of a mammoth ditch that would attract farmers from all over. That meant homes and fences around their crops and the end of the open range. Worst of all, this damned ditch was in his very backyard.

Yank did not know just what to do. He had married Mary Jane Akers in 1857, the same year he had acquired title to his government land. Together, they had carved out their little empire in the foothills of the Sierra. When he had driven a herd of cattle to Los Angeles and brought Mary back some oranges as a gift, she had saved the seeds and later planted a small orchard. It was her world, and that of their children, he was fighting for, also. If she counseled him now against violence, he would have paid no attention. He was a family man and did not want trouble, but a man did what he must do.

Meanwhile, the Easterby farm was progressing handsomely, as reported in the *Expositor*, May 15, 1872:

> From Mr. M. J. Church we learn that the crops on the Easterby farm are looking as well as could be desired. The growing grain looks rank and luxuriant and promises as well as any field of grain in the State. The crops of the other farmers in that vicinity look equally well.

And, if some of the stockmen were upset at the farmers invasion of their territory, there was evidence that others realized the futility of trying to impede agricultural growth in the county. Writing to the *Expositor* later that same month, Easterby reported that a group of cattlemen not only warned the local farmers of a cattle roundup, or rodeo, to be held, but stationed their cowboys around the farms to make sure no crops were trampled.

Moses Church was supervising his ditch work one day when a group of horsemen galloped up. Wiping his brow, he looked up and asked what he could do for them. When a bottle was produced and Church was directed to take a drink, he shook his head.

"I thank you, but I never drink," he replied.

"Boys," responded the cowboy leader, "let us all take a drink to convince this old man that we are not going to poison him." Displaying a rope, he continued. "We'll convince him that we'll drag out his existence over the plains if he don't obey our orders."

"And just what are your orders?" asked the puzzled Church.

"That you leave this county at once!"

Church looked around at the men in alarm. He had seen most of them in the stores and saloons at Centerville. He knew several to be herders for Hazelton, but other local ranchers were represented in the group, also. Taken by surprise, Church still stood his ground.

"By what authority do you give me such orders as this?" he asked.

"I am Yank Hazelton's vaquero," responded the leader. "I am representing him. He owns this county and therefore you must leave."

Although intimidated by the hard-looking cowhands, Church stood firm.

"If he owns the land it is unnecessary for you to make any such demonstrations. All I want is to be convinced that he owns it and I will have to see him and make the arrangements."

The riders had obviously been told to see if they could scare off the intruder, and after glancing at each other, they now wheeled their horses and galloped off. Church stared after them. He could only hope the warning would be carried no farther. He probably regretted now, that he had located only a mile from the Hazelton property.

GRAIN. The first grain ever exported from this county to the San Francisco market, was from the farm of Mr A. Y. Easterby on Fancher Creek, and sent forward by rail last week. This is but the beginning, as we are informed quite a number of the farmers in that vicinity contemplate shipping their grain to the market below.

The dreaded news that spelled the end of the cattlemen's open range in Fresno County. *Fresno Weekly Expositor*, July 3, 1872.

It was a few days later that another cowboy delegation appeared and galloped up to where Church was directing a large group of Chinese working on his ditch. Although Church did not know him by sight, Yank Hazelton himself headed the group that reined up and partially surrounded him. Yank looked down at his adversary.

"You have been ordered to leave here several days ago and have had ample time to get out of this country. If you don't obey orders and go, we will have to do what we came here to do and drag your existence out over the plains with that rope. I have had full possession here for seventeen years and I own this land."

Church now realized he was face-to-face with the cattle king, himself. Some years later he recalled using a sarcastic tone when he made his reply.

"From the demonstrations you have been making, I am satisfied you own the land. Now, what are your orders?"

"You see that band of sheep over yonder?" responded the cattleman. "We found your boy with them and we ordered him to get behind them and not stop until he was out of the county and he is obeying like a little man. You must get in behind them and get out as fast as you can. I am Yank Hazelton."

Church felt helpless and could do little but glower at his tormentors.

"Your request, Mr. Hazelton, is unreasonable and unjust. I can't leave my house, my horses, and grain. Besides, it is nearly night."

Yank turned to his men.

"Well, boys, this is pretty plain talk. What should we do with him?" Paul Stover, a German carpenter in Hazelton's employ, grinned. "If he no go, his cattles is all dead. If he stay I be the carpenter and I makes his little house for him"—a reference to a coffin.

Church reiterated his position, adding that a nearby friend was witnessing what was taking place.

"Give me a reasonable time to gather my things and I will go."

Yank (center) and his vaqueros working cattle. An undated photo, but probably in the 1880s. *Hazelton family collection.*

"I'll give you until tomorrow morning at nine o'clock," replied Yank. "We will be here and if you are not gone, we'll carry out our designs so as not to be bothered with you any longer."

Wheeling his horse, the cattle king galloped off at the head of his men.

Early the next morning Church rode off to make preparations to move. He had no intention of leaving the area, planning merely to shift his location. He returned to find several tons of his hay a smoldering pile of ashes and his house and barn torn down. He knew now the cattlemen meant business, but he still determined to stay.

After moving to a new location, he resumed his ditch work, but tried to keep his guard up. He had heard the rumors of dead men being found in the hills from time to time. "Rustlers," the stories always went. Still, he was going to stay.

One day Church had a clandestine visitor. He was one of Hazelton's men named Ayers and he warned of a plot on the ditch builder's life. Bill Caldwell, one of the Glenn boys, and a man named Hutchison were also involved in the plan. Church didn't place any credence in the story until a few days later when another of the cowboys warned him again. This time details of the ambush were spelled out.

They were to lie in wait for him in Centerville at Jacob and Silverman's store. When Church came in to pick up his mail, Glenn was to spit tobacco juice in his eye and when the ditch man resented it in any way, they were to shoot him down and claim self-defense. Again, Church assumed they were only trying to frighten him. One day while picking up his mail, however, he saw Glenn in the store. Slipping into a back room, Church made a hasty exit via a rear door and quickly made his way out of town.

Later, Church was once again warned of a pending assassination plot. This time Bill Caldwell and Glenn were to ride over to Church's house, call him out to their buggy, and Glenn would insult him. Knowing the scenario, when the two men appeared in a buggy one day and called for him to come out, Church sent his wife

The Centerville Hotel was a prominent stopping place in the upper Kings River country.
Fresno City and County Historical Society.

and daughter out instead. The two ranchers were caught off guard. As the women bantered with them, Church strolled out and asked what they wanted. Caldwell immediately accused him of trying to steal a horse, but Church made light of the accusation, and the two men gave up and drove away. They couldn't start anything as long as Mrs. Church and her daughter stood by watching everything.

In early July of 1872, John W. Ferguson, the *Expositor* editor, rode over from Millerton to where a new town was being built along the railroad. The new station was called Fresno, and along with a collection of tents, a hotel, several stores, and a stable were in operation. Other construction was underway, and two more "horse restaurants" were contemplated, along with a butcher shop. The editor also drove over to the nearby Easterby farm and described the operation:

> ... Here, stretching away in every direction as far as the eye can reach is one grand field of grain. Three herders and a steam thresher and upwards of fifty hands have been at work for several weeks in harvesting the crop and there is still some three weeks work left on hand. Forty tons of wheat per day is being shipped to San Francisco by rail... A branch of the Fresno Irrigation Company's ditch extends through the farm...

Although Church had no doubt informed Easterby of the threats and harassment of Hazelton and other ranchers, there was little they could do. Besides being politically powerful, the ranchers were very careful about any overt acts of violence.

On August 14, 1872, the *Expositor* announced the arrival of some of the local absentee landowners on a visit:

> On last Saturday morning a party of the large land owners of this county arrived at Fresno on the train from San Francisco. They were met at the depot by Mr. M. J. Church and immediately started on a tour of inspection along the canal of the Fresno Irrigation Company. Among the party were Messers A. Y. Easterby and W. S. Chapman. This grand irrigation enterprise is attracting much attention from those searching for places to settle...

One day Church and Easterby rode into Centerville to pick up their mail. The village at this time consisted of two general stores, a hotel, Leonard Farrar's saloon, a blacksmith shop, and a wheelwright shop. The latter also did duty as an undertaker and coffins were manufactured as needed. "The town presented a lively appearance," noted an early resident. "Mustangs were tied to every available fence post and quite a motley assortment of men, each one with an old fashioned six-shooter belted to his waist, left no doubt of its pioneer characteristics."

The two farmers had no sooner entered the store than a crowd of stockmen came in, led by Bill Caldwell and Tom Bates. Caldwell immediately accused Easterby of stock theft, which Easterby hotly denied. It was just the opening Caldwell was looking for, and he knocked Easterby into a stack of canned goods. Scrambling to his feet, the farmer dodged out a back door, leaving his partner alone in the store. Caldwell now attacked Church, knocking him against a

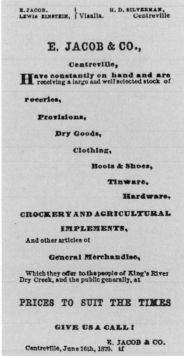

A sampling of the stock of a general store on the frontier appears in this advertisement for the E. Jacob & Co. store, where Church's big fight took place.
• *Fresno Weekly Expositor*, October 2, 1872.

counter with a haymaker to the jaw. Looking up, the ditch man now saw a pistol in the hand of his antagonist, and he quickly dodged behind a counter. Rushing towards the nearest exit, Church was grabbed violently by a cursing Tom Bates. Not caring for the general atmosphere in the place, Church pulled away, leaving most of his shirt and coat sleeve in Bates' hand.

Outside, Church saw a friend in a wagon and ran over and explained the situation as he climbed aboard. An old newspaper account described what happened next:

> ... They then began hunting for Easterby and found him one of the maddest men in the county. The cowboys had gone and Easterby immediately sent for Lawyer Brown of Visalia and Judge Sayle of Millerton. They both came, but nothing was done. Nothing could be done at that time with safety.

If Easterby wasn't convinced of the dangerous resolve of some of the stock raisers before, he certainly was now. He was probably relieved when business dictated he catch the next train back to the Bay Area. Church went back to work, not knowing just what to expect next.

Later that same month, a final confrontation took place. Again, the battleground was the dusty village of Centerville. Church's buggy rattled into town and pulled up in front of Jacobs and Silverman's store. After tying his team, Church entered the store and walked

Bill Caldwell's home in Centerville.
Author's collection.

One of the Easterby and Church ditch-digging crews stop to pose for the photographer.
Fresno City and County Historical Society.

toward the post office, which was located in the rear. Bill Glenn eyed the ditch man with disdain. The German Paul Stover sat on the counter, while George Smith lounged near the rear post office door. It was no time to hesitate, and Church proceeded on his course toward the rear of the store. As Church walked down the narrow aisle, Smith suddenly threw a handful of sand into his eyes, then struck him a powerful blow in the face. Staggered, Church managed to stay on his feet, while rage and self-preservation took over his actions. Attacking Smith with fists flying, he forced his antagonist back toward the post office door. Stover was still sitting on the counter, and as the struggling men passed before him, he kicked Church in the jaw, knocking him off balance. Ignoring his new attacker, Church kept on battling Smith and had nearly forced him back to the rear door when Bill Glenn took a hand. Standing on top of a pile of sacks, Glenn aimed a vicious kick at the ditch man's head, only to have his foot grasped and to be flipped onto the floor.

Rushing past the surprised Smith, Church ran out the back door and around to the street, where he confronted another group of cowboys. His shirt was ripped, and he was covered with blood, but he must have been so battered he no longer cared what happened.

"If you want to kill me," he shouted, "why don't you do it? If you want to whip me, why don't you come one at a time? Now's your opportunity and I'll give you the best I've got."

An account of the confrontation doesn't say how the stockmen responded to the challenge, but they must have been caught off balance. Tom Bates and Alburtus Akers walked toward him, reportedly with pistols in their hands. As they neared Church, however, they suddenly parted and walked over to Len Farrar's saloon. The rest of the crowd followed.

William Glenn was involved in the Centerville fight with Church. *Author's collection.*

Church didn't expect the group to do any soul-searching in the gin mill. He had a strong suspicion they were going to tank up and be meaner than ever. He heard them call for whiskey as he climbed into his buggy and clattered off down the road. On the way back to the head gate of his ditch, he stopped at the home of a friend and explained what had happened. F. E. DeWolf was shocked at his friend's appearance. After listening to the story, DeWolf rushed into his house and returned carrying a pistol.

"Here, take this. Do not disgrace it, nor allow yourself to be disgraced while you carry it."

Church accepted the weapon with reservations. He had never carried a pistol, but the events of that day certainly had been excuse enough for arming himself. As he shoved the weapon in his coat pocket, he could see a dust cloud toward Centerville, and he knew what that meant. Thanking his friend, he again clattered off down the road.

William Alburtus Akers was another Hazelton ally involved in the cattlemen-farmers fight. *Author's collection.*

As the camp of his ditch crew came into view, Church knew he had won his race. Pulling his lathered horse up before W. S. Powell, his foreman, Church jumped down and explained what had happened. Some dozen white men and seventy-five Chinese workers leaned on their shovels and wondered what was happening. Telling Church to get down in the ditch, Powell ordered his workers to

Moses Church had many friends and a successful business career. Today, he is known as the father of irrigation in the county. *Fresno City and County Historical Society.*

arm themselves if they had weapons, as there was going to be another confrontation with stockmen.

Reining up, the riders called for Powell and the foreman walked over and asked what they wanted. "We're looking for Church," yelled several of the group. Powell told them he was nearby and the riders decided on diplomacy. Producing a bottle, one said:

"Where is he? We want to treat him."

"Well," growled Powell, "Mr. Church don't drink. I would advise you to go away peaceably, for if you attempt any injury to him or his property you will be riddled with bullets. Every Chinaman here is armed with a pistol and they will use them if any violent demonstration is made against Mr. Church."

It was a sobering comment. As the stockmen looked around, wondering what to do next, Powell took a healthy pull on the proffered bottle, then passed it back. The stockmen exchanged confused glances and muttered curses, then spun their horses about and galloped off. Climbing out of the ditch, the battered Church watched the cavalcade disappear toward Centerville.

On August 28, 1872, a letter appeared in the *Expositor* giving an account of the brawl in the Centerville store. It was signed "An eyewitness." On September 11 another letter was published, giving the stockmen's version of the incident:

> ... If "Eyewitness" was so informed his informant was either a stupid jackass that knew nothing of what he was talking, or a wilful and malicious liar. We say we were not following Church, that we called upon Powell as friends, in a friendly manner... "Eyewitness" says that there was no cause for the attack on Church, but the energy displayed by him in taking out the waters of Kings River. If

"Eyewitness" does not know of any other cause he had better quit slinging ink on the subject. Church and Smith have had a long and bitter contest on a pre emption claim in which as it now stands Smith believes he has been, through false swearing and otherwise, wrongfully worsted ... This was the cause of the attack, and had "Eyewitness" been a fair-minded man he could easily have known it before he rushed into print to vilify the character of those who have been, and are desirous of, having peace in this neighborhood.

A. W. Akers, B. Akers, Thos. Bates

Yank's wife, the former Mary Jane Akers, had arrived in California by wagon train in late 1852. She had accompanied her parents, five brothers and three sisters, most of whom settled in the Kings River area. Late of Kentucky and Texas, the Akers boys were tough and rowdy frontiersmen who quite naturally sided with their brother-in-law, Yank Hazelton, in his troubles with Church. Tom Bates, another of the local stockmen, had been involved in several of the Church incidents, also.

William Hazelton lost his feud with the homesteaders, but won the respect of his neighbors. The Hazeltons and their rancher allies have always been prominent Fresno County citizens. *Hazelton family collection.*

Records in the state assessor's office in late 1873 show just why the stockmen feared and resented the farmers in the area. While Church held only 800 acres, W. S. Chapman owned over 100,000 acres, Easterby over 2,500 acres and another owner had over 128,000 acres. Listed were more than ten farms of over 20,000 acres each. Although rancher John Sutherland, on the lower Kings River, held over 12,000 acres, most of the cattlemen held much smaller land parcels; Hazelton 2,143 acres, Jesse Blasingame 871 acres, and Tom Fowler 6,380 acres. The days of the open range were clearly, and rapidly, coming to an end.

When the "No Fence Law" was passed in California in 1874, the restrictions on the cattlemen were such that they were forced to fence in their stock and limit their acreage. Yank Hazelton and others had already dabbled in farming for their own purposes. Now many men began farming more extensively, some even bringing in sheep. Hazelton's home faced his ten acres of orange groves and other crops. Always a leader of his community, Yank established the first schoolhouse in the area. In the autumn of his life he took great pride and pleasure in his family and the empire they had created. When he died in July of 1906, the *Sanger Herald* noted: "He will be missed by home circles of relatives and friends for he was a kind and obliging father and neighbor."

Moses Church also went on with his successful career as a farmer, mill owner and irrigation pioneer. Worth nearly half a million dollars at one point, at the time of his death on March 20, 1900, he had lost most of his holdings and was living quietly at a mountain sanitarium he had established. His place in California history was emphasized by the first line of his obituary in the *Fresno Morning Republican:*

> M. J. Church, the father of irrigation in this county, died at 5 o'clock yesterday morning at his home at Oakdale, Calaveras County. He passed away, full of years, and with his children about his bedside.

Hazelton's granddaughter, Sophia Hazelton Gerner, once commented on the celebrated confrontations between Yank and Moses Church: "I guess grandfather was a pretty strict old man, but there wasn't the feeling between the two men after the confrontation that there had been. Grandfather asked Moses Church to dinner, and he came and Grandfather entertained him in his home after they had settled their differences. ...Whether they really settled up their troubles, at least, they weren't enemies."

And maybe that was the best you could hope for in the sometimes deadly conflicts between the cow and the plow.

DOCUMENTS

Document, Register of San Francisco U.S. Land Office, one hundred and eighty-six acres to William Hazelton, November 16, 1857

Humphries, J. W., "Mono Trail," unpublished manuscript by the son of an early sawmill operator on Pine Ridge, who supplied the lumber to build Centerville. June English Collection, Special Collections, California State University Library, Fresno

Russell, Fern Brophy and Diane Tjerrild, "Moses Joshua Church, The Father of Irrigation in Fresno County," Typescript in collection of author, courtesy the late Judy Hazelton Hill

Chapter 3
NOTES

BOOKS

Clough, Charles W. and William B. Secrest, Jr. *Fresno County: The Pioneer Years.* Fresno: Panorama West Books, 1984.

Elliot, Wallace W., publisher. *History of Fresno County, California.* San Francisco, 1881.

Hull, Donna M. *And Then There Were Three Thousand.* Fresno: self-published, 1975.

Thompson, Thomas H. *Official Historical Atlas Map of Fresno County.* Tulare: Thos. H. Thompson, 1891.

NEWSPAPERS

Fresno Bee, February 19, 1956

Fresno Times, February 4, 1865

Fresno Guide, August 18, 1971

Fresno Weekly Expositor, February 22, March 15, 22, 29, November 22, 1871; May 15, 22, June 5, July 3, 10, August 14, August 28, September 11, September 18, October 2, 1872; November 3, 1873

Fresno *Daily Evening Expositor*, December 25, 1895, October 24, 1926

Fresno Morning Republican, March 21, 1900; October 24, 1926

Millerton *Expositor*, March 1871

Sanger Herald, July 1906

OTHER SOURCES

Author unknown. "Centerville's History Contrasts Serenity and Turmoil." *Fresno Past & Present*, Journal of the Fresno City and County Historical Society, June 1970

Cowbelles, Fresno County. "Cattle and Courage: Fresno County's Cattle History." *Fresno Past & Present*, Journal of the Fresno City and County Historical Society, June 1967.

Gerner, Sophia Hazelton. "William Hazelton, My Grandfather," *Ash Tree Echo.* Fresno Genealogical Society, Sept.–Oct. 1966.

Patterson, William B., "All Hail Father of Irrigation," undated clipping, the *Fresno Bee.*

Wardlaw, Muriel. "Personal Interview with Fresno County Pioneer Sophia Hazelton Gerner,." *Ash Tree Echo*, Fresno Genealogical Society, January, 1983.

Author's interviews with the late Judy Hazelton Hill, who also read the preliminary manuscript in September 1994.

Chapter 4

Deadlines and Detectives

Mark Twain's Feud with the San Francisco Police

Samuel Clemens, an erstwhile Mississippi river-boat pilot, traveled west in 1861. He was accompanied by his brother, Orion, who had been appointed secretary to the governor of Nevada Territory. As he rumbled over the wide plains and mountains of the West in mud wagons and the big red Concord stagecoaches, the twenty-six-year-old Sam Clemens had much time to think. He only planned to stay in the West for three months. His brother's destination was Carson City, the capital of the new territory. Young Sam was ostensibly to work for his brother, but he was much more interested in seeing gold mines, Indians, buffalo, bears, and mighty rivers. Then, he would return to his home, and civilization.

Arriving at Carson City in August 1861, young Clemens was strangely fascinated by the barren wastes surrounding the capital. He was well aware that this was mining country. Some twenty miles to the northeast was the booming silver camp of Virginia City and various surrounding mining towns. This was the fabled Comstock Lode. Marked by the 8,000-foot Sun Mountain, the area was fabulously wealthy, with a steady stream of wagons leaving town carrying bullion to the banks of San Francisco.

With little to do at his job, young Sam Clemens began prospecting with friends, participating in the stampedes to the new discover-

Carson City at about the time Sam Clemens and his brother arrived in town. *Author's collection.*

ies at Humboldt and Esmeralda. Soon the three months had languished into six. In the evenings, the budding miner wrote letters and kept his journal. He also wrote several amusing letters to the Virginia City *Territorial Enterprise*. In early 1862, Sam was surprised to see them published under his pseudonym, "Josh." He was prospecting in Aurora at the time and when *Enterprise* editor Joe Goodman offered him a job as a stringer, or correspondent, he jumped at the opportunity.

Writing appealed to the erstwhile miner. Back home in Missouri he had done some writing and set type at a local newspaper. During his riverboat days as a pilot on the Mississippi, he had once written and submitted a humorous article to the New Orleans *Crescent* describing the high water of the river. He had signed his long piece, "Sergent Fathom," and it is reportedly his first published work. When Goodman offered him a job on the *Enterprise* at twenty-five dollars a week, Sam moved to Virginia City and happily took up his new career.

The budding reporter, Sam Clemens. *California State Library*

Although he complained at first about the lack of excitement in the silver town, 1863 was to be a premier year for knifings and shooting scrapes. There was much other news, however. Besides political and mining reports, local gossip, fires, theater reviews, and new gold and silver strikes, Clemens and fellow newsmen Dan DeQuill, Joe Goodman, and

Rollin Daggett delighted in perpetrating hoaxes and creating other literary mischief. They were a rowdy crew. All were young men in their prime and having the time of their lives. Clemens, particularly, was not as concerned with "who, what, where, and why" in his reporting as he was with the entertainment value of his writing. It was a time in which the more daring of the *Enterprise's* editors and reporters delighted in making a full column of a mere paragraph's worth of news, padding it out with their imagination and wit.

Dan DeQuill (William Wright) had a strong influence on young Clemens' philosophy and style. *California State Library.*

A rival reporter was not amused at Clemens' imaginative reporting style, however:

> His satire tends to the amusement of his publishers only, when he ornaments a church item with such a remark as 'dusty old Christian'; or when, in describing a public school, he rides to the humorous necessity of mentioning 'an auburn-haired juvenile, who wiped his nose with his fingers in so audible a manner as to require due castigation from the teacher...'

Despite his critics, these formative days on the *Enterprise* were the mold from which was to spring one of the most prodigious and enterprising humorists this country was to produce.

In February 1863, while in Carson City to cover the political scene, Clemens had an idea. As an attention-getting device, he wanted to sign off his dispatch with a pseudonym, rather than his real name. "Josh," his previous pen name, did not ring any bells, nor did "Sergent Fathom," his Mississippi cognomen. This latter appellation, however, reminded him of an old riverboat pilot named Isaiah Sellers. In various news items Sellers sent to the New Orleans *Picayune*, he ascribed the source as "Mark Twain." It was an old river term used in reporting the depth of water. Clemens later wrote that he "had laid violent hands on it [Sellers' sobriquet] without asking permission of the proprietor's remains." There are other stories of the origins of his pseudonym, but from the time he first signed his new pen name, Sam Clemens became spiritually, and irrevocably, the superlative Mark Twain.

By early 1864, "Mark Twain" was an experienced reporter. When editor Joe Goodman decided on a Lake Tahoe vacation, Mark was given the editorial chores with which to wrestle and apparently did a creditable job. But, it just was not his cup of tea. When the added responsibilities cut into his drinking time, he began sending telegrams to his boss pleading for an early return. Goodman ignored the queries. He was thoroughly enjoying his richly deserved outing. This prompted more serious action by his proxy editor, or, so the story goes.

When Goodman received a copy of the *Enterprise* containing a collection of libelous articles concerning Virginia City's most prominent citizens, he gasped in amazement. He nearly fainted when he noted the same page featured an editorial piece labeling the city's most distinguished and charitable women as something less than virtuous. The horrified editor leapt on his horse and made better time between Tahoe and Virginia City than a Pony Express courier.

Confronting Twain with the offending edition, Goodman was alternately relieved and furious to learn that only the one copy of

Virginia City, when Sam Clemens knew it, was the richest and most boisterous boom town in the West. *California State Library.*

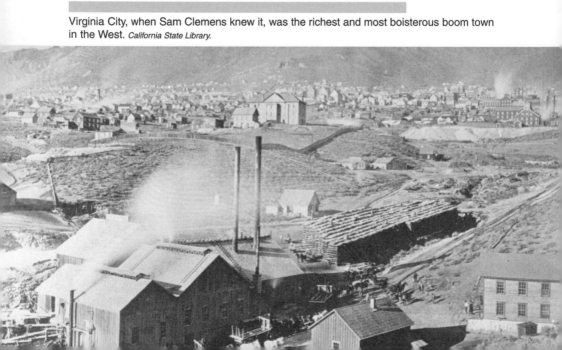

the *Enterprise* he had received had been printed and sent to him at Tahoe. The type had then been reset and the regular edition set up and run off. We can assume that Goodman stayed close to the office for a long time after this incident.

But Twain was becoming restless. Perhaps the mining news, the shootings, and politics had a repetitive and too familiar ring. Or, perhaps his mother's suggestion that he move to San Francisco was beginning to make sense. He had visited the Bay city on several occasions and was indeed charmed. Still, he hesitated to leave his friends. Stories later circulated that he left town because of involvement in a Daggett-inspired duel, but this seems unlikely. Twain himself later wrote that he planned to go to New York to sell some local mining stocks. After arriving in San Francisco in May 1864, however, the bottom fell out of his Comstock stocks and he was forced to reassess his situation. Out of necessity, and a sense of impending hunger, he found himself a reporter on the San Francisco *Daily Morning Call*. His pay was thirty-five dollars a week.

Rollin Daggett was another fun-loving *Enterprise* reporter who taught Sam Clemens the business. *California State Library.*

As the newspaper's "Locals Editor," Mark scarcely had time to enjoy his new position. At nine in the morning he had to be in police court where he made notes on the previous night's events. Next, he visited the higher courts and recorded all the recent decisions. During the rest of the day he scoured the town for news. The upside of this was that much of the news could be found in the better-class saloons.

In the evenings he attended the city's six theaters and scribbled critiques of the performances. By eleven at night he began writing up all his notes to meet a two o'clock deadline. "It was fearful drudgery," Twain later commented, and if he had not been able to add his own brand of color and humor to his reporting, the job would have been intolerable. He was only half joking when he once suggested, "If there were no fires, we started some." And this is where the trouble originated.

Twain was no longer in a rowdy mining town. Candor was wanted in the Bay city, and the endless pumping up of mediocre news and trivializing of important items were frowned on by the *Call*'s management. "That kind of reporting," recalled James J. Ayers, one of the *Call*'s owners, "in a civilized community, where the plain, unvarnished truth was an essential element in the duties of a reporter, could hardly be deemed satisfactory."

An example of Twain's reportorial style was his article describing the city's earthquake on June 22, 1864: "...We are happy to state that they are shaking her up from below now," he wrote. "The shocks last night came straight up from that direction; and it is sad to reflect, in these spiritual times, that they might possibly have been freighted with urgent messages from some of our departed friends..."

Ayers and the other owners of the *Call* began dropping hints to Mark that he could perhaps do better if he looked for work elsewhere. Feeling no doubt that he was unappreciated, the locals reporter began to get sloppy. Besides spending too much time on his write-ups, he was spending too much time in saloons between assignments. After composing an item about a Chinese man being assaulted by some white thugs while a police officer stood by, he found the article had been relegated to the culled stack. Puzzled, Twain asked managing editor George Barnes why his

Old San Francisco during Civil War days, when Mark Twain was warming up the town with his pithy columns deriding Chief Burke and his police.
California State Library.

piece had not been printed. The Irish residents of the state hated the Chinese, replied Barnes. The Irish were also big subscribers to the *Call*. Any future articles on such subjects, cautioned the editor, must be carefully phrased. Mark Twain was not happy. In October 1864, he resigned from the *Morning Call* and looked for an employer more receptive to his own ideas about creativity and morality.

This was the best thing that could have happened to him. Although out of work for several months and continually stalked by creditors, Mark gradually began submitting articles to other newspapers and journals—stories on his own subjects and in his own style. Eventually, the *Golden Era,* the *Californian,* and the *Sacramento Union* all entertained their readers with his unique style of writing and subject matter. He also served as the drama critic for the new *Daily Dramatic Chronicle* and was the Coast correspondent for his old employer, the *Territorial Enterprise* in Virginia City.

Now he was free. He knew the ropes and where to find news, but he could write on any subject that could be made amusing through the use of his bottomless supply of wit and irreverence. Although whispering groups at church socials might be aghast at his columns, the fancy saloons and clubs on Montgomery Street echoed with the laughter engendered by his criticism of municipal politics, personalities, fashion, or opera. Still, he wanted more. Even during his newspaper career, Twain had experienced feuds with rival reporters. It was something about which everyone in town was aware... and enjoyed thoroughly. That was what he needed now. All he required was a target.

Just what crystallized Mark's antagonism toward Police Chief Martin J. Burke and his men is not clear. Indeed, several *Call* articles indicate he admired the man. That admiration undoubtedly had its genesis in Burke and his police force's generous contributions to the Sanitary Commission, the care of wounded soldiers during the Civil War. This would soon change, however.

Burke, a London physician, had emigrated to America and practised medicine in Milwaukee before joining the California Gold Rush in 1850. On the Coast, he operated two successful drugstores and a foundry. Dr. Burke's membership in the 1856 San Francisco Vigilance Committee undoubtedly influenced him to run for the office of police chief, and he was elected in 1858.

Few could deny that Burke was an untiring and efficient officer, but Mark Twain came to view him as a rather pompous dictator who maintained his police empire by high-handed tactics. And he was right, up to a point. Burke was a good politician. He preserved his position by obtaining as much good press as was possible, by utilizing the services of many of his men during election campaigns and by weeding ambitious officers from the department. He also saw to it that his detective force—one of the finest in the country— was thrust into the limelight as often as possible.

The genesis of Twain's animosity toward the police might very well have been generated during his days on the *Call*. His daily attendance in police court was an extremely sordid experience as evidenced by his description of the place.

Police Chief Martin Burke.
Robert Chandler collection.

If I were Police Judge here, I would hold my court in the city prison and sentence my convicts to imprisonment in the present Police Court Room. That would be my capital punishment...

The room is about 24 x 40 feet in size, I suppose and is blocked in on all sides by massive brick walls; it has three or four doors, but they are never opened... There is not a solitary air-hole as big as your nostril about the whole place. ...Down two sides of the room, drunken filthy loafers, thieves, prostitutes, China chicken-stealers, witnesses and slimy guttersnipes who come to see, and belch and issue deadly smells, are...packed, four ranks deep— a solid mass of rotting, steaming corruption...

Here he observed the raw workings of the law: the lying witnesses, grubbing attorneys, and limitless shady dealings that passed for law in old San Francisco. Also, as a reporter he had seen much of the back-alley side of police work. Officers were frequently involved in returning stolen property, then splitting rewards with the thief. And, it was not uncommon for policemen to inquire about the availability of rewards before even trying to recover stolen goods. Twain accepted as fact an assertion in a local publication that a retired policeman had recently built a $25,000 home on his own lot. The Chinese incident which the *Call* refused to print, also still rankled and helped shape the feud he now deliberately fomented with Chief Burke and his minions.

Personal matters also contributed to his sour and surly temperament. His father had left a substantial piece of Tennessee property to his children, and Mark wanted his brother to sell the property to a large wine-making operation. His share would be about $100,000 and would allow the budding humorist to not only return home, but to do so in the style befitting a blossoming (and perhaps even successful) writer. In a later letter to his brother, Mark would pen his feelings that he was "tired of being chained to this accursed desert. I want to go back to a Christian land once more."

His brother, a temperance man, would not consider such a sale, and Mark was left to stew in his San Francisco creative juices. This added to a newly-formed, skeptical outlook on life that spared neither morals or religion. Fortunately, Mark was able to successfully encompass his new outlook on life into his writing.

As early as June 19, 1865, Mark had initiated his criticism of the San Francisco police. His article in the *Daily Dramatic Chronicle* was mild in tone and likely was not intended as the beginning of a feud.

> We regard Mayor Coon's proposition to reduce the pay of policemen as shockingly immoral. How are the policemen going to live on less than $125 per month? Does Mayor Coon wish to drive the police to the necessity of practising the arts for which it is their duty to protect society against? We understand that there are not more than a dozen policemen who have accumulated $100,000 worth of real estate on salaries of $125 per month. This is creditable. But if

their salaries are reduced, of course they will be obliged to make up the deficiency 'outside.'

It was not so much that Mark was mad at the police, mind you. It was just that he wanted to do something to stir things up. He was weary of reporting. There was only so much you could do to liven up the news. He wanted to entertain, not merely inform. Most of all, he wanted to become known and to call attention to himself and stir up the public's interest.

When several friends chuckled over his police article, Mark got an idea. There was little to criticize in 1860s San Francisco. It compared favorably to any city in the nation. In fact, only New York, Boston, and New Orleans could boast a larger share of the country's foreign commerce. Farm products and local industrial goods were being shipped to New York and all parts of the Pacific. The city was booming. But the police might very well be worth writing about. He recalled how a friend of his had been mistreated by an overzealous police officer in June of 1864. The police, he decided, were long overdue for a roasting that would net himself some deserved notice as well. But Mark was writing for various newspapers and publications at the time and it was not until late in the year that he dashed off the following epistle to the *Territorial Enterprise*, for which he served as a correspondent:

THIEF CATCHING

One may easily find room to abuse as many as several members of Chief Burke's civilian army for laziness and uselessness, but the detective department is supplied with men who are sharp, shrewd and always on the alert... An ordinary policeman is chosen with special reference to large stature and... muscle, and he only gets $125 a month, but the detective pays better than a lucky faro bank. A shoemaker can tell by a single glance at a boot whose shop it

Frederick L. Amling was a San Francisco police officer in the days when Twain was making a living belittling Chief Burke and his men. *Kevin Mullen collection.*

comes from, by some peculiarity of workmanship; but to a barkeeper all boots look alike.

Detective Rose can pick up a chicken's tail feather in Montgomery street and tell in a moment what roost it came from at the Mission...

Detective Blitc can hunt down a transgressing hack-driver by some peculiarity in the style of his blasphemy...

The forte of Lees and Ellis is the unearthing of embezzlers and forgers. Each of these men are best in one particular line, but at the same time they are good in all... The detectives are smart, but I remarked to a friend that some of the other policemen are not. He said the remark was unjust—that those other policemen were as smart as they could afford to be at $125 a month. It was not a bad idea. Still, I contend that some of them could not afford to be Daniel Websters, maybe, for any amount of money...

Writing under the name "Fitz Smythe," *Alta* editor Albert S. Evans was Twain's nemesis. *Courtesy the Bancroft Library.*

This was pretty tame stuff, but it seemed to indicate Twain's criticism was directed towards Chief Burke and his regular officers. The detectives usually received more cautious treatment.

Captain of Detectives Isaiah W. Lees had been on the force since 1853 and was famous across the country. Henry Ellis and others of the sleuthing corps were equally noted. For some reason, Twain genuinely admired George Rose, referring to him as "one of the coolest, shrewdest members of the detective force." On several occasions he played up the detective's exploits in his articles. Several years later, however, Rose was dismissed from the force for neglect of duty. The erstwhile lawman moved to Utah where he was later a suspect in a train robbery.

Mark was an equal opportunity feudist, however. When he noticed Albert S. Evans, city editor of the *Daily Alta California*, consistently praising the police under his byline of "Fitz Smythe," Twain began lambasting him, as well. The two newspapermen were just getting warmed up by each other's insults, when Mark decided a rowdy bender was in order. Accordingly, one night he and several friends engaged in a campaign to seriously diminish the city's liquor supply. It was a dandy of a carouse. When he woke up in the city prison the next morning, he had trouble focusing his blurred vision on the countenance of "Fitz Smythe," as his rival leered at him through the prison bars. Mark knew he was in for it now and Evans did not disappoint him.

Mark Twain during his salad days in San Francisco. From here, greatness would be thrust upon him. *California State Library.*

In several letters to the Nevada *Gold Hill News* later that month, Fitz started the ball rolling by suggesting that "sagebrush Bohemians" (his favorite term for Twain) could avoid spending nights in jail if they sought the company of gentlemen when on a toot, rather than "Pacific Street Jayhawkers." Fitz cautioned that when being taken to the Station House "...do not lay down on the ground and compel them to drag you... Dragging your legs on the sidewalk always aggravates a policeman, and you are apt to get kicks for your pains... When you have been searched, and your tobacco and toothpick [knife] safely locked up, go quietly into the cell and lay down on your blankets, instead of standing at the grating cursing and indulging in obscene language until they lock you up."

No one was surprised when Twain ignored his transgression and merely stepped up his campaign against both Fitz and the police. Now, however, he had something to really be mad about! In a letter dated January 11, 1866, and published in the *Territorial Enterprise*, Mark served up the following delicious attack on both the police and his arch enemy, Fitz Smythe. The main point, of course, was to ridicule what Twain considered editor Evans' constant lauding of local police work:

GORGEOUS NEW ROMANCE BY FITZ SMYTHE!

The usual quiet of our city was rudely broken in upon this morning by the appearance in the *Alta* of one of those terrible solid column romances about the hair-breadth escapes and prodigies of detective sagazity [sic] of the San Francisco police—written by the felicitous novelist, Fitz Smythe. It is put up in regular chapter, with subheadings, as is Fitz Smythe's custom, when he fulminates a stunning sensation.

Chapter I is headed "The Koinickers"—dark and mysterious.

Chapter II is headed "A New Koinicker in the Field"—the plot thickens.

Then comes Chapter III "The Police after him!"—exciting times.

Chapter IV "The Decoy Duck"—more mystery.

Chapter V "The New Decoy"—the red hand of crime begins to show—somewhere.

Chapter VI "The Arrest"—startling situation, thunder and lightning—blue lights.

Chapter VII "The Queer Obtained!"—thrilling revelations.

Chapter VIII "The Conviction"—closing in, closing in; the wicked are about to be punished...

Chapter IX "Conclusion"—The scattered threads are drawn together into one woof; the bad characters are sent to prison, to go thence to hell; detective Lees marries detective Ellis; Chief Burke elevates his eyes and hands over the two kneeling figures and says unctuously, "God bless you my children—God bless you!" All the characters are happy, even down to Fitz Smythe and his horse—the former in a chance to go through a Chinese funeral dinner, and the latter in the opportunity of eating up a tank of warm asphaltum while the workmen are gone to dinner.

William Farrell, alias Minnie Price, the counterfeiter alluded to by Twain. *Author's collection.*

The long article detailed Captain Lees and his men's unraveling of a counterfeiting operation by using several snitches and stool pigeons to gain the confidence of, and capture, the gang. Twain complained loudly (and humorously) about the police using criminals and jailbirds in the course of their work, but in the end had to admit the "two pigeons worked the case through to a successful conclusion." Twain continued:

Farrell's counterfeit money was captured and Farrell himself sent to the penitentiary. As is entirely proper, Fitz Smythe gives the credit to detective Lees, and glorifies him to the skies. There is the romance—all there is of it worth knowing or printing—yet it is turned into a novel of ten distinct chapters...

On January 21, 1866, another scathing attack was published in the San Francisco *Golden Era*, as reprinted from the *Territorial Enterprise:*

WHAT HAVE THE POLICE BEEN DOING?

Ain't they virtuous? Don't they take good care of the city? ...Isn't it shown in the fact that although many offenders of importance go unpunished, they infallibly snaffle every Chinese chicken thief that attempts to drive his trade, and are duly glorified by name in the papers for it? And ain't they spry? ...Ain't they friskey? Don't they parade up and down the sidewalk at the rate of a block an hour and make everybody nervous and dizzy with their frightful velocity? ...Don't they smile sweetly on the women? And when they are fatigued with their exertions, don't they back up against a lamp post and go on smiling til they plumb break down?

...Now when Ziele broke that poor wretch's skull the other night for stealing six bits worth of flour sacks, and had him taken to the Station House by a policeman and jammed into one of the cells in the most humorous way, do you think there was anything wrong there?

...And why shouldn't they shove that half-sensless, wounded man into a cell without getting a doctor to examine and see how badly he was hurt... Besides, had not a gentleman just said he stole some flour sacks? Ah, and if he stole flour sacks, did he not deliberately put himself outside the pale of humanity and Christian sympathy by that hellish act? I think so, The Department thinks so, Therefor, when the stranger died at 7 in the morning, after four hours of refreshing slumber in that cell, with his skull actually split in twain from front to rear, like an apple, as was ascertained by post mortem examination, what the devil do you

Captain Isaiah Lees was once called "the greatest criminal catcher the West ever knew."
Courtesy the Bancroft Library.

want to go and find fault with the prison officers for? ...Can't you find somebody to pick on besides the police?

I know the Police Department is a kind, humane and generous institution. Why, it was no longer than yesterday that I was reminded of that time Captain Lees broke his leg. Didn't the free-handed, noble Department shine forth with a dazzling radiance then? Didn't the Chief detail officers Shields, Ward and two others to watch over him and nurse him and look after all his wants with motherly solicitude—four of them, you know—four of the very biggest and ablest-bodied men on the force... at a cost to the city... of only the trifling sum of five hundred dollars a month... But don't you know there are people mean enough to say that Captain Lees ought to have paid his own nurse bills, and that if he had had to do it maybe he would have managed to worry along on less than five hundred dollars worth of nursing a month? I can't think how it aggravates me to hear such harsh remarks about our virtuous police force...

HEAVY ON THE POLICE.—Mark Twain, in his last letter to the Territorial Enterprise, bears heavily on the San Francisco police. Mark says: "Why, what can Dr. Rowell expect his resolution calling for inquiry into alleged misbehavior on the part of the police to result in? What have the police been doing? Ain't they virtuous? Don't they take good care of the city? Is not their constant vigilance and efficiency shown in the fact that roughs and rowdies here are awed into good conduct?—isn't it shown in the fact that ladies even on the back streets are safe from insult in the day time, when they are under the protection of a regiment of soldiers?—isn't it shown in the fact that, although many offenders of importance go unpunished, they infallibly snaffle every Chinese chicken-thief that attempts to drive his trade, and are duly glorified by name in the papers for it?—isn't it shown in the fact that they are always on the look out and keep out of the way, and never get run over by wagons and things? And ain't they spry?—ain't they energetic?—ain't they frisky? Don't they parade up and down the sidewalks at the rate of a block an hour and make everybody nervous and dizzy with their frightful velocity?

San Francisco *Daily Morning Examiner*, January 19, 1866.
California State Library.

It was Twain's strongest and most provocative article to date. Nonetheless, it was as terribly exaggerated as it was humorous. It was typical Twain, overdone with little attention to the facts. The unfortunate burglar was drunk and attempting to flee when the proprietor chased and struck him down with his cane. Far from cleaving his skull from "front to rear," the mortal wound was more like two inches long. A doctor had been summoned when it was determined the thief might be seriously injured. A coroner's jury found it a case of justifiable homicide.

The comment on Captain Lees was a particularly cheap shot. Lees had been investigating a murder some miles out in the countryside in July 1863. As he was returning to the city, the king bolt came out of his buggy and in the resulting accident, the detective's ankle was seriously broken. The injury was dangerous enough that at first amputation was feared and he was bedridden for some time. The four officers, noted by Twain, were not nurses, but served in shifts, primarily to do his secretarial and legwork, since Lees was second in command of the Department and involved in many on-going investigations. As it was, he returned to duty on crutches too soon and a year later was still using a cane and was referred to in the press as a "cripple." Fortunately for the department, in time, Captain Lees fully recovered.

But it made good reading. Best of all, most of Twain's attacks on the police in the *Enterprise* were picked up by the San Francisco press and widely published in other newspapers. And it was making a reputation for a tousle-haired reporter just now beginning to receive Eastern acclaim for a story about a celebrated jumping frog in some place called Calaveras County, across the continent in California.

Occasionally, in his pungent distaste for Chief Burke, Mark would hastily scribble off a bit of correspondence to the *Enterprise* that was not sufficiently thought-out. After one such article, in which Chief Burke and a dog were concerned, Twain was required to write an "explanation" to quiet an outraged and noisy delegation of the chief's friends. In reprinting the offending article in the San Francisco *Daily Examiner* on February 7, 1866, Mark hastened to correct his faulty phraseology and turn tragedy into triumph in his own hilarious manner:

> Editor Examiner: You published the following paragraph the other day and stated that it was an extract from a letter to the Virginia Enterprise, from the San Francisco correspondent of that paper. Please publish it again and put in the parenthesis [sic] where I have marked them, so that people who read with wretched carelessness may know to a dead moral certainty when I am referring to Chief Burke, and also know to an equally dead moral certainty when I am referring to the dog:
>
> "I want to compliment Chief Burke—I do honestly. But I can't find anything to compliment him about. He is always rushing furiously around, like a dog after his own tail—and with the same general result, it seems to me; if he (the dog, not the Chief) catches it, it don't amount to anything, after all the fuss; and if he (the dog, not the Chief) don't catch it, it don't make any difference because he (the dog, not the Chief) didn't want it anyhow; he (the dog, not the Chief) only wanted the exercise, and the happiness of showing off before his (the dog's, not the Chief's) mistress and the other young ladies. But if the Chief (not the dog) would only do something praise-

worthy, I would be the first and the most earnest and cordial to give him (the Chief, not the dog) a compliment that would knock him (the Chief, not the dog) down. I mean that it would be such a first-class compliment that it might surprise him (the Chief, not the dog) to that extent as coming from me."

I think that even the pupils of the Asylum at Stockton can understand that paragraph now. But in its original state, and minus the explanatory parenthysis, there were people with sufficiently gorgeous imaginations to gather from it that it contained an intimation that Chief Burke kept a mistress! And not only that, but they also imagined that Chief Burke was in the habit of amusing that mistress with an entertainment of the most extraordinary character! ...Certain friends of the Chief's were really distressed about this thing, and my object in writing this paragraph now, is to assure them emphatically that I did not intend to hint that he kept a mistress... I am a little at loggerheads with M. J. Burke, Chief of Police, and I must beg leave to stir that officer up some in the papers from time to time; but M. J. Burke, in his capacity as a private citizen, is a bosom friend of mine, and is safe from my attacks. I would even drink with him if asked to do so. But Chief Burke don't keep a mistress. On second thought, I only wish he did. I would call it malfeasance in office and publish it in a minute.

Mark Twain

But Mark was running out of steam. He was enough of a reporter not to overdo a good thing. And, he was becoming restless. In a letter home he even complained about having nothing to write home about. His feud with Fitz Smythe was also becoming stale. Burke, Lees, and others on the force were quite prominent locally and Mark must have been getting a lot of scowls around town by now. He wanted to wrap things up and, after getting off a hurried letter to the *Enterprise*, he began putting his affairs in order.

A trip to Sacramento netted the humorist a commission from the *Daily Union* to visit the Sandwich Islands (Hawaii) and write a series of articles describing the trip in his own inimitable fashion. Twain was delighted and arrived in the islands on March 18, 1866. It was the first of his trips to faraway places which were to furnish the basis for so many of his future lectures, articles and books. He had found a profession that suited him perfectly, even though he regarded humorous writing as "undistinguished."

Sam Clemens, the young man who had trouble finding his station in life, was now Mark Twain, a successful reporter and foreign correspondent. He could at least attach some credit for this transformation to his feud with the San Francisco police. He had found some chinks in their municipal armor, but was he fair to Burke and his men? The San Francisco police had their failings, but certainly no more than any other metropolitan force of the time. Actually, a recent article in the *Journal of Social History* concluded that "San Francisco during the nineteenth century quite possibly had the most efficient, most 'professional' police department in the United States."

Revenge, ambition, and peevishness had fostered Twain's sour attitude toward the city's police, and his attacks were of the surface, rather than in-depth variety. He was not an "investigative reporter," being content to publish hearsay and half-truths of which he often had scant firsthand knowledge. But he successfully augmented and masked his lack of facts with his humor in a fashion that caught the fancy of California, and later the world. He admitted his police feud shortcomings in one of his last articles on the subject to the *Enterprise.* The article, dour and almost humble, was reprinted in the *Examiner* on February 10, 1866:

> I have abused the department at large because I could not find out who were the guilty parties and who were the innocent. I knew there were many honest, upright, reliable and excellent men of the police, but then, on account of the questionable surroundings it would have been a hard thing to prove it! Therefore, I refrained from asserting the presence of this virtue—I had a delicacy about making a statement which would be difficult to substantiate,

Harbor scene in 1860s San Francisco. The time seemed right for Mark to make a change. A paid trip to Hawaii would be nice.
California State Library.

and perhaps impossible. It was safe enough to say that in general they were rather a hard lot, because that didn't require any proof! Some of the policemen are very tender about their character—then why do they sit still and see their brethren bring them into disrepute? Why don't they root out the bad element from the force? ...So far from trying to purge their ranks of men who disgrace them, they are ready at a moments notice to shield such men and hush up their malpractices, if common report be true.

Mark was preparing to leave for Hawaii when he learned that his police feud had borne unexpected fruit. On February 21, the *Alta* heralded "The Charges against the Police Department—Testimony before the Commissioners." Fitz Smythe grudgingly made the following unmistakable reference to Twain in the lead paragraph:

> As some little noise has been created by certain irresponsible scribblers, unconnected to any legitimate newspaper enterprise, concerning alleged misconduct on the part of the Police and general mismanagement in the Police Department throughout, the Board of Supervisors some weeks since appointed an investigating Committee...

Of course, everyone who had any grievance against the department now came forward, and although the hearing dragged on for some time, little was accomplished. Twain went off to Hawaii and his reports in the *Union* were eagerly read by the public.

When he returned, Mark gave a lecture on his trip to a packed San Francisco house. Amelia Neville was in the audience and recalled when he "made his debut as a lecturer and amused us to hilarity with the story of his trip."

Twain then joyfully headed East to immortality. And, whether he took himself seriously or not, Mark Twain probably had as much to do with the defeat of Martin Burke at the next election as any other element in the Bay city. The doughty physician, foundry owner, vigilante, druggist, and ex-chief of police decided it was time to try his hand at real estate. Like his tormentor, Dr. Burke was also very successful.

BOOKS

Ayers, Colonel James J. *Gold and Sunshine*. Boston: The Gorham Press, 1922.

Anderson, Frederick, Frank, Michael B., and Sanderson, Kenneth M. (editors). *Mark Twain's Notebooks and Journals, Vol. I, 1855–1873*. Berkeley: University of California Press, 1975.

Beebe, Lucius. *Comstock Commotion, The Story of the Territorial Enterprise and Virginia City News*. Stanford, California: Stanford University Press, 1954.

Branch, Edgar M. (editor). *Clemens of the Call*. Berkeley and Los Angeles: University of California Press, 1969.

Drury, Wells. *An Editor on the Comstock Lode*. New York, Toronto: Farrar & Rinehart, Inc., 1936.

Fatout, Paul. *Mark Twain in Virginia City*. Bloomington: Indiana University Press, 1964.

Lyman, George D. *The Saga of the Comstock Lode*. New York, London: Charles Scribner's Sons, 1946.

Lewis, Oscar. *The War in the Far West: 1861–1865*. Garden City, NY: Doubleday & Company, Inc. , 1961.

Smith, Henry Nash and Anderson, Frederick (editors). *Mark Twain: San Francisco Correspondent, Selections from his Letters to the Territorial Enterprise: 1865-1866*. San Francisco: The Book Club of California, 1957.

Taper, Bernard. *Mark Twain's San Francisco*. New York, Toronto, London: McGraw Hill Book Company, Inc., 1963.

Twain, Mark. *Roughing It*. New York and London: Harper & Brothers Publishers, 1913.

Walker, Franklin (editor). *The Washoe Giant in San Francisco*. San Francisco: George Fields, 1938.

Weisenburger, Francis Phelps. *Idol of the West, The Fabulous Career of Rollin Mallory Daggett*. Syracuse, New York: Syracuse University Press, 1965.

NEWSPAPERS

San Francisco *Daily Alta California*, January 7, 8, 10, 12, 1866

San Francisco *Daily Dramatic Chronicle*, June 19, 1865

San Francisco *Daily Evening Bulletin*, March 13, 1872

San Francisco *Daily Morning Call*, August 24, 1864; February 3, 1866

San Francisco *Daily Morning Examiner*, January 17, 19, February 5, 7, 10, 20, 21, 1866

The *Golden Era*, January 21, 1866

Nevada *Gold Hill News*, January 29, 1866

Nevada *Territorial Enterprise*, December 11, 19, 1865; February 6, 15, 1866

New Orleans *Crescent*, May 17, 1859

OTHER SOURCES

Burke, Martin J. Dictation, the Bancroft Library, University of California, Berkeley

Daggett, Rollin M. Scrapbooks, California State Library, Sacramento

Ethington, Philip J. "Vigilantes and the Police: The Creation of a Professional Police Bureaucracy in San Francisco, 1847–1900," *Journal of Social History*, Winter 1987

Chapter 5

Shootouts & Shouting Matches

Those Feuding De Young Boys

On July 27, 2000, a legend died. On that date the San Francisco *Chronicle* was sold to the Hearst Corporation. It was truly the end of an era. First issued in 1865, the *Chronicle* was established by two teenaged boys long on newspaper savvy, but short on business morals. The De Young brothers were indeed a feisty crowd and in the early days they scratched, clawed, and shot their way to the top of their profession in the rowdiest city on the Pacific Slope.

Having emigrated to America from Holland at an early age, Michael De Young operated a jewelry store in Baltimore for many years. He moved to New York with his wife, Amelia, and several children in the 1830s. By 1838 the family had moved to Saint Louis where De Young operated a dry goods shop, but soon the family moved on to Texas and Louisiana. By 1850, the family was living in Cincinnati with their eight children. The census of that year lists five girls in the family and three boys: Gustavus, seven years old and born in Louisiana; Charles, five years old and born in Missouri; Michael, three years old and born in Louisiana.

In 1854, the family was again on the move, this time to Gold Rush California. They were aboard the Mississippi River steamboat *Tecumseh* in April of that year when the father was suddenly stricken and died from apoplexy. The grief-stricken mother and her brood probably continued to New Orleans where they caught a ship for California. They took up residence in San Francisco later that year.

Although there was undoubtedly some money in the family, the frugal mother never remarried and the boys went to work early to keep the family solvent. Somehow they managed to obtain an education and in 1860 both Michael and Charles were working for a small Jewish newspaper as typesetters. By 1864, Charles was a compositor at the *Alta California* newspaper, while the other boys kept busy at various odd jobs.

Late that year, the boys discussed the idea of a newspaper of their own. Michael had been clerking recently and had some idea about keeping books. Both boys had much typesetting experience, while Gus could sell advertising. They would start small. All agreed that a four-page tabloid, filled with advertising and distributed free to all the hotels, theaters, and saloons in town would have the best chance of succeeding. The ads would be mostly theatrical in content, and they would sell contracts to print programs in the paper.

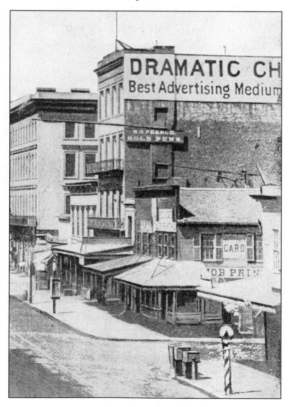

There would also be a sprinkling of reviews and local news. From the beginning, Charles De Young was the guiding editorial force behind the enterprise.

They named their new paper the *Daily Dramatic Chronicle*, but the boys had one problem. Having always given their meager salaries to their mother, they had no money. Their mother's landlord sympathized with the

The advent of a brand new newspaper and style of journalism is announced on the side of the De Young boys' office building in 1865. *Author's collection.*

Michael De Young and his brother brought their own style of confrontational journalism to San Francisco. *California State Library.*

youngsters' ambitions and that far-sighted gentleman offered them a twenty-dollar gold piece. A local job printer fulfilled the balance of the dream with a desk, some type, and some space in which to work. The first issue of the *Chronicle* was distributed on January 17, 1865, and although quite ordinary in style and content, it was impressive enough for a couple of boys barely out of high school.

And savvy boys they were. Although the city was already chock-full of newspapers of every variety, the new *Daily Dramatic Chronicle* reportedly gathered a circulation of some 2,000 in the first month. The *Alta* would later comment ominously on the new paper's beginnings:

> ...Other newspapers had been long and firmly established and were sufficient to satisfy the actual demand of the public... To follow a quiet life would have been death to this paper; novelty was the only thing that could keep it alive; sensation was the only process for novelty, and sensation was necessarily scandalous...

Their first big break came the following April. Mike De Young dropped in for a visit with the local telegraph operator and was asked if he had heard the news. "What news?" he responded. The president—Mr. Lincoln—had been assassinated. When De Young was shown the dispatch, he memorized it and raced back to his brother at the *Chronicle* office. They quickly put together an extra which was greedily gobbled up by the public. They had scooped the city's big dailies by hours.

An example of the boys' choice of sensation and scandal to fuel their new enterprise came when the *Chronicle*'s alcoholic drama critic criticized the performance of an overweight Matilda Heron as Camille at Tom Maguire's Opera House. Maguire, whose programs were published in the *Chronicle*, tore up his contract and told the boys and their critic they were no longer welcome at his place. A tough little ex-hack driver from New York, Maguire no doubt thought he could easily buffalo his young antagonists. It was a bad mistake.

The *Chronicle* kept up a running attack on Maguire's Opera House, maintaining that respectable women patrons ran the risk of being seated next to the prostitute mistresses of gamblers who worked next door. Female performers at Maguire's, they alleged, were regularly drugged, assaulted, and outraged behind the stage. When Maguire had finished with his performers, they were passed on to his employees who

Matilda Heron was one of the more popular actresses on the Coast. *The Annals of San Francisco.*

frequently fought over the actresses' favors. Maguire sued the boys for libel, but they apparently were pretty much on target since they beat him at the preliminary hearing and kept up the assault.

When they had played this scenario for all it was worth, the boys attacked from another direction. A principal advertiser of the *Chronicle*, and a rival of Maguire's, was the Metropolitan Theater. When the Metropolitan had a minor fire, the De Youngs intimated that Maguire was to blame because he loved to see the firemen running down the street pulling their hose and ladder wagons. The outraged

Tom Maguire quickly learned that the De Young boys played a tough game of hardball. *California State Library.*

Maguire sued, but again it was the De Young boys' day in court. Even more personal attacks followed and eventually Maguire's theatrical empire collapsed. Although the public loved these squabbles, the boys gained little respect from their peers. And it was this type of journalism which resulted in the De Youngs' need to begin carrying pistols.

By the summer of 1868, the brothers were ready to expand into a regular, daily newspaper, and it worried Loring Pickering. As an owner of the *Daily Morning Call*, Pickering saw the potential of the De Youngs and their *Chronicle* and he sought to head off the competition. When he offered the boys a half interest in the *Call* if they abandoned their own paper, he met with a cocky rebuke. They were not, they lectured the veteran newsman, in the business of making other persons' fortunes for them. The new *Daily and Evening Chronicle* was first issued on September 1, 1868. The claimed circulation at the end of the first year was 16,000.

Charles De Young knew controversy sold newspapers, but he didn't realize just how tough the game could be. *California State Library.*

When a school director named Richard Sinton charged the *Chronicle* with criminal libel, the case was heard before Judge Delos Lake. The boys had their work cut out for them since they had campaigned against Lake in a recent election and defeated him. On election night the defeated judge had growled, "I'll land those De Youngs in San Quentin yet!"

Mike and Charley were astounded when a friendly mayor appointed the defeated Lake to a newly created municipal court. Mike De Young later recalled:

> After our bitter attacks on Lake, it was a mean trial. It was, in fact, one of the most remarkable cases ever tried in San Francisco. We declined to question the jurors, just let them come into the box. We accepted them as drawn. We knew we could prove our assertions. Judge Lake ruled out everything that came up in our favor. He evinced bitter feeling from the bench. He even interrogated the witnesses himself and suggested points to the prosecuting attorney. He could hardly be called a fair judge. But we fought him right

down the line. The jury went out for ten minutes and came back and said, "Not guilty!"

We had called Sinton a bully and a blackguard and we had proved it. Judge Lake nearly fainted at the verdict.

Judge Lake's run for reelection caused the *Chronicle* to change its independent status. When the paper suggested lawyer M. C.

Blake as an opposition candidate, the local Republican Party made it official. Judge Lake was shattered when he lost the election by a 2,000 vote margin.

Lake's term had only a few weeks to run when he noticed the De Young boys' names again on his calendar. It was the latest in a string of cases all won by the newspaper. Mike and Charley, busy at their work, paid little attention to the matter and when the case was called, their attorneys asked for a continuance to subpoena their witnesses.

Judge Delos Lake was a hefty opponent in more ways than one.
California State Library.

With his tenure to run for just a few more days, a beaming Judge Lake announced, "No, you cannot have a continuance. Please proceed to trial."

Going to trial without witnesses, the De Young brothers asserted they had acted in the public good, insisting the plaintiff was as they had maintained. Judge Lake was thunderstuck when the jury quickly agreed. Once again, the brothers were vindicated as Judge Lake brooded in his quarters.

Several hours after the acquittal Charles De Young was approaching the *Chronicle* office when Judge Lake rushed from a doorway across the street wielding a heavy whalebone cane. The judge aimed at his head, but Charley managed to take the blow on his arm, which shattered the cane and paralyzed his arm. Using the stub of cane as a sword, Lake now tried to stab the newsman, who desperately parried the attacks with his good arm. As the two men clinched, Lake drew a derringer and De Young threw up his arms shouting he was unarmed. Charley weighed some 140 pounds, but he now grabbed Lake's gun arm and heaved the 240-pound jurist over his shoulder. As both men went down in a heap on the pavement, Lake pressed his derringer against the newsman's head and fired. The bullet merely grazed De Young's temple and plowed into the thigh of a bystander across the street.

A policeman came running up at this time and, with the help of a spectator, managed to separate the combatants. Hauled into court on an assault charge, Lake insisted his weapon had merely gone off accidentally during the struggle. Despite the spirited interference of political cronies, on December 30, 1871, he was stuck with a $300 fine, which his friends cheerfully paid. The De Youngs had won again, and Judge Lake was now out of office.

No strangers to political fights, earlier that year, the De Young brothers took an interest in a campaign within the local Republican County Committee to pack the August convention. Bill Higgins, and several other political hacks, sought to connive their way into appointments that would enable them to secure tribute from those who required their services. When the *Chronicle* exposed the plan, one of the gang sued the newspaper for libel, while Higgins attacked Gus De Young as being the party who supplied the information to his brothers. Gus and an attorney friend were pretty roughed up when Higgins pulled a pistol, but the brawl was broken up a moment later. Higgins later apologized, saying he was drunk, but another assault was expected.

William T. Higgins, described as a "ward manager" for the Republican party, had filled various minor political posts, but was seldom seen to work. The 225-pound bruiser liked to cruise Montgomery Street with prizefighter friends, and had once shot and killed a hack driver in a squabble over a boxing bet. Those who expected further trouble weren't disappointed.

On the evening of May 7, 1871, Mike and Charles De Young were in the billiard room of the Lick House for some relaxation. Charles was talking to several friends as Mike played a game of pool, when suddenly Bill

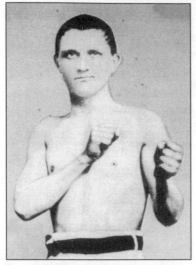

Tommy Chandler was a popular local prizefighter who had once whipped the brutal "Chicken" Devine. *Author's collection.*

Higgins entered the room with Tommy Chandler, a local prizefighter. Carrying a heavy cane, Higgins walked quickly over to where Mike De Young was preparing to take a shot. Seeing Higgins with his up-raised cane from the corner of his eye, Mike barely had time to duck and raise his cue for protection. Higgins' cane shattered the cue, but Mike recovered and attacked with what was left of his splintered cue. "Mr. De Young," noted a newspaper report, "...immediately rushed upon his brutal assailant and struck him in the face and about the head. The two then clinched, and both fell after a short struggle, Mr. De Young uppermost."

Charles had quickly rushed over and pulled his brother off the politician, as Chandler and others hauled Higgins to his feet. The battered Higgins now pulled a revolver, as the surrounding crowd began backing away. Chandler, however, quickly seized his friend's hand and forced it down. After a brief struggle, Chandler secured the weapon.

"If you are a good friend of mine," shouted Higgins, "give me my pistol."

Pocketing his pal's weapon, Chandler now led Higgins outside, as friends of the De Youngs crowded around talking excitedly. Mike did not have a mark on him, but Higgins' face was considerably scratched up. Fortunately, Higgins gave up his retaliatory efforts.

In 1870, one Benjamin F. Napthaly was released from the local boys' reformatory. Applying to the *Chronicle* for work, he was given the job of cleaning up the place, and when he showed some aptitude for reporting, the brothers gave him the chance. Everything went smoothly for awhile, but eventually there was a dispute and Napthaly was dismissed. It was the beginning of a feud that would have tragic repercussions many years later.

In time Napthaly hitched his star to that of a disreputable character named R. F. Fitzgerald and the two managed to acquire *The Sun*, a feeble and dying tabloid barely able to publish from day to day. When the pair attempted to beef up their paper's foundering revenues by blackmailing insurance companies for advertising, a victim complained to the *Chronicle*. The response in that journal on April 31, 1874, was direct and to the point:

> ...He asks what he "had better do about it." We reply, do not give them a cent, and if they annoy you, hand them over to the police and send them to San Quentin where they of right belong. Fitzgerald, the publisher... is, by his own confession, a thief, a liar, a bigamist and... a scoundrel. B. F. Napthaly, the nominal editor, is a graduate of the Industrial School, a professional blackmailer, a hanger-on of the lowest gambling houses and dens of prostitution, and generally, one of the most degraded specimens of hoodlumism...

This left little to the imagination and all hell broke loose. That afternoon *The Sun* came out with a blistering attack on the De Young family, including some sizzling accusations against the mother and sisters. The brothers promptly obtained a warrant charging criminal libel, then girded themselves for war. The public smelled blood and grabbed up *The Sun* as fast as it appeared on the streets. Newsboys were charging as high as $2.50 for the last issues of the paper, the final copies being rented for twenty-five cents an hour.

The San Francisco City Hall, Courts and Police Station was the former Jenny Lind Theater. *Author's collection.*

It was late in the day when word was received that the issue was to be reprinted and Gus De Young burst into the *Sun* office and caught Fitzgerald bending over a printing form. Knocking the publisher across the room, Gus was coming at him with a pistol when several pressmen scooted their boss out a back door and disarmed his assailant.

Captain Isaiah W. Lees was chief of the San Francisco Police detectives for over forty years. *Author's collection.*

While either Mike or Charles De Young, or both presumedly, were hunting for Napthaly, police rounded up all the *Sun* employees and hauled them into court where bonds were fixed at $2,000 each. Gus, meanwhile, did his best to wreck the *Sun* office, breaking furniture and scattering type. When dismissed by the judge, the *Sun* employees returned to their shop and began cleaning up the mess.

Sunday morning dawned the next day and church bells tolled across the city. Police Captain Isaiah Lees was having his morning coffee at headquarters and looking over the past night's criminal activities. As head of the detective force, Captain Lees kept a close eye on San Francisco, and his wife had long ago accepted his erratic and long hours. He had known the De Young boys for some years and was aware they often went about armed. Watching their newspaper grow and flourish, he had admired the abilities of the spunky young men.

As he looked over his reports, the detective was surprised when Mike and Charles De Young asked to see him. Lees had heard of the raucous happenings of yesterday and quickly ushered the excited young men into his office. Word was out that the *Sun* was again preparing to issue their offensive edition of the previous day and the De Youngs were on their way now to stop it.

"Is there going to be trouble?" queried the Captain.

"We don't know, but if that type is being reset there might be. We are going to swear out another warrant at least, if it is."

Thinking he had better go along in case he could circumvent a disturbance, Lees accompanied the brothers to the *Sun*'s upstairs address, but found the door locked. The detective was apparently prowling around looking for another entrance when Mike knocked out a door panel and the brothers burst into the room, followed shortly by Captain Lees. It was quickly determined that the offensive story was again being readied for publication, so Lees herded the printers into another room under the care of a police sergeant, while he and Charles De Young sought a judge and a warrant.

When Captain Lees returned with a warrant, the printing staff was hauled off to the city prison while calls were again sent out for bail bondsmen.

The press of the city was aghast at the sudden assaults of the two papers. Under the headline, "Yesterday's Furor," the *Alta California* commented:

> ...Severe as was the attack in the *Chronicle*, the evening issue of the *Sun* electrified every one by the method it adopted of retaliating for the attack made upon it by the morning paper. The news ran abroad that the editors of the *Sun* had a scathing editorial of a column and a half purporting to be a history of the lives and times of the proprietors of the *Chronicle*, but worse than all, had resorted to the degradation of introducing into the account a mention, in unpardonable terms, of the mother and sisters of the publishers of the *Chronicle*. The affair soon became noised about, and... soon the first edition was exhausted...

The next morning Ben Napthaly, who had

Scene on Kearny Street in the days when the De Young boys were kicking up their heels.
Author's collection.

been named in the indictment, made his way to the police court and asked an officer to escort him inside so he could post bail. At this moment Gus De Young spotted him and opened fire. As Napthaly sprinted for his life, Gus emptied his pistol, but only managed to singe the ear of a policeman. The officer seized the gunman and took him into police headquarters for booking.

As the desk sergeant wrote up Gus, Mike and Charley walked in the door. The brothers were arguing at the desk when the unlucky Napthaly strolled in to surrender. Right there in police headquarters, Mike De Young went for his pistol, but was quickly pinned against a wall by an officer and disarmed. Charley then had to cough up his derringer. The three brothers were all charged for their actions and bail was set at $27,000. Ben Napthaly was offered bail by friends, but decided a stay in the city prison might be much better for his health.

The charges against the De Youngs worked their way up to higher courts, where they were ultimately dismissed. In the course of the trials, the *Chronicle* was forced to print all the nasty *Sun* charges and countercharges the same as the other dailies. The *New York Times* later reported:

> ...De Young's aged mother never saw a line of these proceedings, for a special edition of the *Chronicle*, consisting of one paper, was struck off and sent by special messenger to her home every day. The forms were then lifted from the press, the full "news of the day" was then inserted, and the regular edition was printed as usual.

The libel actions against the De Youngs by Fitzgerald, however, were another matter. The judge ruled:

"This does not hold water. The character of that person [Fitzgerald] being so infamously bad, by his own admission, he is not susceptible to damage by libel."

Unable to make much headway against the De Youngs, Napthaly pressed charges against Captain Lees for unofficerlike conduct. The canny detective, who once commented that he prized his honor above his life, wasn't about to be cornered by someone of Napthaly's character.

Acting as his own attorney in a hearing before the Police Commissioners on April 2, Napthaly called Charles De Young as his first witness. The story of that Sunday morning was recounted, with De Young stating that Lees was not present when his brother Mike broke in the door. If Captain Lees had not been there, insisted De Young, serious trouble might very well have resulted.

During the examination of several typesetters, all admitted that nothing was broken after Lees entered, that he treated everyone properly, and no violence was offered to anyone.

When the detective captain quoted various passages from legal journals justifying his actions, Napthaly saw his case go out the window. The commissioners unanimously agreed to dismiss the charges.

The *Sun* had "set" for the next few months, but eventually staggered to its feet again. When Napthaly decided to liven up his pages with a few mild cracks about the De Youngs, he got more than he bargained for.

The *Sun* editor was talking to a friend on Montgomery Street on June 15 when Charles De Young spotted him. Noticing the *Chronicle* man just as he was closing in, Napthaly made a dash for the police station, only a block away. De Young rushed after him, trying to get a clear shot as he ran, but when he tripped on a cobblestone his quarry rushed into Dunbar Alley and into the back door of the police station. Running through the station, Napthaly was screaming, "I am unarmed and he's after me again with a pistol!"

De Young arrived seconds later and saw that his target had eluded him. He sat down and watched a poker game in the station rather than continuing his pursuit.

The next day Charles was a little more careful. Posting himself outside the new Appraiser's Office Building, he leaned against a fence in a heavy overcoat with the collar turned up and a scarf further hiding his face. Napthaly came out of the post office and walked right past De Young, who quickly fired and missed. Standing behind a lamp post, De Young fired several times at the dodging *Sun* editor, who seemed to be doing a jig in the middle of the street. By now, Napthaly had his pistol out and the two men exchanged six or seven shots, without scoring a hit on each other.

Pedestrians scattered in every direction during the firing, but the only casualties were a young girl who fainted and a Western Union boy who took a bullet in the leg. Napthaly finally made it into a building and, as De Young yelled for him to show himself, both were arrested and hauled off to Police Court.

At their preliminary hearing, both men claimed the other had fired the first shot and they had merely responded to the attack. Napthaly did a creditable job as his own counsel and charges were dismissed against him. De Young was held for trial, but some months later Napthaly had the charges dismissed. He admitted at the time that he actually admired the De Young boys and, in later years, would become a good friend of Mike.

The press generally agreed that although the *Sun* overreacted to the original *Chronicle* article, certain aspects of such "disgraceful journalism" made some kind of sense. Others saw some poetic justice in the whole thing. The *Daily Oakland News* commented:

> A fine illustration of the tendency of chickens to come home to roost is the tribulation of the *Chronicle*. Of course the *Sun* article was as vile and scurrilous as words could make it, and had the persons attacked been other than the De Youngs, shooting would be none too bad for the author. But that the *Chronicle* people should raise such a howl at getting a dose of their own medicine is of a piece with the conduct of a joker who loses his temper at a witty repartee. The *Chronicle* has carried the reputation of a merciless scandal-monger, and does not deserve the least sympathy.

The San Jose *Mercury* agreed:

> The *Chronicle* publishers, who have never let an opportunity pass to assail the private character of those whom they don't like, ... made a most unprovoked attack through their paper, on the editor of the *Sun*. The *Sun* came back at them the same day in a manner that was calculated to astonish... The De Youngs can now ruminate on the delight of having their own private affairs paraded before the public as they have often served others...

So far as the public was concerned, it was pretty much a case of "a plague on both your houses." But the boys had drank too deeply from the cup of power and they continued their rowdy ways. In April of 1874, they lost a slander suit against a woman that cost them $3,000.

San Francisco police officer Edward Byram showed his own distaste for the brothers in his notebook. The book, devoted solely to a listing of criminals, is a clear indication of the officer's disdain for the owners of what would someday become one of the world's most influential newspapers:

> De Young, Charles - age 32 in 1877.
>
> De Young, Michael Harry - age 30 in 1877.
>
> De Young, Gustavus - age 34 in 1877.
>
> Jewish proprietors of the San Francisco *Chronicle*, a notorious, libelous sheet."

In October of 1876, the *Chronicle* referred to the Duane brothers as "squatters" (one of the nicer things they could have called them), resulting in John Duane punching out Charley De Young when he caught him on Clay Street. It cost Duane $250, but was probably worth it to him. Charley Duane had been shipped out of town by the Vigilantes in 1856 and had been involved in several shooting scrapes.

The following year there were libel suits in Stockton and Placerville. When Congressman H. F. Page sued the De Youngs in a Placerville court, a great many public officials were called to testify. In October of 1878, a hung jury resulted in their release, but they were already being sued by Dr. C. C. O'Donnell. The doctor, a member of the new legislature, resented being called an abortionist and had Mike and Charley hauled into Police Court where they secured bonds of $1,000 each. The case was dismissed on December 23, 1878, when the De Youngs easily proved their case and wrecked the doctor's burgeoning political career.

John Duane (above) and his brother, Charley, were two of the worst thugs in the city. *John Boessenecker collection.*

But circumstances that would disastrously affect the *Chronicle* were already in place. In June of 1879, the De Youngs printed a small item in reference to the coming city elections. The heading read—

"Reprinted from the Wichita, Kan., *Herald* of June 29, 1879:"

The Reverend Ike Kalloch of Boston scandal fame, who achieved some notoriety in this state as a self-adjustable lawyer, preacher, politician and common barroom loafer, who smoked poor cigars and drank poorer whiskey, and who jumped Leavenworth and Lawrence, leaving a long list of creditors to mourn his untimely departure, is Kearney's candidate for Mayor of San Francisco.

The 1870s had been difficult years for the country. Depressions and labor troubles had resulted in unemployment, strikes, and riots in various large cities, and San Francisco did not escape. Here, the Chinese were a ready scapegoat and were blamed for much of the unemployment, although they frequently held jobs that white men wouldn't consider. The match to start the conflagration was one Denis Kearney, a San Francisco teamster.

By the summer of 1877, Kearney had become the leader of a mob of unemployed who gathered on the city sandlots to hear his radical, socialist speeches and denouncement of the Orientals. "The Chinese must go!" became a rallying cry, as thugs and hoodlums infiltrated the unemployed workingmen's ranks. In July a meeting of some 6,000 unemployed persons was held at a sandlot near City Hall, and it quickly erupted into a riot. Thousands ranged through the streets for the next few days, burning, looting, and fighting a combined force of police, national guard and citizen volunteers. Out of this inferno was forged the new Workingmen's Party, headed by Denis Kearney.

Kearney's speeches became more and more radical and violent.

It was first thought that the new political party would be a source of release for some of the agitators, but when a Workingmen's Party candidate was actually elected to the state legislature, it became a wake-up call for the city.

The *Chronicle*, one of the few newspapers tolerant of the new party and its talk against corporations, now suddenly saw a monstrous serpent straddling the Golden Gate. "If Denis Kearney and his gang obtain control of San Francisco," warned Charles De Young, "there will be given to the city to regret and lament the worst spectacle of misgovernment ever seen in the Republic."

The man heading the Workingmen's slate for local offices was the sleazy Reverend Isaac S. Kalloch, labeled by the De Youngs as a "tainted preacher." And tainted he surely was.

Charley De Young shot Kalloch down in front of San Francisco's huge Baptist Metropolitan Temple. *Author's collection.*

Kalloch had come to California in 1876. His appearance alone made him a striking figure: at some 240 pounds, with a great mop of flaming red hair and matching whiskers. In Boston at age twenty-three he had been minister of the famous Tremont Temple, said to be the largest church in the country. When he was discovered in a hotel room with a parishioner in the winter of 1857, a sensational trial barely acquitted him, and he left town.

He turned up in a New York pulpit sometime later, but before long was caught with a choir girl with the same moral ideas as his own, and again fled. This time he headed west, where he founded a college, a town, a railroad, and a newspaper in Kansas. Cheating Indians out of their land and being elected to the state legislature went hand-in-hand to Kalloch. His pseudo-legal operations and swindling schemes quickly wore thin, however, and he was compelled to move west again.

In California, Kalloch soon wheedled himself into being pastor of the huge Baptist Metropolitan Temple, between Market and Mission streets. When he espoused the Workingmen's cause, his colorful oratory and church following made him an ideal candidate, and he found himself on the ticket as the mayoral nominee. Kalloch was indeed nominated and the De Youngs unleashed a bitter name-calling campaign, culminating on August 20, 1879, with a two and a half column report of his old adultery trial headed, "The Record of a Misspent Life." A raw and outrageous biography of Kalloch in which he was referred to as the "Sorrel Stallion," the article was also a declaration of war.

Kalloch was furious, but he had an idea. An aide had dredged up the old *Sun* article on the De Youngs and now the fiery minister called a meeting for the evening of August 22, 1879. He would read that discredited *Sun* article in retaliation against the *Chronicle*, apparently not knowing, or caring, that Napthaly had long ago retracted the offensive report. A huge crowd attended the meeting, Kalloch having to give one speech inside and another outside on top of a piano crate.

Only brief excerpts of Kalloch's speech were printed in the city newspapers, but he apparently didn't recite from the old *Sun* article. He did, however, refer to the De Youngs as "hybrid whelps of sin and shame," a characterization from the hated *Sun* article. Everyone knew the De Young brothers idolized their mother, and one paragraph of Kalloch's speech was designed to jab the De Youngs where it really hurt:

> In maligning the reputation of my father, who has filled an honored grave for many years, these journalistic vipers have rendered the most vicious retaliation on my part necessary and justifiable. Their disgraceful records in this city make such retaliation possible, and I am justified in pronouncing them the bastard progeny of a prostitute.

Not content with this outrageous accusation, the crowd now called for Kalloch to read the old *Sun* article, but the minister only smiled and raised his hands. He wasn't going to expend all his ammunition at once. Besides, he intended reprinting the old article in the next issue of the Workingmen's Party newsletter. He would then comment on the article in his next speech. The news was soon passed on to the *Chronicle* owners.

The next morning Charley De Young called a cab and picked up a messenger boy from the local telegraph company. He drove out to Kalloch's Mission Street home, but the minister was absent and the newsman drove straight to the Temple. Here, Kalloch was seen at the curb preparing to get into his buggy. The unsuspecting messenger boy was then sent out to tell the minister that someone wanted to speak to him in the cab. Upon receiving the message, Kalloch looked up, then began walking towards the cab.

Isaac S. Kalloch left a trail of moral and financial destruction from one end of the country to the other. *Kansas State Historical Society.*

It was a deadly ambush! Poking his pistoled fist from the cab window, De Young fired point blank at the approaching clergyman. The huge figure dropped to the ground, but immediately staggered to his feet as De Young stepped from the carriage and fired again. Hit in the left side and thigh, Kalloch was helped into his temple as all hell broke loose outside. The *Bulletin* reported:

Mike De Young's shooting of Kalloch as depicted in *Frank Leslie's Illustrated Newspaper*, September 13, 1879.

...At this stage of the proceedings a large crowd had gathered about the coupe and several attempts were made to drag De Young from the carriage. He sat there, however, with his pistol extended and cocked and threatened to shoot any man who laid hands upon him. In a few minutes an officer came up and arrested De Young, getting into the carriage with him. Thereupon the crowd, which was every moment growing larger and more excited, attacked the coupe, overturned it with its occupants, and seizing De Young,

Charles De Young met the same fate he had tried to delegate to Isaac Kalloch. *Author's collection.*

dragged him from the wreck and began to beat him with fists, boots, etc...

It was shortly after ten o'clock in the morning when Captain Lees received a telephone call advising him of the shooting. He immediately sent all available officers under Captain Short to the Metropolitan Temple, then rushed into Police Court and ordered all the officers and clerks there to follow. Back at the temple, another policeman ran up and both officers rushed the publisher through a building to Market Street, where another cab was commandeered for a fast trip to City Hall. Lees himself was just heading for the door when he saw the cab carrying De Young and the two officers pulling up at the curb. The publisher was rushed into a cell as mobs began filling up the street in front of police headquarters.

Huge crowds quickly gathered on various sandlots in the city, fiery speeches were given, and it seemed a bloody riot was inevitable. Kalloch's son, Isaac M. Kalloch, also a minister, counseled against any mob action, but stated that if justice could not be had, "I will see that De Young is killed." Various speakers demanded the crowds break into the city jail and lynch De Young, while several citizen groups offered their services to Police Chief John Kirkpatrick. The chief and Captain Lees both knew that any real trouble would result only if Kalloch died, so they awaited medical reports and advocated caution.

Late that night physicians announced that Kalloch was conscious and not in any great pain. Although first reports stated the wounds were mortal, physicians later revised their diagnosis to say there was a good chance he would recover.

A strange story surfaced at this time, based partially on poor people's distrust of the police and on Captain Lees' known friendship with the De Youngs. It was rumored that the captain of detectives had been with Charley De Young when he had shot Kalloch. The *Bulletin* printed the rumor even though none of the eyewitness reports of the incident had mentioned Lees being present. Still the rumor persisted.

That night, the head of the Police Commission investigated, but found no substance to the rumor. When Lees was advised of the heresy making the rounds, he promptly called for another meeting of the Police Commission. He detailed his movements on the day in question and sixteen officers testified to his being at his office at the time of the shooting. Despite the detective's insistence on an investigation, the commissioners decided the rumors were groundless and any further inquiry would be a waste of time.

When it was announced that Kalloch was out of danger, Charles De Young was released on bail. At the time of the election, Kalloch was still bedridden and managed to win by a margin of some 1,500 votes. Although the Workingmen's Party won many of the major city offices, they won only two supervisor seats.

The new mayor was continually under attack by the city press after stating in his inaugural address that "the people expect their officials to steal." Continually under fire and defending itself, Kalloch's weak administration found any solid accomplishment impossible. There was constant talk of impeachment. The mayor was further disturbed to know that Charley De Young was conducting business as usual and obtaining constant delays in his trial which had recently again been postponed until May 3, 1880.

Young Isaac Kalloch, meanwhile, had become a clerk in his father's office, but soon left the city and was preaching to a small congregation at Healdsburg, some miles to the north. In early April he returned to San Francisco and began drinking heavily. Of a naturally quiet demeanor, the young minister seemed to be brooding over the troubles and

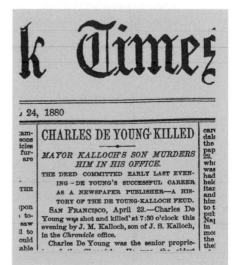

De Young's death made headlines around the country. It was front-page news in the *New York Times*, as shown here. *Author's collection.*

111

constant criticism of his father. He was also undoubtedly convinced that Charley De Young was never going to be punished for his attempted murder of the elder Kalloch.

In April, there were rumors that a booklet was to be published detailing again the old *Chronicle* account of Kalloch's Boston troubles. It was more than the young Kalloch could endure. On the evening of April 23 he walked rapidly down Bush Street towards the big, new *Chronicle* building.

Kalloch's son, Isaac, shown here at the time of the murder, ambushed Charley De Young, just as his father had been gunned down. *California State Library.*

It was a quarter to eight when Charley De Young walked into the *Chronicle* office. He began chatting with two friends just inside the door. Clerk Willie Dreypolcher was behind the counter engaged in a conversation. De Young, still talking with Gus Spear and Ed Read, moved toward the counter, where their discussion continued. When the door opened and closed rather noisily, clerk Dreypolcher glanced up and his blood ran cold:

> ...When I looked up and saw Kalloch he had a pistol in his hand and almost at the same instant he fired a shot. Mr. De Young looked up and saw him at the same time I did, and after the first shot was fired he ran back towards the gate (leading behind the counter). He was about to the gate when the second shot was fired and he got down behind it at the third shot. He was right at the corner when the fourth shot was fired...

Scrambling desperately for cover, De Young clawed back his overcoat, trying to draw his own pistol, and dodged behind a desk near the gate. Young Kalloch had been following closely on his heels and now as De Young looked up from the floor to see where his assailant was, he stared into the barrel of Kalloch's pistol. Dreypolcher continued:

> Just then, as De Young was down and Kalloch was stooping over him, he fired again, and that is the shot that hit him in the mouth. The pistol was within two feet of his face...

Charley had finally got his pistol out, but it was too late. As Kalloch turned and ran towards the door, the publisher didn't have the strength to raise his weapon. Friends rushed to his side as he slumped to the floor. His powder-burned face looked up, but he couldn't talk. He had been shot in the upper lip and the blood now gushed from his nose and mouth. He was dead at seven minutes past eight o'clock.

By the time the coroner arrived at nine o'clock, huge crowds filled the streets, mostly noisy and jubilant Workingmen's Party members. The *Alta* reported on the ugly scene:

> ... a boisterous, ruffianly mob drew in from all quarters of the city, cheering and hooting in exultancy... When the coffin was brought out and placed in the deadwagon, the mob made louder the cheers and hoots, and at every step launched foul oaths at the man who had been murdered by the son of their reverend leader...

A guard of policemen with drawn clubs escorted the wagon to the morgue. Kalloch had been immediately captured and taken to police headquarters, but steadfastly refused to make any statement. His legal defense team went quickly to work, however.

On Sunday morning, April 25, 1880, morbid, sight-seeing crowds began filling the street before the De Young Eddy Street address. Hordes of friends and associates were present at the one o'clock funeral, while the outside crowds were held back by police. Great mounds of flowers covered the casket. The mother, Amelia De Young, was noticeably absent, but friends knew that she preferred to remember her son as he was in life. Although his mustache neatly hid the ugly bullet wound, the powder-burned face would have been more than she could bear to see.

It took twenty days to select a jury for young Kalloch's trial. The defense was, of course, self-defense. Kalloch's tale was

At his brother's death, Michael De Young felt the full weight of the business upon him, but he was equal to the task. *California State Library.*

that he was upset at the publication of the new booklet on his father and went to the *Chronicle* office to complain. He was talking to De Young when suddenly Charley pulled his pistol and began shooting. To bolster their case, Kalloch's attorneys produced a witness who corroborated this scenario, although all the other witnesses denied this had happened. Tests proved Charley's pistol had not been fired, but the defense stubbornly stuck to their witness, even though he was a convicted perjurer and had been brought into court in handcuffs from San Quentin.

Amazingly, after some twenty-eight days of argument and testimony, young Kalloch was acquitted. There were great celebrations in the streets, but Mayor Kalloch lost the nomination to run for re-election and both he and his son soon moved to the Northwest.

Michael De Young now assumed the editor's chair at the *Chronicle*. Chastened and saddened by his brother's cruel death, he nonetheless continued the policy of sensation-based journalism which had built his newspaper into one of the most powerful organs in the West. And, more trouble was just around the corner when Mike decided to tackle the powerful Spreckels family a few years later.

Born in 1828 in the political turmoil of what is now Germany, Claus Spreckels emigrated to the United States at the age of seventeen. With only a dollar in his pocket as he stepped ashore in New York City, in a few years Spreckels had parlayed his funds into his own grocery store in Charleston, South Carolina. He came to California in 1856 and opened another grocery store in San Francisco, soon buying a local brewery, as well. He sold these two ventures to establish the Bay Area Sugar Refinery, which processed mostly imported raw sugar cane. The refinery was highly successful and in 1866 he built a larger San Francisco plant that produced sixty tons of sugar per day. Quite wealthy by now, Claus and Anna Spreckels had thirteen children over the years, but only five lived to maturity.

In 1865, Spreckels spent eight months in Germany studying beet sugar farming and technology. By 1872, he had invested in sugar beet planting near Santa Cruz. He induced other local farmers to plant sugar beets after guaranteeing to buy their crops, then built a beet refinery. Soon sugar beets were a major crop of the coastal area.

Not content with his highly rewarding San Francisco and coastal sugar refining operations, Claus Spreckels now gazed with covetous eyes on the Hawaiian Islands. When the price of Hawaiian sugar cane increased by two cents a pound in 1876, Spreckels quickly moved into the new territory. Through loans to King Kalakaua and his kingdom, he acquired vast economic and political power. His Maui plantation at Spreckelsville was the showplace of the islands, but despite his money and influence, there was trouble in Spreckels' Pacific paradise.

Adolph Spreckels took the *Chronicle* more seriously than did his father, who, however, spared no expense in his son's defense. *California State Library.*

For some time, the *Chronicle* had been accusing Spreckels of monopolistic policies and other transgressions. One article insisted Claus used slave labor, and even lepers, to work in his Maui plantation sugar fields. Another article reported that Spreckels had provided women from the mainland for the king, in exchange for his plantation property.

When first issued in 1882, public stock of the company sold for around sixty dollars. By late 1884, however, the operation was heavily in debt and the stock had diminished to twenty-five cents a share. With a $1,000,000 personal loan and other machinations, Spreckels began slowly moving the price upward.

Following an investigation, the *Chronicle* determined that the sugar company's manipulations were an attempt to bilk the public. On November 17, 1884, just prior to a stockholders' meeting, the *Chronicle* published a particularly nasty article:

> The case of the Hawaiian Commercial and Sugar Company is the old story. All that is of value will be gobbled by Sir Claus Spreckels...

> It seems doubtful whether the Commercial ever made any money at all. On August 31, 1882, it seems to have had $17,569 in the bank, on the strength of which the Directors declared a divi-

dend of $50,000. After paying the dividend the company was indebted to the bank [in the amount of] $55,333, thus increasing its indebtedness to the bank to $122,600. Not only was all the dividend money borrowed, but the receipts from all sources continued to fall short of the expenditures... Of course somebody knew that the company, instead of making money and earning dividends, was really falling behind all the time... The Directors... can be indicted and convicted...

Claus took all this in stride, striking back with personal attacks on Michael De Young in a friendly local weekly newspaper. His son, Adolph, at this time secretary of the California Sugar Refinery, had been pushed to the edge, however.

In a scenario strikingly similar to his brother's assassination, Mike returned to the *Chronicle* business office a little after five o'clock on the evening of November 19, 1884. A number of employees were in the office as De Young entered, made his way past the counter, and pushed open a swinging brass gate. He had just reached a desk when he heard someone call from behind him.

"Mr. De Young! Mr. De Young!"

Turning, the newsman's eyes widened in terror. Adolph Spreckels had followed him closely into the office and was just a few feet away, pointing a pistol directly at him. With a dozen witnesses in the office, the *Chronicle* account of what happened next is probably as accurate as any:

> Another instant, and without another warning, Spreckels fired. With the sight of the flash Mr. De Young felt a jar in the left side, and running quickly by the end of the desk, tried to put it between himself and his assailant. Spreckels dashed open the little gate, cocking his pistol as he came along, and, coming up in a few rapid strides to that corner of the desk at which Mr. De Young had first stood, passed it and leveled his weapon again. By that time, however, Mr. De Young had given up trying to get out of the way of his desperate pursuer, and on reaching the end of the third side of the desk, he turned to grapple with the would-be murderer.
>
> As he did so his foot slipped and he fell forward in a half-stooping posture. While in this helpless position, Spreckels turned his pistol on him and fired the second shot.

De Young felt another stab of pain, this time in his left shoulder.

Michael De Young at his desk in the editorial rooms of the *Chronicle*. *California Illustrated.*

By this time George Emerson, one of the clerks, had snatched a pistol from a drawer and fired at Spreckels at almost the same time as De Young received his second shot. Spreckels was hit in the arm, just as two other clerks rushed up and seized the gunman. When a police officer burst into the smoke-filled room, the excitement was over.

Medical bulletins were issued to the press for the next few days, but it quickly became apparent that De Young's wounds were not serious. Spreckels' injury was slight, also. The press almost universally condemned the assault, particularly since the De Young attacks on the sugar company had nowhere near the bite of previous feuds. "So far as we have been able to judge," said the *Napa Daily Reporter*, "that paper [the *Chronicle*] has confined its strictures and comments upon Claus Spreckels with the proprieties of honorable and legitimate journalism." Most other papers agreed. Perhaps the *Chronicle*, like the city in which it was spawned, was beginning to grow up.

The trial of Adolph Spreckels lasted over six weeks, beginning in June 1885. Spreckels fielded a team of four prominent attorneys, headed by the formidable Hall McAllister. The prosecution boasted the talents of Judge Alexander Campbell and Reuben H. Lloyd, both very skilled lawyers of long experience.

THE acquittal of A. B. Spreckels was followed by scenes that do not speak much for the judgment of his friends and relatives, who are described as having rent the air with shouts of joy, and later on the Spreckels mansion was illuminated, a brass band engaged to blow sounds of joy over the result, while the friends and sympathizers assembled within the house and were wined and feasted in honor of the event. Naturally, Mr. Spreckels' friends were glad to see him escape punishment, but a regard for decency would have suggested a less demonstrative manner of expressing their feelings.

Young Spreckels' acquittal for the DeYoung shooting was condemned in most of the press, the Fresno *Daily Evening Expositor* taking its criticism one step further. *Author's collection.*

Claus Spreckels and his other offspring were in court every day. And, despite the constant and overwhelming references in the press to the "cowardly" and "brutal" assassination attempt, the defense managed to stall, confuse, and overload the case with extraneous detail which slowly wore down the prosecution. Interest in the case was so widespread that the *Folsom Weekly Telegraph* devoted its whole front page to trial testimony.

Judge Alexander Campbell.
Author's collection.

The defense pled both insanity and self-defense and somehow made it work. Despite a herd of witnesses who testified De Young was given no chance in the encounter, the defense brought in a witness who testified De Young had fired first; this, despite the fact that the victim denied even carrying a weapon that day. And no witness saw him draw a pistol, which he certainly would have done under the circumstances.

Still, the jury returned a verdict of "not guilty." We can only speculate if it would have been the same had the *Chronicle*'s reputation been better.

The feuding frontier days were coming to a close, in the larger cities at least. Slowly, the surfeit of newspapers in San Francisco was modified, and most were weeded out, until only the larger dailies survived. In September 1913, the *Call* was purchased by the *Chronicle*, reminding the oldtimers how that newspaper had tried to buy out the De Young brothers at the beginning of their career. The acquisition was perhaps all the sweeter for some since the owner was now John D. Spreckels, another of Claus' sons.

Inspired by his brother's memory, Michael De Young plunged ahead to make the *Chronicle* into one of the great dailies in the country. Instead of involving himself in feuds, De Young became active in community affairs, associating himself with charitable endeavors and public events.

Michael De Young died in 1925, leaving many memorials to civic achievement, along with memories of California's violent, feuding, and colorful newspaper past.

UNPUBLISHED SOURCES

Byram, Edward, *Record Book No. 1*, a listing of criminals and companion volume to his personal journals. Collection of John Boessenecker

BOOKS

Bancroft, Hubert H. *History of California*, Vol. VII, 1860–1890. San Francisco: The History Company, Publishers, 1890.

Bruce, John. *Gaudy Century, 1848–1948*. New York: Random House, 1948.

Chapter 5 NOTES

Gagey, Edmond M. *San Francisco Stage: a History*. New York: Columbia University Press, 1950.

Issel, William and Cherny, Robert W. *San Francisco 1865–1932*. Berkeley, Los Angeles, London: University of California Press, 1986.

Wheeler, Keith. *The Townsmen*. Alexandria, VA: Time-Life Books, 1975.

Young, John P. *Journalism in California*. San Francisco: Chronicle Publishing Company, 1915.

_____. *San Francisco: A History of the Pacific Coast Metropolis*, 2 Vols. San Francisco, Chicago: The S. J. Clarke Publishing Company, 1912.

NEWSPAPERS

Butte *Record*, December 9, 1871

Fresno *Daily Evening Expositor*, November 20, 1884; July 3, 1885

Fresno *Weekly Republican*, April 2, 1881

Folsom *Weekly Telegraph*, July 18, 1885

Grass Valley Union, June 1, 1873

Merced *San Joaquin Valley Argus*, September 20, 1879

New York Times, April 24, 1880

San Francisco *Chronicle*, May 9, 1871; January 31, 1874; April 26, 1880; November 17, 20, 21, 22, 23, 1884

San Francisco *Daily Alta California*, May 8, December 31, 1871; February 1, 2, 4, 6, 1874; October 22, 25, 1876; April 3, 2, 4, 15, 26, 1880

San Francisco *Daily Dramatic Chronicle*, May 24,1865

San Francisco *Daily Evening Bulletin*, February 2, April 3, 1874

Shasta Courier, August 30, 1879

Visalia *Weekly Delta*, May 28, 1876; May 27, 28, June 3, 1874; April 30, 1880

OTHER SOURCES

Adler, Jacob, "The Sprecklesville Plantation: A Chapter in Claus Spreckles' Hawaiian Career," *California Historical Society Quarterly*, March 1861.

Rosenwaike, Ira, "The Parentage and Early Years of M. H. DeYoung," *Western States Jewish Historical Quarterly*, April 1975.

Chapter 6

Vengeance and Vendettas

The Coates - Frost Feud

"**I** looked around and saw Wesley Coates going out and Duncan behind him. Wesley Coates got in about six feet of one of the little oaks, turned 'round pulling off his coat. About the time he got his coat off, or laid it down, Duncan struck him with his pistol. Wesley Coates fell, as near as I could see. Duncan pursued him and they all began to pile in..."

And so began one of the most deadly gunfights in California history as recounted by an eyewitness. It was the culmination of a bitter feud that would fester and inflame, rotting families from within until members turned on each other. It was a vendetta in which the carnage reached truly epic proportions.

Situated some twenty miles north of Ukiah, in Mendocino County, Little Lake Valley was settled in 1853. Mendocino was a wild place then, with redwood forests, roving Indian tribes, wild animals and wilder roving white hunters competing for the land. When the Baechtel brothers established a cattle ranch in Little Lake Valley, it was not long before a village grew up among the scattered oaks lining the principal road of the area. A saloon was probably the first building put up in 1859; the "spiritual" needs of the budding community must be looked after first and foremost. A social hall, school, and store soon followed. The rough village of Little Lake lay within the confines of the present city of Willits.

The Frost family arrived in Little Lake Valley about 1858 from Davis County, Missouri. The head of the family, Elijah Frost, was called "Old Man" or "Pap" by his children and relatives. Born in Tennessee in 1800, "Pap" and his wife, Elisabeth, raised a family of nine children in Missouri before heading west. Two of the girls, Phoebe and Polly, had married and stayed behind, but Elisha, Isom, Martin, James, Catherine, Elisabeth, and Lavisa settled in California with their parents. The oldest son, Elisha, and his wife, Amanda, had seven children. Daughter Catherine later married Frank Duncan in Little Lake. Benjamin Frost, a cousin, also lived in Little Lake.

Southerners and Democrats, the Frosts were also highly partisan secessionists in their politics. They were hard-working sheep and hog raisers, but would fight at the drop of a hat and were usually armed. Oldtimers related how two of the Frost boys, on a drunken spree, shot up a local Indian rancheria and chased the natives off. Some days later two Indian women, one of them blind, were found in the hills in a starving condition. It was said that no Indian ever again set foot in the valley. It was also said that during inner-family quarrels, old Pap Frost would take down his shotgun and threaten to shoot the first one of his boys who drew a weapon.

The Frosts first ran afoul of the Coates family during the Civil War days. Abner Coates and brothers Thomas and George were natives of Pennsylvania. The same age as Pap Frost, Abner lived in Indiana and Wisconsin before joining a wagon train for California in 1859 with his wife, Cecelia, four sons, and three daughters. Two brothers, Thomas and George Coates, were with Abner and his family when they settled in Mendocino County. Abner farmed in Rock Tree Valley east of Little Lake, while brother George opened a grist mill in town. George's sons, Wesley, James, and Henry, presumedly helped out at the mill. Republicans in politics, the Coateses supported President Lincoln and the Union cause during the course of the war.

The children of both families attended the Little Lake school in the early years of the war. Most accounts agree that a Frost boy and a Coates boy had a disagreement and during recess, went into the school yard to settle the dispute. Given the times, the argument was probably over politics. In any case, the teacher broke up the scrap

A typical schoolhouse during California's frontier days. The school in this undated photo was at Knight's Ferry, in Stanislaus County. *Author's collection.*

and whipped both boys for their infraction of school rules.

Far from settling the matter, that night the boys complained of the incident to their fathers. Both men called on the teacher, each insisting his son should not have been whipped since the other boy was in the wrong. "To maintain discipline in the school," argued the teacher, "boys must be punished for infractions of the rules." While Coates came around to the teacher's way of thinking, the Frost father insisted the schoolmaster had erred and he took the matter before the school district board of trustees. A hearing was held and when the board sided with the teacher, Frost stomped out, vowing to see that none of the members would be reelected at the next election.

The Frost boy was no longer allowed to attend the school, and much of the community began taking sides in the matter. Threats between the two families made the situation even worse. Although the matter was eventually settled, bitter feelings had been engendered and some worried that the valley could never be the same.

Frank Duncan, Catherine Frost's husband, particularly disliked Wesley Coates, and the two frequently threatened each other. When they met one day in Little Lake, a verbal exchange was rapidly evolving into a gunfight when friends managed to separate them. Each vowed vengeance, as they were dragged off in separate directions.

In the waning years of the war, the two families engaged in several confrontations and brawls. Abraham Coates and Martin Frost met in Little Lake in the fall of 1866. Both were in their early twenties and they came together like two maddened bulls. Several of the other Coates boys joined in the brawl and Frost was badly beaten. A year later in early September 1867, Elisha Frost and one of the Coates men engaged in a violent argument at the polls. Members of both families now circled the two men, but the sheriff arrived in time to break up the fight. As the crowd began to leave, Frank Duncan shouted, "I can whip any abolitionist in Little Lake, or any Black Republican of the Coates name." The threat soon reached the ears of Wesley Coates.

A little over a month later a judicial election was being held in the Little Lake social hall. It was a warm afternoon, October 16, 1867, and all day voters had drifted in and out of the hall and Baechtel's general store and saloon. Up the road there was a small hotel and various travelers and voters had gathered there to pass the time. E. R. Budd, editor of the Ukiah *Mendocino Herald*, was there and later recalled that day:

> It was too warm to play cards any longer, so we concluded to sit under the shade of the overhanging awning and calmly await the cool of the evening. We had been there but a short time when we noticed a cloud of dust down the road which meant that somebody was coming to town. This was a relief, for in those days news from the outer world was scarce and every stranger was at least about to tell us something we had not heard before. We little thought any of us were about to witness one of the most speedy fights that ever took place in this or any other country.

The cloud of dust was Abner Coates' big farm wagon, filled with nine of his sons and relatives, who were on their way to vote. Abner always carried his shotgun when he traveled, and Wesley and Abraham were both wearing their pistols. Wesley was still smarting from Frank Duncan's "Black Republican" comments at the previous election.

Three of the Frost boys were lounging about Baechtel's store after voting. Elisha, the oldest of Pap's sons, was the father of seven young children, while Martin and Isom were in their early twenties and unmarried. Frank Duncan was sitting on the store counter when Henry and James Coates walked in. Henry and the Frosts exchanged a few words just as Henry's father, George, entered. He had heard the comments and said, "Henry, it's time to leave."

As Henry was ushered out by his father, he snarled, "I can't get any fight out of any damned big man."

Outside, Henry told his brother Wesley Coates that Duncan and the Frosts were inside. Brushing by his brother, Wesley entered the store and walked up to where Duncan still sat on the counter. Owin Whitcomb was in the store and described what happened next:

> Mr. Duncan was sitting on the counter in the jew store. Wesley Coates came in and said to him that he (Duncan) had said that "he could whip any Republican at Little Lake." Duncan said, "What he said, he had said out there before all, and that he did not take anything back." Wesley Coates then said "Do you say it now?" Duncan replied, "If it comes in the way I can." Wesley Coates then replied, "I am your man, just walk out and try it." Duncan kind of paused, that is [he] did not start at the challenge. Coates made some remark which I did not understand. Duncan said "I can do it damned quick, jumped off the counter and started out the door.

Wesley Coates followed Duncan out, stripping off his coat as he walked into the street. As Coates was laying his coat on the ground, Duncan turned and pulling his navy pistol, leapt forward and brought the weapon down on Wesley's head. Young Coates went down, but quickly tried to get to his feet as Duncan again struck him on the head, breaking his pistol in the process. Somehow Wesley remained conscious and struggled desperately with his enemy. He managed to grab a knife from Duncan's belt and stabbed him several times in the chest. Others rushed into the fight now, including the three Frosts and Abraham and Henry Coates. The men flailed with their fists and drew weapons, and it appeared as if the gates of hell had opened.

Duncan scrambled to his feet and ran, and Wesley followed and stabbed him again in the shoulder. Martin Frost's navy Colt was in his hand now and he shouted, "Stand back! Stand back!" Now gunfire erupted and clouds of powder smoke mingled with the dust kicked up by the struggling men.

A bullet struck Abraham Coates in the chest. He staggered to cover behind a pine tree, before collapsing. Martin Frost shot young Henry Coates next, his shot ripping into Henry's lung. Martin then fired twice at Albert Coates, who turned and ran since he was un-

The big Coates-Frost battle took place just across the road from these barns and outbuildings on the old Baechtel ranch, shown here in the 1890s. *John Boessenecker collection.*

armed. Albert had only gone a short distance when Elisha Frost shot him twice, the second round piercing his heart. "Oh, my God!" he gasped, and then he died.

Wesley Coates pulled his six-shooter and fired at Elisha, but missed. A moment later Martin Frost shot Wesley through the chest, giving him a mortal wound. Abner Coates now got into action and shot Elisha with both barrels of his shotgun. Frost died in the road with some thirty-eight pieces of lead in his body.

As the unarmed, elderly Thomas Coates tried desperately to stop the fight, he was interrupted by the crack of the pistols and he looked about, wide-eyed. Isom Frost quickly shot him twice in the chest and he dropped to the ground. Young James Coates was shot a moment later by Martin Frost and staggered into the store with a mortal wound.

Although badly wounded, Abraham Coates now crawled from behind his pine tree and shot at Martin Frost. Returning his fire, Frost's bullet ripped into Coates' shoulder and ploughed into his chest. Coates' return fire was the last shot of the battle, but it was ineffectual and he rolled over, mortally wounded.

As the dust settled and powder smoke slowly drifted away, spectators gasped at the scene before them, their gasps mixing with the groans of the dying and wounded. Some twenty shots had been fired in just fifteen seconds, and six men were dead or dying, with three others seriously wounded. The dead were:

Albert Coates, age twenty-two; Henry Coates, age twenty-five; Thomas Coates, age sixty-three; Wesley Coates, age thirty-three; Elisha Frost, age forty-three.

Abraham Coates died the next day, while James and Abner Coates and Frank Duncan all eventually recovered from their wounds. It had been a bloody day.

The services were held the following day, members of both families moving among the caskets wailing and sobbing uncontrollably over husbands, brothers, and fathers. The bodies were then loaded on wagons and taken to the graveyard, as reported in the *Mendocino Democrat:*

> The funeral procession was conducted with great order and judgement. The first wagon moved up and took off the oldest, Thomas Coates, and as it moved off five elderly gentlemen, all about the same age as the deceased, served as pall bearers, and walked along with the wagon to the grave. The next that followed was Elisha Frost, who was next in age. A like number of similar pall bearers took charge of his remains. The same ceremony was observed in each case. The funeral procession was about three quarters of a mile in length. They were all buried in the same graveyard, a few feet only from each other.

The fallen warriors, who had hated each other with such vehemence in life, would in death spend eternity in the company of each other's bones.

The toll of the deadly

battle was so horrifying that the two families seemed to carefully avoid each other from that day on. Fatherless children and their widowed mothers could only wonder in stunned silence how such mindless violence could happen. If only they had voted in the morning, instead of the afternoon. If only... , but there was no use wishing things had been different. Their lives had been changed forever.

Hiram Willits was a member of the coroner's jury after the big street fight between the Frost and Coates families. *Author's collection.*

As if the terrible tragedy had somehow un-leashed a curse on the two families, the Frosts and Coates would now begin a series of domes-tic squabbles within their own families. Frank Duncan, Catherine Frost's husband, was one of the early victims. When he got into a squabble with brothers-in-law Martin and Isom, he knew better than to hang around, and he left the valley with his family.

The Coates family also had brother-in-law troubles. Abner

Coates' daughter Mary had married a reckless character named Samuel Besse. The couple had a livestock partnership with Abner, who had allowed them to live in a house he owned in Scott's Val-ley, some twelve miles east of Little Lake. Abner and his son-in-law owned adjoin-ing land claims, the house being on Abner's property. When the two men had a dispute, Besse was ordered to leave the house, but he refused to do so.

After a period of time, Abner deter-mined to evict Besse from the house. On February 1, 1872, he sent sons John and William Coates over to help enforce the eviction. The two armed men were sent

Elisha Frost's grave in the Little Lake Cemetery. *Author's collection.*

as a precaution. Besse was known as a violent man who had frequent troubles with the law and had once been indicted for assault to commit murder. John Coates was tubercular and had been at the big street fight at Little Lake, but had not gotten involved. He disliked Besse and probably relished being able to evict him.

They found Besse in the woods near his home, hauling rails with his team. When they served him with the eviction notice, he read it, then tore it up. What happened next was reported in the *Petaluma Crescent on* February 7, 1872:

> The matter in dispute was brought up, when hard words and mutual accusations and recriminations ensued. The quarrel became so intensified that Besse drew a butcher knife and made an assault upon J. Coates, who drew a revolver and fired five shots at his antagonist, killing him instantly. The two brothers then returned to their home and at last accounts had not been arrested, though they were making no endeavor to evade the officers... Besse leaves a wife and several children... .

Arrested for the killing, John was indicted, tried, convicted, and sentenced to San Quentin state prison for three years. Because of his health he was pardoned by Governor Newton Booth in March 1873.

When Amanda, Elisha Frost's widow, died in 1870, her children were virtual orphans. There were two daughters and five sons, Asbury, David, Elijah, Jimmy, and Taylor. The oldest daughter's husband, James McKindley, was appointed guardian of the younger four boys, but he found it a tough and thankless task. Twenty-one-year-old Elijah was a particular nuisance. He seemed hell-bent on constantly getting into trouble.

Working with a pal named Bob Reynolds, Elijah stole a wagonload of

William Coates was present at the killing of his brother-in-law, Samuel Besse. *John Boessenecker collection.*

apples worth some fifty dollars. The pair were caught and arrested, but old court records indicate charges were dropped for lack of evidence. Taking his brother Taylor along, Elijah and Reynolds next stole

Hell-raising Elijah Frost and his faithful, but foolhardy wife, Mary. *John Boessenecker collection.*

some hogs and changed their ear brands. Once more they were caught, but again, they were released for lack of evidence.

Since he seemed to be getting away with his various transgressions, there was little reason for Elijah to clean up his act. And, he did not. In September 1875, Elijah and his fourteen-year-old brother took off on a horse-stealing expedition in northern California. Not content with putting his younger brother in harm's way, Elijah also drug his own wife, Mary, along when they stole sixteen horses from Joseph Brock's Shasta County ranch on Pit River.

Driving the stolen animals toward Red Bluff, the rustlers crossed the Sacramento River, heading south. Rancher Brock, a day behind them, reported the theft to Tehama County deputy sheriff O. A. Lovett. Tracking the stolen stock towards Oroville, Lovett and Brock teamed up with Butte County sheriff S. L. Daniels and arrested the three horse thieves a few miles from town.

In jail at Redding, the Frosts maintained they had bought the horses from "a Spaniard," but they were charged and indicted for grand larceny. Both Mary and fourteen-year-old Jimmy Frost were released, but Elijah stood trial in December 1875 and was convicted and sentenced to four years at San Quentin. If Little Lake residents hoped Elijah's enforced vacation might change his criminal tendencies, they were disappointed. When he was released on August 18, 1878, he returned home meaner than ever.

Taking up with Abijah Gibson and Tom McCracken, two young thugs of his own stripe, Elijah now embarked on a campaign of thievery and vandalism. Besides robbing chicken coops and smoke houses, and cutting up harness belonging to local farmers, the gang's drunken howling and shooting off of their pistols in town terrified the local populace. One night a flock of geese were stolen and found dead the next morning, their heads tied between the rails of a fence. A man who protested against the thugs found his barn burned one morning.

Caught red-handed stealing a set of harness in September 1879, Elijah and his pals were ironed and placed in a guarded room in Brown's Hotel since there was no jail in Willits, a village one mile north of Little Lake. A preliminary hearing was quickly scheduled for September 4. Meanwhile, the prisoners were foolishly making threats, promising to retaliate against those who had been involved in their arrest. It was a bad mistake.

On the morning of September 4, attorney J. A. Cooper was on the stagecoach heading for Willits to defend Frost, Gibson and McCracken. Near town he was stopped by a rider who was going to Ukiah to summon the coroner. The lawyer was told his services were no longer needed. The reason was explained in an article the following day in the *Ukiah City Press:*

> The prisoners were in bed, handcuffed (two together, one singly) in a small room opening out of the office of Brown's hotel. J. Tatham and Davis were guarding them. Between one and two o'clock A.M., Thursday morning, about 25 men with feet and heads muffled in sacks, walked in on them without ceremony, tied and gagged them [the guards], aroused and served the prisoners in the same way, and marched the whole party out in the street and through town to the bridge, about 400 yards off. Then ropes were placed on their necks , tied to the side rails, and the three pushed over. Two were hanged manacled together on one side, and one lone corpse

This 1888 Willits street scene shows the hotel, at far right, from which Elijah Frost and his pals were taken and lynched in 1879. *Courtesy Rena Lynn Moore.*

swung on the other side. The neck of one was broken, but the other two seemed to have died of strangulation. So quiet were the whole proceedings that they were in the house and out before anyone was alarmed, and then nothing wrong was suspected. The Coroner's jury found no one in particular guilty.

The vigilantes were apparently from Little Lake, and although several press notices decried the extralegal proceedings, few citizens complained. Before the prisoners were lynched, the vigilantes demanded they tell where all their stolen loot had been hidden. They steadily refused until the ropes had been put around their necks, then they quickly blurted out a location where much stock and other stolen items were located.

"One of the unfortunates," wrote a contemporary, "belonged to a younger generation of the Frost family. Some of the good people of Little Lake declare to this day [1899] that the leading regulator was a Frost, and an uncle to the boy he ordered hanged." It was known locally at the time that Martin Frost had been one of the vigilantes and the lynched Elijah's four brothers were very bitter toward their uncle. James "Little Jimmy" Frost, now seventeen years old, was a hard case, as was his brother, Taylor, and more trouble was expected.

Oddly enough, while the Frost family was turning on itself, a newspaper item in the *Democrat* announced that, among others, "M. Frost and Chas. Coates" had been appointed as assistants to Ukiah city marshal J. A. Jamison for the duration of the local county fair.

But Martin Frost's placid streaks were short-lived. It was just a year later that he and one of his brothers rode over to Ukiah on a Friday night for some recreation. According to the local press he was "armed and well equipped for a good time." He made the rounds of the saloons, filled himself with "tarantula Juice" and whooped it up generally before staggering to bed late that night.

The next morning he was considerably hungover and thought a little whiskey would improve what ailed him. That first drink was so good he took a little more and by nine o'clock in the morning he was thoroughly plastered again. His loud shouting and careless handling of his pistol began to alarm his brother, who snatched his English bull-dog revolver away from him to prevent any trouble. When

Martin promised to start for home right away, his pistol was returned, but he quickly back-peddled on the agreement.

Taking up a position on the sidewalk in front of the People's Hotel on State Street, Frost began flourishing his pistol and forcing pedestrians to the middle of the road. When some affronted citizens complained to Marshal Jamison, the lawman quickly made his way to the hotel. He found a drunk and raging Martin in the hotel's saloon, but before he could come up with a strategy to handle him, the bad man grabbed him by the coat and pulled him into the room. He accused the marshal of trying to arrest him and threatened to kill him if he tried anything. The Ukiah *Democratic Dispatch*, October 29, 1880, related what happened next:

> Mr. Jamison at once saw the condition Frost was in and tried to quiet him, and finally persuaded him to sit down and have a talk. He remained seated but in a moment, when springing to his feet, he declared that no man could make him sit down and then stepped back a few paces, put his hand to his hip pocket and ordered the official to remain seated. The Marshal, seeing there was likely to be trouble, in order to gain time and get nearer to Frost, rose up slowly, saying that he could not sit there without someone to talk to. Without further ceremony, Frost drew his revolver and attempted to level it for the purpose of firing, when Jamison sprang upon him, grasping him around the body with his right arm, and with his left hand

Ukiah in the 1880s, when Martin Frost "hurrahed" the town. *Mendocino County Historical Society.*

seizing the pistol. They had quite a scuffle, Frost endeavoring to get the pistol in position to shoot, and Jamison doing his utmost to frustrate him. Seeing that his life depended on disarming his antagonist, the officer pushed him backward toward the fireplace, in which there was a good fire burning at the time, intending to shove him into it and then force him, by means of the fire, to give up the revolver. But just as the contestants reached the fender there was an explosion, and a

The local fire department poses on Ukiah's State Street, with the People's Hotel in the background. *Robert J. Lee collection.*

moment later Frost relinquished his hold on the revolver and began to sink, and would have fallen into the fire had the officer not prevented him.

Frost had accidentally shot himself, the bullet burying itself in a bone of his right foot. It was a painful wound and a physician was immediately sought. The newspaper thought it strange that none of the bystanders in the saloon had helped the marshal, but obviously none cared to invite the enmity of the dreaded Frost family. The next day Martin insisted he had no recollection of his escapades, "which," commented the press, "is undoubtedly true, as he was perfectly crazy with liquor."

Apparently no charges were filed against Martin Frost, although he should have been prosecuted for assaulting an officer. Perhaps Marshal Jamison was on good terms with Frost when he was sober, or perhaps he, too, disliked the idea of getting on the wrong side of the Frost family. As a "peace" officer, this tactic seemed the practical thing for the marshal to do, especially since the town had no jail.

However, Martin Frost seemed incapable of staying out of trouble for long. In early March 1882, Martin and his cousin, forty-six-year-old Benjamin Franklin Frost, took a drove of hogs over to the coastal village of Mendocino. After disposing of their hogs, the boys had a few drinks and slept that night in town. They were up early and started on the return trip home. John Robertson, who had brought a wagonload of turkeys over to the coast, had met the Frosts in town and was returning to Little Lake with them. Robertson was riding horseback, while a young boy was driving his wagon. Ben had brought along a bottle and was having trouble staying on his horse by the time they neared home. The *Mendocino Beacon* reported on March 18:

> When somewhere near the observatory on the Little Lake road, Ben Frost, who was intoxicated, came near falling off his horse, when his brother and Mr. Robertson came to his assistance, and in the scuffle which ensued in trying to keep him on his horse, which was skittish and wild, a pistol which Mr. Robertson had in his pocket was discharged accidentally, the bullet taking effect in Ben Frost's body, killing him almost instantly, he only living long enough to exclaim "Who fired that pistol?"

Martin Frost, perhaps the most deadly of all the Frost family gunmen.
John Boessenecker collection.

Ben was placed in the wagon and taken home to his widow and four children. At the inquest, Martin and Robertson told a somewhat different story of what had occurred. Ben had lost his hat and was trying to retrieve it without dismounting and fell to the ground. As Martin and Robertson were helping him remount, there was a pistol shot and Ben fell forward and was dead in a few moments. Testimony brought out the fact that the pistol had been fired from inside a saddlebag on Robertson's horse when the animal had shaken itself, or perhaps made a jerky movement. Whatever had happened, it was a peculiar incident, but the coroner's jury agreed it was an accident and the matter was closed.

Meanwhile, bad blood still simmered between the younger Frost boys and Martin and Isom. Twenty-two-year-old Jimmy Frost had not forgotten the lynching of his brother, Elijah. And, although he married Alice Whitcomb in 1878 and had two children and every-

"Little Jimmy " Frost had his pistol out and ready when he outshot his uncle Martin.
John Boessenecker collection.

thing to live for, Martin continued on his own path to self-destruction. When he quarrelled with Jimmy Frost over a parcel of land, Martin threatened to kill his nephew, and Little Lake Valley waited to see what would happen next.

Andreas Hamburg was a quiet, respected local rancher who operated a sheep ranch in nearby Scott's Valley. Hamburg and Martin Frost were business partners and the German immigrant soon found that Martin's problems were his, also. One night Jimmy and Taylor Frost went to Hamburg's home and called for him to come outside. Suspicious about the late-night callers, the German asked his wife to see who was there. The response was "Mart and Isom Frost." Hamburg knew better and had his wife tell them to come back the following day.

When Hamburg told his partner what had happened, Martin was angry. He was sure the young Frost boys were looking for an excuse to kill his partner. Taking along Alf McCabe and Charlie Bean, two enemies of the Frosts, Martin rode out to look for his nephews. They were not at Taylor's ranch, so they rode over to James McKindley's, the former guardian and brother-in-law of Jimmy and Taylor. As they rode up to the house, they saw the two nephews standing near the well, close by the kitchen door. It was four o'clock in the afternoon. Twenty-year-old Sarah McKindley recalled what happened next:

> Martin Frost spoke to Taylor and James Frost who were standing near the kitchen door and also near the well. Taylor and James spoke then in a low tone and nodded their heads. Seeing that the parties did not speak to each other, I stepped to the kitchen door and spoke to Uncle Mart and invited him in. Mr. McCabe remarked that they would not have time. Mart Frost remarked to me that Taylor and James Frost would not speak to him. He got off his horse and came to the kitchen door and shook hands with me and stated that he was a friend to me, but that the boys had not treated him right or were not friends to him or some such remark. I remarked to him that it was best to have peace between all and he remarked that... they were the cause of all the trouble.

When Charlie Bean walked up to the Frost boys, Taylor pushed him away saying he did not want any trouble. Turning to Martin, Taylor said, "No Mart, I am not the cause of any trouble."

"You are a damned lying son-of-a-bitch!" snarled Martin.

"By God, you are another!" returned Taylor, as their uncle reached for his hip pocket.

Jimmy had already quietly drawn his pistol and was holding it behind him. Now he swiftly swung the weapon around and shot Martin in the head, the bullet exiting just behind the right ear. He was dead when he crashed into the well platform.

With his pistol still smoking, Jimmy then cursed and shouted for Bean and McCabe to get out of there, to which they promptly responded. The killer then rode to Ukiah and turned himself in at the county jail. Asked if Martin had drawn his pistol during the fight, Jimmy replied, "No. If he had, I would not be here to tell it."

Aurelius O. Carpenter was foreman of the jury that freed Little Jimmy Frost. Carpenter later co-authored a history of Mendocino and Lake counties. *Author's collection.*

The *Ukiah City Press*, January 4, 1884, reported:

> The east side of Little Lake Valley has been the scene of another Frost tragedy. Last Friday afternoon Mart Frost went to the residence of Mr. McKindley, and there, meeting Taylor and young James Frost, a quarrel ensued during which James Frost shot Mart through the head, killing him almost instantly. James went immediately to Ukiah and gave himself in charge. Mart was buried last Sunday in the burying ground north of town. His remains were followed by a large concourse of his neighbors, notwithstanding the rain. He leaves a wife and two children.

Young Frost was charged with first degree murder, and his trial began on July 8, 1884. His defense was that he had shot to protect his brother and, taking Martin's reputation into consideration, the jury returned a verdict of not guilty.

There were some who relished the passing of Martin Frost, but his brother Isom was not one of them. Convinced that a terrible injustice had taken place, Isom now swore revenge against the younger Frosts who had killed his brother. Grieving and furious that Jimmy was free, Isom tried to drink up all the liquor at the house of Old Jim Frost (his only remaining brother). Two of Jim's ranch hands, Isaac Smith and Jose Sicotte, were helping in Isom's drinking project and later in the evening the tanked-up trio made their way down the road to Tom Gibson's cabin. Gibson was an old friend of Isom's and a brother-in-law of Andreas Hamburg.

George Gibson found himself drawn into a deadly, no-win situation. *California State Archives.*

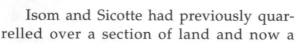

Isom and Sicotte had previously quarrelled over a section of land and now a squabble broke out between the two ranch hands on one side, and Isom and Gibson. As Gibson snatched Sicotte's rifle, Isom pulled his Bowie knife and stabbed both men, inflicting only minor wounds. Sicotte and Smith then fled, but armed themselves and returned, firing some twenty rounds into the cabin. Gibson and Frost returned the fire, Isom receiving a shot in the knee.

Old Jim's two ranch hands were arrested and tried on assault to murder charges. Each received six years in San Quentin state prison. Isom, however, still hungered for revenge.

The last of Isom's brothers, Old Jim, was sixty years old. He also despised the overbearing young Frosts, but preferred to stay in the background and let others do the dirty work. Tom Gibson also refused to get involved, even for the $500 Isom offered.

Isom did not want to tackle Jimmy alone, because of his brothers. Taylor was as tough as Little Jimmy, and brothers David and Asbury might very well figure into the equation when the chips were down. It was too risky. Isom needed a partner and Tom Gibson's younger brother, George, now seemed to be the most likely candidate.

Like his brother Tom, George Gibson had grown up with the young Frosts and knew them well. There had been a rupture in their relations, however, when Taylor Frost had roughed him up at a dance one night. The Frosts had resisted any effort of Gibson's to make peace and had continued to harass him at every opportunity. When Gibson settled on a piece of public land in 1883, the Frost boys contested his claim, threatening to kill him if he didn't give it up. One day when riding into town, Gibson noticed Little Jimmy and a pal named Les Case riding in the opposite direction. Then, returning to his claim the next day, he again encountered Frost and Case, who were riding into town.

"When I got there [to his claim]," recalled Gibson later, "I found my house, with all I had in it, burned to the ground. I turned around and saw a little tree with a piece of paper stuck on it. I walked up to the tree and counted twelve bullet holes fired into the tree, one right over the other. I took the paper down and there was a coffin drawn with a lead pencil, and my name right in the center... ." Gibson got the message and never returned to the claim. Later, the Frosts acquired the land.

Perhaps things might have ended there, but the Frosts continued their harassment and bullying of young Gibson. Isom also kept up his pressure for Gibson to join his assassination scheme. Gibson steadily refused, but Isom and Old Jim kept reminding him of threats against him made by the young Frosts. They told him repeatedly, Gibson reported later, "If I didn't go, I would be killed anyway." Finally, he agreed to go along with a plan to kill Jimmy and his brothers.

It was known that the Frost brothers were to attend a sheep rodeo beginning on April 8, at Hamburg's place in Scott's Valley. Although Hamburg had been Martin Frost's business partner, business came first and no trouble was expected. The sheep roundup would last for several days and Isom's plan was to ambush the Frosts as they rode up the Rocktree Grade on the way to Hamburg's corrals. On the appointed day, Isom and Gibson were lying in wait, but none of the younger Frosts appeared.

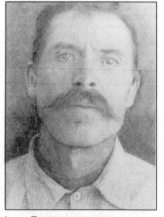

Isom Frost. *Author's collection.*

They finally realized the victims had already passed by. Returning to Old Jim's place, the two ate a noon meal, then Gibson said he "had had enough," and he rode back to Hamburg's corral where he worked the rest of the day separating and marking sheep. That evening he rode back with Old Jim.

At the turnoff for Jim's place, the old man asked him to come and stay the night. Gibson said his wife was expecting him, but Jim again began insisting that he stay and go with Isom in the morning to "kill them damned Indians." He kept up his arguments until Gibson followed him up to the house, where they joined Isom and a friend named Ed Jewell.

The next morning Old Jim went back to Hamburg's, while Isom and Gibson followed a short time later. Both men carried 45-70 Marlin rifles. They tied their horses a mile and a half from the corrals, then walked the rest of the way. Taking up positions under a fir tree on a ridge, they saw some fifteen men working among the sheep about 130 yards below. Only Jimmy and Dave Frost were armed with pistols.

As the two assassins watched, Little Jimmy Frost walked from the corral to the wool shed. "When he comes back," Isom hissed, "I'm going to kill him. You shoot Dave." Pulling a sheep by a hind leg, Jimmy reappeared and deposited the animal inside a corral. As he stepped to the side of the gate, Jimmy rested his hands on the fence and Isom drew his bead. The shot was hardly audible to those

Sheep shearing season in old Mendocino County, probably Anderson Valley. It was during such an occasion that "Little Jimmy" Frost was killed.
Robert J. Lee collection.

below as the bullet ripped through Jimmy's back and, bursting out of his chest, ploughed into the fence. An account in the *Mendocino Beacon* described what happened next:

> James Frost was seen to suddenly stop his work and throwing up his hands he exclaimed, "I am shot!" Strange to say, no report of a firearm was heard, and from the course taken by the ball it is thought that the shot was fired from the hill nearby. Frost fell to the ground mortally wounded, but he immediately drew his revolver and shot Hamburg, the bullet entering his abdomen. Hamburg also fell, and Dave Frost, who was armed, shot him through the heart. The Frosts then emptied their revolvers at whoever chanced to show themselves, Tom Lynch being the only person struck. James Frost, helpless and evidently near his dissolution, prayed that someone would reload his revolver that he might kill another of the cowards... .

Sheriff Jeremiah "Doc" Standley.
California State Library.

Isom and Gibson watched as Dave Frost grabbed one of Hamburg's horses and rode away. They quickly walked back to their own mounts, keeping under cover as best they could. Once out of the valley, Isom stopped near Old Jim's place where he turned to young Gibson.

"Don't you chirp this now," he growled. "If you do, I'll blow the top of your head off, too!"

Gibson quickly rode to his home in Little Lake. "I was between two thorns," he would later comment, "and didn't know which would stick me first."

As word traveled to Ukiah concerning the shootings, Isom talked two friends and neighbors, Ed Jewell and Jake Dunn, into swearing that he had been at Old Jim's all morning. By ten the next morning, County Sheriff Jeremiah "Doc" Standley was at the scene of the murders. Nicknamed "Doc" because he had nursed an animal back to health when he was a mere boy, Standley was elected sheriff in 1882, had served several terms and was one of the best of California's pioneer lawmen. At the scene, Standley placed a rod in the bullet hole produced by the ball that had killed Jimmy Frost. It pointed straight to the ridge from where the shots were fired. After climbing the hill, Standley found broken twigs and other evidence that someone had been there recently.

After interviewing those present during the shooting, the sheriff talked to the two elder Frosts, as well as Jewell and Jake Dunn. All insisted Isom had been home all that day. Doc noticed that Jewell appeared to be afraid of Isom, and if he were dealing with a conspiracy, Jewell was the weak link. The lawman had known Isom for a long time and was certain he had killed Jimmy Frost. He watched Jewell for several days hoping to catch him away from the Frosts, but could never do so.

Then Jimmy Frost's brothers threw a monkey wrench into the sheriff's plans. After the investigation had dragged on for some time, David, Asbury, and Taylor agreed to offer a $6,000 reward for the arrest and conviction of their brother's killer. It was just what the sheriff didn't want. As soon as he heard of the plan, he quickly called on the brothers and asked them to rescind their reward offer as that would certainly scare off the suspects. He had a clue as to the guilty parties and he was sure he could arrest and secure their conviction. Standley informed them that he was only waiting for Ed Jewell to leave the Frost house so that he could get him alone and get a confession from him. All he wanted in compensation, continued the sheriff, was enough money to defray expenses, hire a competent deputy as assistant, and employ an attorney. Three thousand dollars would, in his opinion, be more than enough. The Frosts were satisfied to leave the matter in Standley's hands.

Finally, Jewell disappeared. After investigating, Standley learned that Old Jim and Jake Dunn had driven Jewell to Healdsburg in a covered wagon. The sheriff went quickly to work. He hired a Point Arena man, George McMullen, to go to Healdsburg and see what he could discover. When Jewell disappeared again, McMullen traced him to Willows, then over to Marysville. There, he was reported to be working on a Yuba River wharf. After reporting back to Standley, the two men traveled to Marysville, where they learned Jewell was employed by a man named Schimp. The two lawmen explained the situation and Schimp was induced to employ McMullen to work with Jewell and share his room. After the two men became pals, McMullen soon learned the story of the murders.

It was mid-September 1885, when McMullen steered his roommate into a drinking spree. After Jewell was thoroughly plastered, a Marysville police officer put him into a cell where Standley called on him the next morning. It was very simple. Jewell had harbored and concealed the identities of the killers and was an accessory after the fact. For his testimony, however, Standley and the district attorney would request leniency and he would receive a minimum three years in prison. Jewell grimly nodded his head. The first part of the plan had succeeded.

Doc Standley already knew that Isom Frost was herding sheep in the backcountry of Trinity County. Taking the train to Red Bluff, the sheriff rented a horse and proceeded up Cottonwood Creek to where the sheep camp was located. He found the cabin vacant and sat down nearby. Standley had waited an hour when his quarry came walking down the trail toward the cabin with his rifle on his shoulder. Isom didn't see Doc until he was but a few feet away. He was startled when the lawman stood up and said, "What in the devil are you doing here, Isom?"

The bad man instinctively offered his hand which was grasped by Doc's left, his right hand on the butt of his double-action pistol. "Give me your gun," requested the officer. Isom sullenly did as he was told, "You are under arrest for the murder of Jimmy Frost," said Standley. "Are you going to kick?"

"How can I kick?" responded Isom. "I have nothing to kick with."

After returning to Marysville, Standley proceeded to Ukiah with McMullen and the two prisoners. On September 25, he arrested George Gibson at midnight in Little Lake and soon had him jailed with the other suspects. Both Jewell and Gibson turned state's evidence and were given the light sentences they had been promised.

Dave Frost was tried for killing Andreas Hamburg, his defense being that his brother Jimmy had shot the sheep man. Ed Jewell testified that Isom told him that Hamburg had given George Gibson

$1,000 to kill Jimmy Frost, but whether it was true or not, the jury deadlocked and Dave went free.

When Isom Frost went on trial on January 5, 1886, his defense was an uphill battle. After five days he was convicted of first-degree murder and sentenced to life in Folsom State Prison. As to the reward, Sheriff Standley called on the Frost boys and presented his bill. "When we came to settle with him," they later wrote, "although he had our note and mortgage for the whole amount, he delivered to us a full account of all expenditures, which reached the amount of $2,000, which was all he claimed, was satisfactory to us, and which was all we paid him."

After serving eighteen years of his sentence, Isom was paroled in 1904 and returned to Little Lake. He died there on April 29, 1928. A peaceable and chastened old man by this time, he was probably the last relic of the devastating Coates-Frost feud that had cost so much in wasted lives and shattered families.

California's dreaded Folsom State Prison.
California State Library.

DOCUMENTS

Bunner, W. C., "California's Family Feud," Willits, 1899, handwritten document dealing with the feud, in the collection of John Keller, courtesy John Boessenecker

People vs. James Frost, Case No. 2474, Mendocino County Superior Court, typed notes from court record, including statement of Sarah McKindley, Mendocino County Historical Society Library, courtesy John Boessenecker

Chapter 6
NOTES

BOOKS

Bossenecker, John. *Badge and Buckshot*. Norman and London: University of Oklahoma Press, 1988.

Bancroft, Hubert Howe. *The Works of Hubert Howe Bancroft, History of California*. San Francisco: The History Company, Publishers, 1886.

Carpenter, Aurelius O., and Millberry, Percy H. *History of Mendocino and Lake Counties*. Los Angeles: Historic Record Co., 1914 .

Cossley-Batt, Jill L. *The Last of the California Rangers*. New York and London: Funk & Wagnalls Company, 1928.

Nixon, Stewart. *The Redwood Empire*. New York: E. P. Dutton & Co., 1966.

Palmer, Lyman. *History of Mendocino County*. San Francisco: Alley, Bowman & Co., 1880.

NEWSPAPERS

Healdsburg Democratic Standard, October 24, 1867

Marysville Daily Appeal, September 27, 1885

Mendocino Beacon, September 13, 1979; March 18, 1882; May 15, 1886

Mendocino Democrat, February 8, 1872; September 6, 1879

Mendocino Herald, April 24, 1868

Petaluma Crescent, February 7, 1872

Petaluma Journal and Argus, October 24, 1867, November 7, 1867

Sacramento *Record-Union*, April 13, 1885

San Francisco *Daily Alta California*, October 26, 1867

San Francisco*Daily Evening Bulletin*, October 25, 1867; February 8, 1872

San Francisco *Daily Morning Call*, October 22, 1867

Ukiah City Press, September 5, 1879; January 4, 1884

Ukiah *Democratic Dispatch*, October 29, 1880; January 4, 1884; January 29, 1886

OTHER SOURCES

Cornish, Ken, "Little Lake Feud," *Frontier Times*, March, 1977.

Chapter 7

Ambushes and Street Fights

The Walker-Burton Feud

Scrubby oaks and brush, with a scattering of pine, cover the rocky hills of the Kern River Valley. Quaint names, dating from the early days, are sprinkled throughout the area: Oyster Bar, Greenhorn Gulch, Dutch Flat, Hogeye Gulch, and Rattlesnake Creek. It is a quiet, sparsely inhabited area today. Although pioneer stockmen had already invaded the area as early as the 1850s, gold was the real lure. Miners were soon prowling the gulches and hills and the mining camp of Keyesville was established by 1854. The villages of Havilah, Kernville, and Whiskey Flat appeared almost magically in that twilight of the 1849 Gold Rush, during the big strikes in the early 1860s.

Arriving in California at the height of the Gold Rush, William Brannon Walker and wife Mary settled in Placer County where he worked as a miner. Southerners by birth and inclination, Walker and his wife joined many other Rebel sympathizers in the Kern River area. Walker built a house in Keyesville for his wife and son James, who had been born in 1861. A typical pioneer, hard-working and industrious, Walker worked in local mines while always prospecting for that big strike of his own. Benjamin was born in 1865, followed by William in 1867, then came John Newton, Hal, Mary, and Phillip.

Born August 17, 1871, John Newton Walker was always called

"Newt" by the family. When he and his brothers grew older, all worked on nearby farms or cattle ranches and in local mines and sawmills. And all showed a marked interest and proficiency in fire-arms. This was the day of the gun, a time when a weapon meant game on the table, protection from a sometimes hostile nature, and personal defense when a peace officer might be many miles away. All of the boys spent their money on guns and ammunition and their spare time in target practice.

The Gibson and Burton families were neighbors of the Walk-ers, engaged in modest mining and farming operations. The three families were friendly and the boys grew up together, often work-ing, hunting, and fishing together. The youngsters were toughened by their frontier upbringing, but seemed to have gotten along well and by all accounts were popular and good workers.

Sometime in the 1880s, a stranger took up residence on the South Fork of the Kern River. He was a long-haired, buckskin-clad char-acter with the curious name of Jack Spratt. He apparently became

A group of workers in Andy Brown's Kern Valley sawmill in 1894. Newt Walker is at top row, left, while Jim Walker is at bottom, left, sitting. *Merfle Hight collection.*

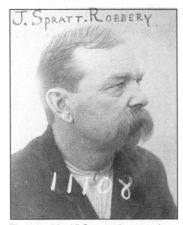

Thomas "Jack" Spratt, the notorious stage robber who would rather have others do his dirty work, when possible. *California State Archives.*

friendly with both the Burtons and the Walkers, despite his having a generally bad reputation. Indications are that his real name was Thomas Spratt, and he was originally from Ohio, but in 1860 he had lived for a time in Forest Hill, in Placer County. After joining the Second California Cavalry Regiment in September 1861, Spratt saw service in the Indian troubles in the Owens Valley area. When he was shot in the head during an Indian skirmish in April 1863, Spratt was sent to recover at the San Francisco Presidio. He was on detached duty at Fort Tejon the following September and in July 1864 was a member of Professor William H. Brewer's exploring party in the Sierra.

Spratt was mustered out in September of that year, but little is known of his movements for the next ten years. Reportedly, he worked on various Kern County ranches, then tiring of that, did some prospecting in the desert country. Several shooting scrapes are suggested as reasons Spratt took to a more lucrative, although less legal, means of earning a living.

Although he was never prosecuted for the job, Wells Fargo maintained that Spratt was the lone robber of the Mohave to Panamint stage on December 8, 1879. The *Inyo Independent* reported:

> There were no passengers or other persons aboard the stage except Miller, the driver, who was driving slowly along when a form arose apparently out of the earth, which without any introductory remarks, ordered him to "Throw out that box!" and to "drive on!" ...both orders were obeyed...

Spratt had netted $3,831 in gold coin and it was suspected the robbery was an inside job. Few clues and a slow response, coupled with the sparsely-settled desert area, resulted in a clean getaway by the outlaw. Wells Fargo later noted that Spratt then hid out with the Indians. By this time, the highwayman was known as John, or "Jack," Spratt, perhaps because his unusual surname reminded others of the John Clarke nursery rhyme which dated from 1639.

On October 12, 1883, Morris Jacoby and two other men were on their way to Caliente from Kernville. They were traveling in a light spring wagon and carrying an undisclosed amount of bullion for Michaels & Company. Suddenly, two highwaymen stopped the vehicle and demanded the bullion. Jacoby was equal to the occasion, however, as recorded in the *Kern County Californian* on October 22:

Wells Fargo's famous detective, James B. Hume. *California State Library.*

(The robbers) were assured, with such an appearance of truth and unwavering firmness that it had been forwarded some days previously in another conveyance, that they shouldered their rifles and withdrew. Jacoby was confident that he knew them, and proceeding directly to San Francisco, sent up a celebrated detective to ferret them out and arrest them... .

Jacoby had recognized Fletcher and Jim Burton, although both boys were still in their teens. He gave this information to the "celebrated detective" brought down from San Francisco, who happened to be James B. Hume, the Wells Fargo operative. Hume and a Kern County deputy sheriff quickly went into action as reported in the *Daily Californian*:

Last Saturday morning a Deputy Sheriff brought down and lodged in jail two men, James and Fletcher Burton, brothers, whom the evidence that they are the would-be-robbers unmistakably pointed out. They had not been long in jail before they weakened, confessing the crime, but alleging that they are not the principals— that it was planned and engineered by another under whose direction they acted. This resulted in the arrest of John Spratt, a resident of the South Fork.

At his hearing on November 15, 1883, Spratt pleaded not guilty and was represented by A. R. Conklin, under whom he had served in the army. Hume assisted the prosecution and trial was set for January 15, 1884. With the Burton boys' testimony and other evidence, Spratt was easily convicted and sentenced to San Quentin for ten years.

Although Spratt tried to implicate the Burtons in other crimes, the two boys seem to have been industrious and honest both before and after the attempted robbery with Spratt. It was unfortunate that a chain of circumstances had been set in motion which would affect their lives for some years to come.

Some of the Walker boys had been on friendly terms with Spratt. Having spent their whole lives in the Kern River area, the Walker boys undoubtedly liked to listen to Spratt's boasting of his Indian fighting days in the army and his travels to Fort Tejon and San Francisco. To the Walkers, it looked like the ex-soldier had taken a rap for the Burtons. A coolness developed between the families, aggravated by a mining dispute which erupted some time later. The Burtons and the Walkers both claimed ownership of a mine near Keyesville, but Jim and Fletcher Burton made it known that they intended working the mine in the face of all the Walkers who trod the earth. Both families had mines in the area, and their muttered threats and curses were soon intensified by armed men going to and from work.

Bill Gibson and his brother Charles were farmers in Hot Springs Valley and also had a part interest in the disputed Walker mine. Dave Burton married Addie, a sister of the Gibsons, sometime in the late 1880s. When the Gibson brothers went into a mining project with the Burtons, the agreement worked well for a time. However, when it appeared that one of the mine properties might be quite rich, there was a squabble about who had done the most work in the partnership.

About November 18, 1892, Bill Gibson filed on the claim in his name, but failed to mark the boundaries or post a notice to that effect. On the 28th, Luther Burton started for Bakersfield with friends, Mr. and Mrs. Robinson. Traveling in a light buggy, Burton was going to town to file his own claim on the mine. On the Hot Springs Grade, they met the Gibson brothers in their own buggy, leading a saddle horse. Both the Gibsons had rifles. The *Daily Californian* reported what happened next:

As they approached, Gibson said to Burton, "Have you recorded that mine yet?" "No," was the answer. "Well, you had better not, or there will be trouble," returned Gibson.

During the talk Mrs. Robinson became frightened and commenced to cry, and finally Gibson said, "Here are two guns. Let the lady drive on and you take one gun, and I will take the other, and we'll fight it out and will settle the thing right here." Burton declined the offer and finally drove on with his party, the Gibsons following for a while. As they finally turned to go away, one of the Gibsons said, "We are going right up to put Fletch off that mine."

Bill Gibson and his brother were victims of misplaced justice. *Jeff Edwards collection.*

That very night of November 28, 1892, Fletcher Burton was busying himself about his mining cabin while his brother Jim went to Kernville for supplies. It was bitter cold outside. Suddenly rifle shots disrupted the calm of the crisp night air and Fletcher Burton sprawled dying on his cabin floor. That same night, as Jim Burton was having a drink in Leon's Kernville saloon, another murderous shot cut him down at the bar. The shot was fired through a window, hitting Burton in the arm, then ploughing around his back and entering his side. Footsteps clattered down the wooden sidewalk and disappeared into the night.

Old Kernville in the days of the Walker-Burton feud. *Author's collection.*

Fletcher Burton was dead, but his badly wounded brother survived the deadly ambush. He told bystanders that Bill Gibson "must have shot him," but since Jack Spratt had recently been released from prison, suspicion immediately fastened on him, also. Officers searched a wide area but Spratt was nowhere to be seen. It was concluded that he had not been near Kernville, and the law soon began looking elsewhere for the killers.

Because of their numerous threats against the two Burtons, Bill and Charlie Gibson temporarily disappeared from the area, only to later surrender themselves to the sheriff in Bakersfield. They were afraid the other Burtons might shoot them on sight. They vehemently denied any knowledge of the crime, even though they were unable to come up with a satisfactory alibi for the fatal night. Sometime during the Gibsons' stay in jail and their prolonged trial, Ben Walker disappeared from home. Little attention seems to have been paid to this circumstance, however, and he never returned to Kern County.

Charles Gibson.
Jeff Edwards collection.

In early 1893, the Gibsons were convicted of first degree murder on circumstantial evidence and sentenced to life in San Quentin. Through it all, they stoutly maintained their innocence.

Meanwhile, Jim Burton recovered from his wounds and further trouble brewed in the hills around Keyesville. Charley Allison had been a mining partner of the Gibsons and had loudly proclaimed their innocence during and after their trial. Burton and Allison were soon discussing each other in unflattering terms, and saloon talk evolved into outright threats.

It isn't clear whether the two partisans met by chance or whether the meeting was a more formal affair. Whatever the circumstances, they did meet one day and both men were armed. A miner, resting beside the Kernville stage road, saw Burton and Allison approach each other near the bridge by the old Greenhorn Trail. He was the only witness to what happened, as reported in the *Daily Californian*:

In the encounter that followed the men circled around each other warily, both seeking for a point of vantage; there was a shot fired and Jim Burton lay dead in the road.

Allison was tried and vigorously prosecuted, but his plea of self-defense was accepted by the jury and he was acquitted. Two Burtons were dead but the feud raged unabated, with both sides threatening vengeance and more bloodshed. The mantle of the Burton family now passed to the two surviving brothers, Dave and Luther.

Over the years, the cause of the Gibson brothers attracted more and more attention. The nature of the circumstantial evidence which convicted them, coupled with Ben Walker's disappearance, combined to convince many people that a wrong had been done. A petition signed by the jury members, county officials, and other prominent citizens was submitted on their behalf, and in 1898, the governor commuted their sentence. The two brothers lived out their lives in peaceful anonymity near Porterville.

Thomas Walker as he appeared upon entering Yuma Territorial Prison in 1899. *Yuma Prison.*

A strained coexistence settled over the Kernville community. The Walkers and the Burtons never had anything to do with one another. Still, a fierce hatred remained, along with the feudists' nagging feeling of an unsettled score. In the mountains, settlers waited and wondered what turn the troubles might take next.

But the Walkers did not need a feud to liven up their existence. On April 28, 1898, Tom Walker was challenged to a fight by one William A. Woods, as they stood in the street at Kernville. Tom did not know the fellow and just walked away. Woods followed him into a saloon, and Woods again accosted him at the bar. When Walker tried to ignore him, Woods became even more obnoxious and he was thrown out of the place by the bartender. Woods shouted that he was going after his gun, and Walker left and called for his horse at the livery stable.

While waiting for his horse to be saddled, Tom saw Woods approaching him again. When Woods resumed his verbal assault, Tom drew and shot him in the neck, killing him. Everyone agreed that "a bad man got what he looked for," and Tom was exonerated by a coroner's jury.

Some months later Tom got into another scrape while working in

The mining village of Havilah as it appeared in its declining years. *Mrs. Marge Powers*

Arizona. Assaulted by a drunk named Bennett in a saloon, Tom swiftly drew and shot him down. Then, as Bennett lay on the floor, Tom shot him in the back, killing him. He was convicted of murder and sentenced to life in Yuma Territorial prison.

James Longstreet Walker was the blacksmith of the family. Jim was a hard working fellow but he too could shoot fast and accurately when he had to. In late 1903, Jim was sleeping in a tent at Kernville when a man named Cortinas entered and stole some money. Jumping up, Jim remembered he did not have a weapon with him and secured a pistol from a nearby friend. He quickly ran after the thief and caught up with him on a mountain trail. Cortinas saw him coming and raised his pistol, but Jim was too fast for him. He put a quick round into the thief, who failed to go down. Two more shots did the trick and Jim ran back to town for the coroner. Although tried for murder, Jim was acquitted and went back to his blacksmithing.

Even the baby of the Walkers, twenty-four-year-old Phillip, was involved in a murder in the Kern River village of Isabella. When he and several friends beat up and robbed an old man named Nichols on October 7, 1904, they were promptly caught and clapped in jail.

Nichols died from his beating and Phil and his pals were charged with murder. It was after attending Phil's trial in Bakersfield, that Newt and his father had their gunsmoke date with destiny.

The town of Havilah was born with the discovery of gold in 1864. Located between Kernville and Walker's Basin, it was a typical mining camp consisting of a dozen or so business buildings, surrounded by scattered tents and shacks. It was never much of a town as mining towns went, and when it narrowly lost the Kern County seat election in 1874, Havilah settled into the slow decline so typical of Western boom towns. By 1900, it was a sleepy little supply center, nestled in the foothills and dozing on the perimeter of a rapidly encroaching civilization.

Phillip Walker was the youngest of the family to do prison time.
California State Archives.

Early on the afternoon of April 24, 1905, the stagecoach from Caliente rattled its way down Havilah's main street and pulled up at the post office. Newt Walker stepped down from the coach and then turned to assist his father. The elder Walker was now seventy-six years old and tragedy no doubt had further lined his rugged, weathered face. The two men were returning from Bakersfield, where they had attended Phil Walker's trial. Phil had confessed to the Nichols murder and was leaving to begin a life sentence at San Quentin. For the father it had been a pathetic and tearful farewell, and their attorney, Rowan Irwin, had reportedly turned to Newt with a stern appeal.

"Newt, let this be a lesson to you. You go home with your father and take care of him and stay out of trouble."

"That's just what I'm going to do," he assertively replied. "If a man was to kick me in the road, I'd let him get away with it. I want no trouble."

As father and son walked across the street to Gus Miller's store for lunch, Newt noticed three men standing in front of W. L. Dooley's saloon. He spoke briefly to S. H. "Bert" Gibson, but ignored Dave

Burton and a companion named George Bagsby. Gibson was a brother of the Gibsons who had recently been pardoned for the murder of Fletcher Burton. He was also a brother-in-law of Burton. Newt and his father went into Miller's store where they purchased a lunch of sardines and crackers from Hannah Miller.

Outside on the street, Gibson turned and went into the saloon while Burton and Bagsby followed the Walkers into Miller's store. A few minutes later Hubbel, Havilah's blacksmith, looked up from his anvil and noticed some men standing on Miller's porch. He watched unconcernedly as two of them walked up the street in the direction of Kernville, followed quickly by Dave Burton and Bagsby.

Hubbel gasped in shocked disbelief as the two groups suddenly began shooting at each other. In a moment the fight was over and two figures lay sprawled in the rutted road. Newt Walker stepped quickly to his father's side as the old man gazed down at the dead, or dying, Burton and Bagsby. After reloading, Newt holstered his pistol and grasped the elder Walker's hand. They talked briefly, then Newt walked quickly in the direction of Kernville.

Walker had no sooner disappeared into the mountains than county officers were on his trail. Deputy Constable Gonzales of Kernville was already tracking him, as Sheriff Kelly and the Kern County coroner hurried to the scene from Bakersfield. Arriving in Havilah at eleven o'clock the next morning, Kelly was joined by Constable Johnnie Swett, and the two men went directly to the

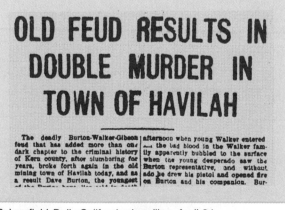

OLD FEUD RESULTS IN DOUBLE MURDER IN TOWN OF HAVILAH

The deadly Burton-Walker-Gibson feud that has added more than one dark chapter to the criminal history of Kern county, after slumbering for years, broke forth again in the old mining town of Havilah today, and as a result Dave Burton, the youngest of the Burton boys, lies cold in death... afternoon when young Walker entered ... the bad blood in the Walker family apparently bubbled to the surface when the young desperado saw the Burton representative, and without ado he drew his pistol and opened fire on Burton and his companion. Bur-

Bakersfield *Daily Californian* headline, April 24, 1905. *Author's collection.*

Walker cabin at Keyesville. It was generally feared that Newt might be joined by his brother in the mountains, and when Jim showed

up in Havilah the day after the shooting, he was detained by the officers.

The *Bakersfield Californian* gave the double killing a big splash and, in the prejudicial reporting typical of the day, tried and convicted Newt before any of the facts of the case were even known. Large black headlines proclaimed him a desperado and murderer, the first reports of the shooting stating that Newt had shot down his victims with no provocation whatsoever.

Meanwhile, Newt was still at large in the hills between Havilah and Kernville. Sheriff Kelly and Constable Swett remained on his trail, amid wild speculation as to what would happen when a confrontation took place.

Within the few preceding years, two of the most desperate outlaws in the West had come to horrible ends and, inevitably, these two men were now compared with Newt Walker.

In 1902, Harry Tracy committed suicide in a wheat field near Creston, Washington. A posse had tracked him down after his escape from an Oregon penitentiary. He had killed ten men during his flight, which had lasted less than two months and was heralded even in the New York City newspapers.

Locally, the desperado Jim McKinney had been shot to death in a Bakersfield Chinese joss house after a wild gun battle in 1903. He killed two officers before he himself died in a blaze of shotgun fire. "When I get started, McKinney won't be in it," the *Californian* quoted Newt Walker as once saying. The story went on to quote one who "knows him well":

The "shootin'" Walker boys livened up the Kern River country for many years.
Author's collection.

If Newt Walker killed those men in cold blood he will never stop fighting until he is killed. He has long had an ambition to emulate Tracy and McKinney and he has boasted that some day he would get a lot of his enemies and make a record that would surpass either of the noted outlaws named.

Kern County sheriff John W. Kelly. *Harold Edwards collection.*

Despite the predicted bloody finale to the Havilah shoot-out, the chase ended quietly when Newt surrendered the day after the shooting. Kelly and Swett had met Joe Ferris, Newt's mining partner, at the Isabella stage station. Ferris informed them that Walker was in the hills and was prepared to surrender himself and his pistol to the officers. At eight o'clock on the evening of April 25, Newt Walker strode up to the sheriff and gave himself up.

"I have lots of enemies in that country," Newt was to comment later, "and I made up my mind not to surrender to any of the officers there. I declared I would surrender to the sheriff and I waited for Mr. Kelly to come and give myself up."

The sheriff was praised in the local press for his wise course of action in hunting the fugitive. A wild-eyed posse almost certainly would have precipitated more bloodshed and brought fruition to the dire predictions of the sensation seekers.

Newt and Sheriff Kelly reached Bakersfield on the same day that the bodies of Burton and Bagsby arrived in town. Dr. Newberry, who conducted the autopsy, declared that all of the men's wounds but one would have been fatal. Burton had been shot twice through the body, the wounds being within inches of each other. Bagsby, too, received two bullets through the body, each wound also being within two inches of the other. A third shot had struck Bagsby in the right hip, inflicting a flesh wound, and the bullet was found in his clothes. By all accounts, some fast and accurate gunplay had been seen that day in old Havilah.

By now it had been established that of the two dead men, only Bagsby had been armed during the shoot-out. Newt adamantly insisted the battle was a case of self-defense, however, and he maintained that when the facts were known it would be found a justifiable shooting. His version of the affair, as given to the press, was as follows:

> We went into Miller's store, my father and I, and bought a can of sardines and some crackers, of which to make a light luncheon. We had paid our fare to Havilah on the stage and expected to walk on to Keyesville. While we were sitting down eating, Bagsby and Burton passed by the door. They saw us inside and came in. They walked around the room and made remarks to each other, Burton to the effect that the Burtons always come out on top and that he was not afraid of anybody. I asked if that remark was intended for me, and he said I could take it as I pleased.
>
> My father said that we did not want any trouble and that we had better go, so we went out into the street and Burton said, "What was that last remark you made?" We had started up the road and they were apparently following us. I was looking back over my shoulder. I saw Bagsby with his hand on his pistol and the weapon partly drawn. I turned and fired at the two men in quick succession, killing them both.

From the ground, Bagsby had fired three shots before dying.

When questioned, the sheriff stated that there had been three witnesses to the shooting but that none of them had yet been located. "From what I could gather of the statements that the three other men had made," said the lawman, "their story tallies with that told both by the old man and by Newt himself."

Walker's arraignment and preliminary examination were held early in May and the case was called in Superior Court on June 5, 1905. After various delays, a jury was selected and the trial commenced on June 13. District Attorney Laird and Deputy District Attorney Coil were assisted in the prosecution by special prosecutor G. L. Sanders of Los Angeles, who had been employed by Dave Burton's mother. The law firm of Emmons and Irwin represented Walker, who was to be tried first for the Burton killing. With Burton's mother and two sisters seated behind the prosecution and the elder Walker leaning on the rail behind his son, the stage was set for the final act of the drama. Strangely, Burton's widow was not seated with her mother- and sisters-in-law.

For the next few days, a parade of witnesses told what they knew of the gunfight. L. G. Dye had driven the stage into Havilah that day and had stuck his head out of the stage barn when the shooting started. Both men were already on the ground, and when Bagsby began shooting, Dye ducked back into the barn.

Several other witnesses were called, and the coroner and Dr. Newberry testified as to the wounds the dead men had received. Dooley, the Havilah saloon owner; Hubbel, the blacksmith; and S. H. Gibson all gave their versions of the affair, which in the main veri-

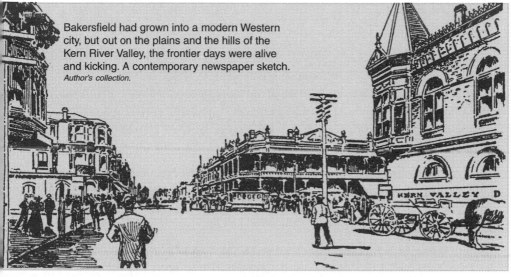

Bakersfield had grown into a modern Western city, but out on the plains and the hills of the Kern River Valley, the frontier days were alive and kicking. A contemporary newspaper sketch. *Author's collection.*

fied the defendant's story. Gus Miller, the storekeeper in whose place the trouble had started, testified as to what he could recall of the incident. The witnesses previously mentioned by Sheriff Kelly were located and their testimony also served to verify the defense's preliminary statement.

On the fourth day of the trial, a mountain resident named Carl Pascoe made some remarks concerning an alleged holdup of the Kernville stage. The incident referred to had taken place the previous March when both Burton and Bagsby had been passengers. It was stated that Newt Walker had tried to stop the coach, but before the details of the incident could be developed, Judge Mahon ruled it immaterial and the question was dropped. More was to come out later, however, as the crowded courtroom waited impatiently for the defense to begin.

On the morning of June 16, the defense fired its first theoretical guns of the trial. The big stumbling block to the defense plea of justifiable homicide was the fact that Dave Burton was unarmed at the time of the shooting. Two witnesses were introduced to prove that Newt Walker had every right to assume that Burton was indeed armed when the encounter took place. William Yates testified that he had been in Havilah that day and had seen Burton and Bagsby at Brown's store. The two men were talking, while Burton held and patted a pistol in his hand. This took place after the stage had arrived.

Another witness, Ephraim Williams, a miner who lived in Havilah, testified that he saw Burton and Bagsby a few minutes before they entered Miller's store and that Burton had a pistol in his hip pocket. This was a strong indication that Burton had given the pistol to Bagsby before entering the store, but, of course, Walker could not have known this.

A hush fell over the crowded courtroom as Newt Walker was sworn in and took the witness stand. He was an imposing figure, and in a clear, firm voice began the story of the events for which he was now on trial for his life.

My name is John Newton Walker. I knew David Burton; we were boys together. I did not know Bagsby [but] had seen him before. Burton and I did not speak, though we met frequently. We had not spoken for twelve years.

I knew Dave Ingram. I had a conversation with him a year ago. Ingram told me that Dave Burton said there wasn't room enough at the bar for him [Walker] and Burton to stand together. Burton said there were trails in the mountains where he would meet him [Walker] and when they did meet, one of them would die and that one would be Walker.

Continuing his recital, Walker told of getting off the stage that day in Havilah and of speaking to Bert Gibson. As the two Walkers strolled over to Miller's store, Newt noticed that Burton was armed with a pistol in his hip pocket.

Burton and Bagsby came in while we were eating lunch. They

Newt Walker as he looked in his prime. Old-timers said, "None of those hi-falutin' newspaper gunmen could hold a candle to any of the Walker boys when it came to fast and accurate shooting." And Newt was the best. *Harold Edwards collection.*

walked around. They bought nothing. They ate no lunch. Burton talked some and took up a paper. Bagsby went to the door and said, "Dave, how would you like to have this tall, gangling _____ hold us up today?" Burton said, "It would be a good time. We've got bullion for him today." Bagsby said, "No Walker _____ could hold me up and get away with it."

I turned and said, "I didn't hold up no stage," and I started on. I saw that Bagsby had his pistol in his hand, the weapon being in his pocket. After I started, Bagsby again said, "Hold on, we want you."

By now Walker had risen from his chair and was actually acting out the movements of that deadly afternoon.

I turned again and Burton then put his hand towards his hip pocket. Then I wheeled and began to, fire. My recollection is that I shot Bagsby first. I thought I was going to be shot down right then and there. I never tried to hold up any stage in March or at any other time.

When District Attorney Laird stepped up to cross-examine the witness, his first questions concerned the stage incident. Although no stage had been held up, the prosecution was evidently trying to prove that Walker had planned to hold up the stage and changed his mind at the last minute. Or that he had planned to take a shot at Burton who, with Bagsby, was a passenger on the coach. Walker calmly related how he had not recognized anyone on the stage that day and had merely stopped by the road to take off his shoes when the stage had passed by.

The prosecutor tried to delve into the Walker-Burton feud troubles of some twelve years past, but the court ruled the questioning irrelevant.

Under rigid cross-examination, Newt stuck steadily by his story.

One point which the prosecution hammered on was the seeming impossibility of Walker's being able to draw and kill both men after Bagsby had already begun to draw his own pistol. Walker insisted, however, that he had not gone into action until Bagsby had started his draw and Dave Burton had reached for his hip pocket. Determined to break down the defendant's story, the district attorney told Newt to stand up and put on his holster and pistol so as to demonstrate the action of that day. The court then witnessed the incredible speed of a skilled gunman.

Details of the demonstration are lacking, but one story has it that to emphasize his point, Newt called to Judge Mahon to take out his handkerchief. As the judge reached for his pocket, Walker drew his pistol and clicked the hammer four times. When the defendant left the stand, the judge, jury and spectators were true believers.

Next day the defense, according to the *Californian*, delivered "one of the most elaborate and logical arguments that has been heard in the local courts for many a day." Attorney Irwin had sought to establish that beyond doubt the shooting was a case of self-defense. Taking up where his partner left off, Emmons now set out to disprove the special prosecutor's farfetched deductions. Praising Sanders' oratory and acting abilities, Emmons declared that the world of the theatre had lost an eminent member when the prosecutor turned his attention to the law.

For the balance of the day, a succession of defense witnesses corroborated Newt's contention that Burton and Bagsby were the aggressors. Joe Gonzales, a miner and resident of Kernville, caused a sensation when he testified that two years earlier, in Bakersfield, Dave Burton offered him $200 to kill Walker. Charles Tibbet, also of Kernville,

The Kern County courthouse, where Newt Walker was tried. *Author's collection.*

164

told of a conversation he had with Bagsby the previous March. Bagsby, while twirling a pistol on his finger, said that he was brought to the area by Burton for the express purpose of getting Newt Walker.

After a three o'clock recess, the elder Walker was called to the stand. The old man's testimony backed up his son's story in all particulars. When he had finished and stepped down, court was adjourned for the day.

Most of the next day, Saturday, June 17, was taken up by the special prosecutor, whom the *Californian* characterized as "actor-orator Sanders." "He has a pleasing manner, a ready flow of language and a happy gift of word painting," stated the newspaper, "but coupled with all these are the traits more ordinarily seen before the footlights than in front of a jury in a court of justice."

Every aspect of the case was acted out vividly by Sanders as he pictured the villainous Walker holding up the stagecoach, which in reality was never held up. According to Sanders, Walker, like a "leopard whelp who had tasted human blood," had been cheated of his game in the stagecoach incident and so had schemed to shoot down his enemies in cold blood that day in Havilah.

Ignoring the fact that Walker had surrendered of his own volition as soon as possible, Sanders bellowed and strutted before the jury box.

"Why did the murderer run away?" he raved. "Why, but for the same reason that Cain, when he felled his brother, hid himself in the hills of Nod, and for the same reason that every murderer from this first shedding of human blood by primeval man down to this day has felt his guilt upon him and run from the scene of the crime."

Sanders' oratory ran the gamut of emotions and the Burton women more than once were seen to lift their veils and dab at their eyes. Through it all Newt and his father grimly watched as the attorney paced before the jury, striving with all his eloquent might to put a noose around the defendant's neck.

The district attorney gave the final summation for the prosecution. He completely dismissed the stagecoach incident as having any relevance to the case. He insisted too that the meeting of the men in Havilah was pure chance and that neither party knew the other would be in town. He argued strongly that murder had been done, however, and declared that Walker's shooting of the victims was inexcusable and not justified by the men's actions. At twenty minutes past five, the jury retired to consider a verdict.

News soon filtered out of the jury room that the panel stood ten for acquittal and two for conviction, but by the time they filed out for dinner they still had not reached a verdict.

After deliberating a little more than four hours, the court was notified that the jury was ready to report. Judge Mahon hastily called court into session and asked foreman Holmes if they had agreed on a verdict.

"We have, Your Honor. We, the jury in the above entitled case, find the defendant not guilty."

Newt Walker had been leaning forward in his chair and he now sat back with a look of relief on his face. As soon as the court formalities had been dispensed with, Newt and his father both stood up and shook the hand of each juror as he left the box. Dave Burton's widow stepped up to Newt and in turn grasped his hand. It was a strange ending to a unique chain of events.

Throughout the trial it had been noted that Burton's widow had clearly been sympathetic to the defense. After the acquittal, she spoke briefly to a newspaper reporter.

"When you write up the trial today, you can say that I am for the defense." Addie Burton smiled and added, "Does that sound romantic?"

It did indeed sound romantic, but it isn't known just what the implications of her comments were. If there was a more "basic" reason for the Havilah shoot-out, it didn't come out at the trial. The widow's candid interview, however, must have set tongues to clacking in Bakersfield and the hills around Kernville.

Walker was scheduled to be tried for the Bagsby shooting also, but the district attorney had no recourse but to have the case dismissed. With Newt acquitted of shooting the unarmed Burton, Laird could hardly hope to convict him for shooting the armed Bagsby, who had been shooting back at him. As he walked down the courthouse steps with his father and attorney Irwin, Newt Walker was a free man again.

Evidently, Newt managed to stay out of trouble for the rest of his life, with two notable exceptions. In the summer of 1924, so the story goes, he had a misunderstanding with one Floyd Fisher when the latter's car was stalled in the deep sand of French Gulch. Newt put two bullets into Fisher, seriously wounding him and necessitating a visit from the Kern County sheriff.

The old Walker cabin still sits at the base of Greenhorn Mountain at the site of old Keyesville. This view was taken about 1900. *Bob Powers' collection.*

The sheriff, Cas Walser, casually called on Newt and suggested that he accompany him to Bakersfield.

"Why Cas, you ain't got your gun," commented Newt, after quickly noting the sheriff was unarmed.

"Didn't figure I needed one," observed Walser, and the wise Western sheriff drove on into Bakersfield with the man who was perhaps the deadliest gunfighter that old California had ever seen. Newt was acquitted of the assault charge, but it was to be the last time he would walk the streets of Bakersfield.

On a Tuesday morning, November 25, 1924, Mr. and Mrs. Walter Armstrong called at the ancient cabin of the Walker family in Keyesville. The sturdy log cabin was one of the few remaining structures in the old mining town and had outlived the Walker parents and two of their sons. Newt still called it home—living there with Tex Roland and Frank Murdock, old-time friends. The Armstrongs wanted some mining information from Newt, and when there was no response to their knock, the couple walked around to the back door.

When they saw Frank Murdock lying on the ground just outside the back door, the Armstrongs first thought that he was drunk. Closer examination revealed the blood and the fact that Murdock was stiff and very dead. Shocked, the couple glanced in the back door of the cabin and saw another body lying amid the debris of an overturned kitchen table. Cautiously, Armstrong stepped inside for a closer look at the shirtless body.

Most of this group are unidentified, but Phil Walker kneels at far left. Newt stands third from the left, while brother Tom stands at far right. *Mrs. Marge Powers.*

Cold in death, with a bullet through the heart, lay the corpse of Newt Walker.

Kernville authorities and the sheriff's office in Bakersfield were alerted. By dusk that evening the county coroner, several deputy sheriffs, and a newspaperman were at the Walker cabin. They were greeted by a houseful of grim mountaineers from the surrounding hills, who showed the officers the scene of the tragedy. Jim, Bill, and Phil Walker were there also, their

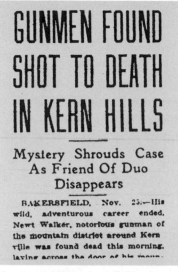

Newspapers throughout California proclaimed the Old West alive and well in Kern County. *Fresno Morning Republican, November 26, 1924.*

faces ashen and hard. All were armed and eager to start the hunt for the killer of their brother. The Walker brothers watched silently as a sheet was placed over Newt's body. A curtain had been drawn on a Kern County legend, and yet a feeling of apprehension seemed to fill the room as if a dreaded anticlimax somehow lurked beyond the cabin door. The "finest pistol shot in the San Joaquin Valley" was dead, but the uneasy glances of his brothers somehow suggested that perhaps a last terrible act was yet to be played.

Tom Walker lived in his own cabin on the hill in back of the family home. He was known to have played poker with Newt, Roland, and Murdock the previous Saturday night, but so far he hadn't shown up at the scene of the crime.

The officers quickly made their preliminary investigation. Newt was barefoot and shirtless, a bullet having passed through his arm and into his heart. Murdock had one bullet in the brain and a bad bruise on the head from a blunt instrument. Some twenty feet from Murdock's body, an empty .38 revolver was found, and it was assumed to be the death weapon.

After questioning the neighbors, officers concluded that the men had been dead for several days, probably since late the previous Saturday or early Sunday morning. A quick gathering of the evidence suggested a quarrel during a poker game had resulted in the shooting. It was feared that Roland, too, might be found dead somewhere in the vicinity, although hope was expressed that he was alive and could shed some light on the mystery.

Inside the house, officers searched for further clues. Under Newt's mattress were found his favorite weapons, a matched pair of long-barreled Smith and Wesson revolvers and a smaller pocket pistol of the same make. Leaning against the head of the bed was a high powered Remington automatic rifle, and nearby was a shotgun.

Tom Walker had still not shown up at the scene of tragedy and no one seemed to know where he was. Several officers, accompanied by Tom's brother Phil, made the trek up the mountain to Tom's cabin, but finding it empty, returned to the murder scene. The officers then gathered up Newt's weapons and discovered that the small Smith and Wesson had disappeared from under the mattress. All attempts to find the weapon proved fruitless.

Charley Woodward, the best of the local trackers, Deputy Phil Fickert, and Phil Walker now traced some footprints to a mine shaft near Tom Walker's cabin. Scarcely knowing what to expect, Fickert and Walker entered the mine and cautiously explored the interior. Suddenly they came upon a body. Huddled against the side of the tunnel lay the corpse of Tom Walker. In his hand was a revolver and there was a bullet wound in his head. Nearby were two empty bottles of moonshine. The corpse was still limp when found.

Tom's body was brought down the mountainside and laid beside those of his brother and Frank Murdock. Now only Tex Roland had to be accounted for, but the mystery of the multiple deaths was as perplexing as ever. "So all the way through it is 'Tex,'" stated an article in the *Bakersfield Californian*. "'Find 'Tex' dead or alive and the mystery is solved,' say the mountain men and all day long they search the thousands of gulches, mining shafts and other holes in which the man might be found—dead or alive."

Today, a few old cabins slumber amid the memories of Keyesville's colorful past. *Author's collection.*

Numerous theories concerning the tragedy were being advanced, but in lieu of anything concrete, hopes for unraveling the killings lay with discovering what happened to Tex Roland. If he were alive, he was obviously the murderer. If dead, a darker solution to the tragedy seemed painfully evident—at least to the mountain people.

It was several days after Newt and Murdock's bodies were discovered that Tex Roland was finally found. Some 300 yards up the mountain in back of Newt's cabin, the body was located in a brush-choked gully. A bloodstained wheelbarrow was hidden nearby. Splashes of blood and ground markings spelled out the story. With all the participants dead, the complete story might never be known, but to the mountain people the tragedy was now an open book and the officers had to concur.

"Tom went crazy mad," they said. "Killers always go that way sooner or later."

The story, as pieced together by the mountaineers, was a grim tale of mass murder, sparked by moonshine. The four men had played poker Saturday night, with Newt and Murdock being the winners. All had probably imbibed freely from the contents of the Walker whiskey still, which was located nearby. Early Sunday morning, Tom had come down from his cabin, hung-over and disgruntled over losses incurred during the game. Roland was in the back yard, perhaps washing up, when Tom engaged Murdock in a heated argument. Newt was still in bed, but coffee was on the stove and the men were preparing for breakfast.

At the sounds of the arguing, Newt got up and pulled on his trousers just in time to see Tom knock Murdock down with his pistol. Yelling at his brother, Newt rushed to the door, but Tom was beyond control and gripped by an insane fury. Tom shot his unarmed brother as he stood in the doorway and watched as Newt crashed down on the kitchen table. Roland, in the background, had witnessed the whole terrible scene and stood rooted to the ground, too shocked to move. Now he scrambled madly to escape, but Tom whirled and stopped him with a shot in the back, shooting him again in the right breast as the dying man fell. Then, stepping up to

Murdock's unconscious form, Tom shot him mercilessly in the head and threw the pistol to the ground.

It was probably a few moments later that Tom came to his senses and realized the enormity of his crime. Panic-stricken, he dumped Roland's body into a wheelbarrow and trundled it up the hill and into a gulch. He then evidently went back to his cabin, where he spent the day in an agony of remorse... and dread. Friends remembered later his insistence that he would never go back to prison. That night, torn by his emotions, he returned to the scene of death, and through the cabin window saw the sheeted bodies surrounded by officers and his armed brothers. He was heard prowling about, and the men rushed out of the cabin with their pistols at the ready, but Tom disappeared into the brushy slopes. Somehow, he managed to obtain Newt's small pistol from under his brother's mattress. Later, he secured more moonshine from the hidden still and went into the mine shaft and committed suicide. It was the only escape possible from prison and his tortured, shattered life.

Today, the ancient home of the Walker clan still stands at the base of Greenhorn Mountain. What a tale that old cabin could tell. Nearby is the lonely Keyesville cemetery. On that haunted, tree-sprinkled knoll, the graves are obliterated and forgotten to all but a few. Only oldtimers now exchange tales of men too good with guns and the terrible twenty-year vendetta in the wilds of the beautiful Kern River Valley.

DOCUMENTS

Thomas Spratt, 2nd Regiment, California Cavalry, Muster Rolls, National Archives, Washington, DC

Federal Census, Placer County California, 1860

Burmeister, Eugene, letter to the author, February 11, 1968

Edwards, Harold, letter to the author, September 12, 2002

Chapter 7 NOTES

Gibson, Vera K., Kern County Clerk, letter to the author, August 19, 1975

Powers, Bob, letters to the author, July 29, 1977, September 12, 2002

Walker, Ardis, letter to the author, February 9, 1968

BOOKS

Brewer, William H. and Farquhar, Francis P. (editor). *Up and Down California in 1860-1864, The Journal of William H. Brewer.* Berkeley: University of California Press, 1974.

Burmeister, Eugene. *The Walker Basin Story.* Bakersfield: Kern Publishing House, 1965.

Cragen, Dorothy Clora. *The Boys in The Sky-Blue Pants.* Fresno: Pioneer Publishing Company, 1975.

Miller, Thelma. *History of Kern County, California.* Chicago: Clark, 1929.

Powers, Bob. *North Fork Country.* Los Angeles: Westernlore Press, 1974.

_____. *High Country Communities.* Spokane: Washington: The Arthur H. Clark Company, 1999.

Scanlan, Nicholas Patrick (editor). Kern *County Pioneer Recollections.* Bakersfield: Kern County Library, 1985.

Walker, Ardis M. *The Rough and the Righteous of the Kern River Diggins.* Balboa Island: Paisano Press, Inc., 1970.

Wilson, Neill C. *Silver Stampede,* New York: The Macmillan Company, no date available.

Wortley, Ken. *Historic Land of the Rio Bravo.* Bakersfield: Sierra Rainbow, 1987.

NEWSPAPERS

The Bakersfield Californian, April 2, 1966

Bakersfield Daily Californian, April 24, 25, 26, 27, 28, 29, June 5, 6, 12, 13, 14, 15, 16, 17, 20, 1905; November 26, 27, 28, 29, 1924

Kern County Daily Californian, October 22, November 3, 17, December 15, 1883;

January 15, 19, 26, February 9, 26, 1884

Fresno Daily Republican, December 1, 1892

Fresno Morning Republican, April 25, 1905; November 26, 28, 29, 1924

Fresno Weekly Expositor, December 7, 1892

Fresno Daily Evening Expositor, March 20, 1895

Inyo Independent, December 1879

San Francisco *Call*, April 25, 1905

San Francisco *Chronicle*, January 17, 1884

OTHER SOURCES

Secrest, William B., "Gunplay!," *Old West*, Summer 1969.

Edwards, Harold L., "Newt Walker's Two Fast Draws." *Quarterly of the National Association for Outlaw and Lawman History, Inc.*, April–June 1998.

Edwards, Harold L., "Newt Walker's Murder Trial." *Quarterly Bulletin Historic Kern*, Kern County Historical Society, Winter 1999.

Palazzo, Robert P., "The Operations of Wells, Fargo & Co.'s Express in Death Valley During the Nineteenth Century," *Proceedings, Fourth Death Valley Conference on History and Prehistory*, February 2–5, 1995.

_____, "A Study of Violence in the Nineteenth Century Death Valley Region," *Proceedings, Fifth Death Valley Conference on History and Prehistory*, March 4–7, 1999.

Chapter 8

The Curse of Chinatown

Opium Dens and Tong Wars

Chinese immigrants to California during the Gold Rush were only temporary sojourners. They had no idea of staying in this land of "foreign devils" any longer than necessary. They were here simply looking for opportunity... and gold. So clannish were these Oriental arrivals that they even shipped the bodies of dead friends and relatives home to China for burial.

These Chinese immigrants were almost wholly men, very few women making the long trip. A few thousand dollars back in their poverty and strife-riven homeland could insure their future. Just a few years' residence in the land of Gum Shan, the "Mountain of Gold," and they would be able to buy some land or start a shop and to care for their families. Like the white man, some found their fortune in gold, while others found success in politics, or shop-keeping. Of course, some found neither.

In late 1849, there were only a few hundred Chinese in San Francisco, but by 1851, the Customs House had recorded 2,716 emigrants. Labor agents in both Hong Kong and Canton, China, recruited coolies for California by parading the streets banging drums and gongs while shouting, "Be rich! Go to the Land of the Golden Mountain!"

By 1852, Chinese immigration in San Francisco had jumped to 20,000. Although most Chinese moved on to the mining country, a

Chinatown quickly developed in the Gold Rush city by the Bay.

Chinese aid societies were quickly established to help the new arrivals. These societies, called companies (wui kun), only provided aid for those from a particular district of China. By 1854, secret societies known as tongs were being formed in California to perform other functions. These tongs dated back as far as 1674 in China, according to some sources. Many of the early immigrants were of the poorest class from Kwangtun Province and not only were illiterate in their own language, but, of course, spoke no English, either. These people needed aid, and the tongs and family organizations helped them as needed.

As more and more Chinese crowded into the Chinatowns across the state, the tongs grew larger in membership. These organizations reflected both the Manchu Dynasty that was in power in China, and the red-turbaned rebel Triad Society that sought to restore the Ming Dynasty during the Taiping Rebellion of 1851. These secret societies had their origins in the haves and have-nots of ancient China. An old Chinese maxim stated that "the Mandarin (wealthy class) derives his power from the law, the people (poor class) from the secret societies."

In the land of Gum Shan, it only remained for the tongs to grow strong enough before they were first recognized in San Francisco. This happened in early January 1854, when the *San Francisco Daily Herald* reported 159 Chinese members of a secret association had been arrested:

The nature of this conspiracy is described as an association whose object and practise it is to demand of each of the Chinese women residing in public houses in this city, the sum of ten dollars every month

Chinese on the Hong Kong docks boarding a Pacific Mail steamship for the trip to the "Mountain of Gold."
Author's collection.

176

Weaverville was already a sprawling village in 1852. *Trinity County Historical Society.*

for the permission of the association to remain in the city, and to force and drive from the city all such as refuse to pay this tribute.

The tongs had arrived in America!

Like other mining towns in California, Weaverville had a Chinese population of over one thousand by 1854. Situated in northern California's Trinity County, two tongs were active in town, each representing a different Chinese mining operation. The Hong Kong Yang Wah Company made up one group, while the Canton City Company was the other. The genesis of the trouble is obscure, but a growing animosity between the two groups reportedly originated from the fact that the Hong Kongs supported the rebels back in China, while the Cantons were loyal to the Manchu government.

Weaverville supported three Chinese dry goods shops, several restaurants, a joss house, and a gambling house called the Golden Gate Saloon. Since the two rival tongs avoided each other, the proprietor of the Golden Gate decided to cater to the larger of the two groups, the Cantons. The favored group was given free tea and cigars, while the Hong Kongs were discouraged by poor service and no free tea and cigars. It was a situation that simmered and finally boiled over.

Feeling they were being discriminated against, not to mention insulted, the Hong Kongs determined to take action. A red-turban rebel fugitive from China, named Charlie Yung, was hired to lead a gang of Hong Kongs who broke into the Golden Gate one Sunday evening. The owner lived on the premises, and when he heard the smashing of furniture and glassware, he burst into the room and was badly beaten.

At a meeting of the Cantons, it was decided that the incident was, in reality, a challenge to fight. The Canton tong now hired one Hi Long Chang, a Manchu killer from China, to lead its members in the impending conflict. Talk quickly spread around town that a war had been declared and preparations were soon underway by the two factions.

John Carr, a local blacksmith, looked up from his forge one morning to see a member of the Canton tong standing in his shop holding a large paper sketch in his hand. It was a pattern for a medieval-type pike weapon that would fit on the end of a long pole. The Oriental explained that he wanted one hundred of the weapons made of steel, then asked the price. When Carr explained that the cost would be one dollar and fifty cents each, he was told to proceed. An hour later the Hong Kong representative appeared and asked what the cost would be for one hundred of the same weapons. Carr no doubt smiled broadly as he realized what was happening:

John Carr, the Weaverville blacksmith who made weapons for the tong war. *Author's collection.*

> I told him one dollar and fifty cents. He told me if I would quit making them for the Cantons he would give me two hundred for his company. I said, "All right, John."

> In a short time afterwards the boss of the Cantons made his appearance, and told me, if I would quit the Hong Kongs' work, he would give me two dollars and a half, and I could make him three hundred more.

Again Carr readily agreed to switch sides, even though the large quantity, in addition to his normal work load, "was crowding things in my line pretty heavily." Other blacksmiths in the area were also busy making pike-type spears, as well as daggers, hatchets, and swords. Continued Carr:

> Some of the queerest things I made for them that I have ever seen or read of—great spears with three prongs, heavy enough for old Goliath to have wielded in his day; others were made some-

thing like brush scythes. And they would take them away from the shop before they were cold, and pay up for them.... In the meantime other Chinamen were in the woods cutting poles fourteen or fifteen feet long, bringing them to town, and dressing them up for handles for the instruments they were making.

Writing on July 18, 1854, Weaverville merchant Franklin Buck was also totally caught up in the drama taking place:

The whole country has been thrown into a perfect cold sweat by the excitement. All the blacksmiths have been busy making weapons. The tinman sold all his tin and sheet iron for shields. We sold all our hatchets and powder and everybody came from far and near to see the battle. Now the cause of this war I have in vain tried to find out. Some say one party is the imperial and the other the rebel, the same as in China. ...Another is that it arose about six bits at a gambling table. Now you know just as much as I do about it.

...On Tuesday the Red Cap party paraded in the street. They numbered one hundred and ten. They charged up and down the street with hideous yells. The parade was made more interesting by the appearance of one of our citizens, Sites, mounted on a fire horse in full regimentals. Sites says he was offered $500 to fight for them, but wanted a thousand.

On Friday both parties encamped within one mile of each other, about a mile from town. On Saturday the fight was to come off and on that day there must have been nearly two thousand persons on the ground. In the morning I visited the camp of the Canton men. They mustered two hundred and fifty warriors. ...Imagine that number of Chinamen armed with long spears with sheet iron helmets and tin shields, enormous squirt guns filled with some infernal liquid, gongs beating and horns blowing, marching into battle. Now they would halt, with their poles upright, looking like a forest of trees. Then, lowering the points of their spears, with awful yells, they would run two or three hundred yards. Then stop, the front rank dropping on one knee, forming a perfect rampart of spears and shields.

Buck then visited the Hong Kong camp, noting they mustered about one hundred and ten men, "but were the best looking party." He also noticed that though they had no iron helmets covering their red turbans, many of the Hong Kongs were armed with revolvers, probably to even the odds. "Everybody seemed to think," wrote Buck, "although the other party outnumbered them two to one, that the Red Caps would clean them out."

179

During the previous few weeks the local sheriff had been trying to dissuade the two tongs from engaging in any conflict. Unkind chroniclers have insisted his motive was a loss of taxpayer revenues, but this hardly seems likely. In any case, everyone in the county, Caucasian and Chinese, wanted a fight, and the sheriff finally just threw up his hands.

At three o'clock on the afternoon of July 14, 1854, the two tongs faced each other on a flat a mile east of town. The two groups had been marching, gesturing, and making noise at each other for some time and the large group of spectators were beginning to think they were all show and no fight. Again, Franklin Buck was on the scene and described the action:

> "The Cantons were divided into three parties; one in front on the bank of a gulch, one in the rear and one on the left. The Red Caps were on one side of this gulch and the Cantons on the other. The leader of the Red Caps very deliberately rolled up the legs of his wide Chinese trousers to his thighs, struck his shield with his sword, gave the word to charge and rushed across the gulch. They charged up the hill right on the spears of the Cantons. The leader of the Red Caps, covering his body with his shield, fought like a lion. The Cantons wavered, broke and ran."

When one of the other Canton groups tried to assist their comrades, miner spectators threw rocks and fired pistols at them under

the pretense of having a fair fight. A Swedish miner named John Malmberg, who fired into the Chinese for no apparent reason, was shot through the head by another miner. Those who saw the killing said he richly deserved it. Several of the wounded were skewered on the ground where they lay. Some eight Chinese were killed and six or eight wounded before the two tongs left the field to assess their casualties. The ground was littered with broken spears, banners, shields, and weapons of every kind.

A newspaper dispatch from Weaverville noted that the fighting was over, "but their differences are in no better condition now than they were before. Neither dare go to work: one is afraid of the other, consequently both are idle. So matters stand at the present." After the funerals on Sunday, Buck reported a party was held and liquor and cigars were passed around to the large crowd of Chinese and white miners. "The wounded are doing well," he stated, "and quiet is again restored in China."

Chinese tong representatives from San Francisco were soon on the scene trying to mediate the situation. They reported that both sides still wanted to fight, but under more controlled circumstances. "They are anxious that each party shall be permitted to select an equal number of men, say 50, 100, or 150, as shall be agreed, and let the whole difficulty be settled by a fair contest, without interference from any source, and they will faithfully abide by the result." Fortunately, the talking seemed to cool the ardor of the combatants and soon all went back to work.

And so the tong wars in California had begun. As if taking their cue from their northern brethren, a month or so later there were various outbreaks, and casualties, in Marysville, Greenwood, and Sacramento. Newspaper interviews with participants indicated that the See Yup and Ning Yung tongs had implemented a tax on other Chinese groups and the trouble started when they met a stiff resistance, instead of payment. Large amounts of armament had been stockpiled by the evening of September 8, 1854, when an incident set off a minor conflict at the corner of Fifth and J streets in Sacramento.

According to Wong Ahong, he had visited some friends at a Chinese gambling house, then later left to return home. He had proceeded a short distance when he was attacked in the street by Chaong Aking, who struck him a glancing blow with a sword. Others would later testify that Ahong had stolen thirty dollars in the gambling

An early daguerreotype shows a Sacramento tin shop that probably made weapons for the tong wars in that area. *California State Library.*

house and he had been pursued and attacked. Whatever happened, Ahong fled and was taken to the police station by a man who noticed his bloody condition. "Thence," noted the *Sacramento Daily Union*, "with a policeman, they proceeded to the Chinese quarter, when a Chinaman was discovered parading the street with a heavy Chinese sword, and was designated by the wounded man as one of the parties for whom they were searching."

The swordsman was quickly in tow, but while taking him to the station, the authorities were confronted by a group of armed Chinese who rushed at them. The policeman's party faced off their attackers and chased them off, then returned to the station. When an armed crowd gathered, several other policemen arrived and began arresting anyone who had a weapon. A battle broke out anyway as reported in the *Sacramento State Journal*:

> They were armed with tin hats, bamboo shields, tin and iron swords and cutlasses, a la pick handles, and proceeded at once to business. They were not separated into different armies, but pitched

in generally, every man apparently on his own hook... They fought some half hour or so, when the police interfered in the sport...

At the station, word was received of the fighting and a contingent of police and reporters, under Deputy Marshal Lambert Welborn, rushed to the scene of action as noted in the *Union*:

> (They) proceeded to the spot and commenced a search through the Chinese tenements for the arms with which we were informed they were well provided. Our investigations... led to the discovery of a very large quantity of knives, swords, spears, shields and helmets... The search occupied about two hours and resulted in the arrest of twenty-eight persons, besides the seizure of about a cart load of warlike implements of a formidable character. The police were aided in their operations by several Chinamen, who were particularly anxious that every dangerous weapon should be discovered and seized.

It seemed the prompt action of the police had averted a more serious clash between rival tongs, although a casualty list was apparently not reported. Court hearings later brought out the fact that groups of Chinese had been filtering into the city for some time in preparation for an armed conflict. A letter, published in the *Union*, indicated that some of the Chinese who had accompanied the police in their search had ulterior motives:

> Yesterday while the honorable police were in search of war implements, three of your police went to the garden and house of Ah-Ki, ...accompanied by about twenty of the said Yue-Ti men, and while the police were in search of weapons, a large number of this gang went out in the garden and destroyed most all of his watermelons and vines... . I think this was very wrong, as he is quite aged in years, and is harmless and inoffensive to any person...

Some twenty-eight Chinese were convicted in the incident, and the po-

A Chinese sword dancer of the early days. Such weapons were often used in tong war battles.
California State Library.

lice kept a wary eye on Chinatown for the next few weeks.

Although there were lesser skirmishes throughout the state, the next clash of any magnitude did not take place until several years later, in Tuolumne County. The initial dispute was a minor affair and could easily have been settled by rational men, if both parties had made any effort. Unfortunately, one of the groups were Sam-Yups, while the others were Yang-Wos.

In mid-September 1856, twelve miners of the Sam-Yap tong were working a claim at Two-mile Bar on the Stanislaus River. Noticing that several large boulders had suddenly appeared overnight on their property, they asked a group of six Chinese miners working an adjoining claim if they knew how they got there. The Sam-Yaps were certain these adjoining miners were the source of the unwanted boulders, and undoubtedly were not very diplomatic in their questioning. They also knew the culprits were Yan-Wos, sympathetic to the Manchu Dynasty. The Sam-Yaps were, of course, a tong sympathetic to the rebel cause, and the resulting brawl between the two groups on the claim resulted in a victory for the more numerous Sam-Yaps. As they retreated, there were dire threats of a grand bloodletting from the temporarily defeated Yan-Wos.

It was Weaverville all over again.

Although the Yan-Wos were the defeated party, it was the Sam-Yaps who quickly initiated a call to war. In their euphoria over the winning of their minor skirmish, the Sam-Yaps published the following challenge in the *Columbian Weekly*, published at the nearby mining town of Columbia:

Challenge from the Sam-Yap Company, at Rock River Ranch, to the Yan-Wo Company, at Chinese Camp.

There are a great many now existing in the world who ought to be exterminated. We, by this, give you a challenge, and inform you beforehand that we are the strongest, and you are too weak to oppose us. We can therefore wrest your claim or anything else from you, and give you notice that it is our intention to drive you away from us, and make you ashamed of yourselves. You are nothing compared with us. We are as durable as stone, but you are pliant as sponge. ...You want to coax us to come to terms. That we refuse. We mean to fight you, and expel you all from your localities. If you don't stand and fight us, we will consider you no better than so many brutes; and as such, we will harness you to our own desires. There are plenty of us, well equipped, and ready, at any time, to meet and fight you wherever you choose; and would make you run into holes and hide yourselves. ...You are perfect worms... If you won't accept the challenge, we tell you, by the way, ...to go to... your houses, shut the doors, and hide yourselves, and we'll kill every man of you that we come across. Shame! Shame!

There seemed to be little doubt about the seriousness of the situation after this announcement. In a replay of the Weaverville scenario, there was a general rush by both groups to stockpile weapons, and the blacksmiths of the area geared up for the business. Unlike the Weaverville hostilities, the Tuolumne County warriors made no stipulation about firearms and many were armed with pistols and rifles. White miners were hired to teach the Orientals the fine points of shooting Colt pistols and muskets. When both sides considered themselves ready, they agreed to meet on a large flat at the foot of the local Table Mountain. A man named Hanley, a local Chinese interpreter, wrote up an account of the resulting battle for the *Sonora Union Democrat*:

> On the morning of the 26th of September, the members of the Yan-Wo, 900 strong, started from Chinese Camp to meet their opponents, who were 1,200 strong, at the place agreed on. About ten o'clock, A.M., both parties came into a collision. They fired in all about one hundred shots and retreated, killing two of the Yan-Wo men, and wounding one. Two of the Sam-Yaps were wounded, one having his nose blown off, and the other his leg broken close by his ankle. As soon as the Sam-Yaps had wounded two of the Yan Wos, they instantly rushed on them—stabbed them all over the body, carried them off on tridents, out of reach of the enemy's bullets, and cut them to pieces as they would a hog, and afterwards carried the remains out of sight, burned them to ashes and scattered them to the winds of heaven. The Yan-Wo men, having but twelve muskets, were unable to compete with the Sam-Yaps... But proposed to fight them with their Chinese arms, and cast their muskets aside. This the Sam-Yaps refused, and retreated to their quarters at Rock River Ranch, about four miles distant.

A posse under Tuolumne County sheriff James Stewart tried valiantly to stop the proceedings, but made no headway and finally let the combatants proceed. Afterwards, some 250 Chinese were arrested, fined, and released. "The expenses incurred by the fight," reported an observer, "cost the Yan-Wos $20,000 and the Sam-Yaps upwards of $40,000, which comes out of the pockets of the miners, who I expect will have to do penance for the next year to come." These expenses must have included all the weapons purchased and used, since one account noted that fines of $40 per head were imposed, which adds up to only $10,000. It was a genuine windfall for the county.

By the early 1860s the Chinese tongs had acquired an ever more ominous presence in San Francisco. The conflicts taking place in the mining country were now being mirrored in the alleys and avenues of the city's Chinatown. Instead of opposing armies in the field, however, the feuds between rival tongs now involved assaults and assassinations in the confines of alleyways and dimly lighted rooms. Occasionally two opposing groups would fight it out, but mostly hatchet men would chop up an unsuspecting enemy in his home or a dark alley, then quickly disappear into the shacks and underground rooms of what was called the "Chinese Quarter."

Not so politically inspired now, the tong clashes had often become territorial in nature. Slave girl prostitutes and gambling were the prizes of conflict, now, and wealthy tong leaders employed bodyguards for protection. The Chinese had originally flooded into the country without women. It was their intention to work for a few years, then return home. Soon "sing song" girls, or prostitutes, were being imported or smuggled into California to service the hordes of single men. Control of these women became immensely lucrative. Gambling,

San Francisco's Chinatown in the days of the tong wars. *California State Library.*

also an important part of these lonesome men's lives, was very profitable and killing a gambling house owner to acquire his territory was well worth the risk. Opium dens were also a source of great profit. The origins of the See-Yup and Hop-Wo tong troubles are not known, but the killing of Ah Cow in Sacramento in the late summer of 1862 resulted in other attacks in San Francisco. Under the heading, "A Barbarous Assault," the Bay city's *Daily Herald* reported:

> Ah Hang made a ferocious attack upon Ah Quan with a hatchet, inflicting two or three severe gashes on the head and shoulder, and cutting the ornamental que of Ah Quan from his devoted head. It was evidently the intention of Ah Hang to decapitate Ah Quan, but the weapon, although new and keen edged, glanced aside from the skull, and his benevolent design was frustrated. Further mischief was prevented by the arrest of Ah Hang by Constable Harding, who handed over the would-be murderer to Capt. Douglass, and he was safely incarcerated in the City Prison. ...The parties in this affair are members of rival Chinese companies between whom there is now a deadly feud existing.

San Francisco's famous detective, later police chief, Captain Isaiah Lees. *Author's collection.*

The seriousness of the situation was indicated by a similar attack which took place at the corner of Commercial and Kearny streets about an hour after the above-noted assault. One Ah Chow slipped up to Ah Tye, known to be a tong activist, and severely wounded him with a hatchet. Amazingly, both victims survived to face their attackers in court.

By late 1864, a new menace had surfaced in San Francisco's Chinese Quarter. Following the defeat of the Taiping Rebellion in China, many of the rebels had fled to California, where they knew they had supporters in San Francisco's burgeoning Chinatown. Sympathetic Chinese in the Bay city generously furnished subsistence to these expatriate rebels, many of whom took advantage of the situation and made no attempt to earn a living for themselves. Isaiah Lees was captain of detectives at this time, and in later years explained this evolution of the tongs he had witnessed:

> They sought no means of self-support; and when the voluntary subscriptions gradually grew less, they resorted to blackmail and

187

extortion, going so far as to organize courts presided over by judges, by whose direction bailiffs seized and brought before these pseudo courts merchants and other Chinese of financial standing, who were required to contribute under threat of dire penalties. Our police authorities succeeded in stopping such high-handed doings, and drove the perpetrators under cover, where they broke up into rival bands and vied with each other in the levying and collection of blackmail from their Chinese brethren.

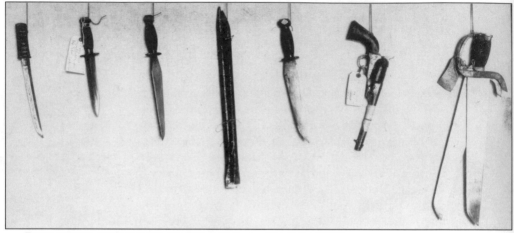

Tong weapons confiscated by the San Francisco police in the 1890s. *Courtesy The Bancroft Library.*

As these thugs and "hatchet men" took over the San Francisco tongs, they quickly established gambling, opium, smuggling, and bordello operations to broaden their power base. Since the Chinese lived within their own world in Chinatown, it was some years before it was known what was going on. Even then, it was difficult for the legal authorities to police the area since the Chinese were so isolated from the rest of the city. By 1866, Chinese were being imported

A gambling den in San Francisco's Chinatown. *Author's collection.*

to build railroads and perform other work at the rate of 1,400 a load on the Pacific Mail steamers. Many were unaware of the shadow that had fallen over San Francisco's Chinatown. The day of the boo how doy (salaried tong soldier) had arrived.

Little was known of the Chinese tongs because of the vast cultural differences between the white and Chinese races. The Chinese Quarter was a bit of China that few whites cared to understand, even though by the late 1880s it was something of a tourist attraction. The fighting men of the tongs, the "hatchet men" or "highbinders," were shadowy killers about whom the police knew little. In early 1891, however, San Francisco police chief Patrick Crowley received a Chinese document from Victoria, British Columbia. It was a contract between a Canadian tong and a highbinder which indicated the sophistication of these organizations. When translated it read:

> To Lum Hip, salaried soldier:
>
> ...Now this Tong appoints salaried soldiers to be ready to protect ourselves and to assist others. This is our object.
>
> All, therefore, who undertake the military services of this Tong must obey orders and without orders you must not dare to act. If any of our brethren are suddenly molested, it will be necessary for you to act with resolute will.
>
> You shall always work in the interest of the Tong and never make your office a means of private revenge.
>
> When orders are given you shall advance valiantly to your assigned task. Never shrink or turn your back upon the battlefield.
>
> When a ship arrives in port with prostitutes on board, and the Grand Master issues an order for you to go down and receive them, you must be punctual and use all your ability for the good of the commonwealth (or state).
>
> If in the discharge of your duty you are slain, we will undertake to pay $500 sympathy money to your friends.
>
> If you are wounded, a doctor will be engaged to heal your wounds, and if you are laid up for any length of time you will receive $10 per month.

Labeled as "Typical highbinders" in an 1891 issue of *Californians* magazine, this is apparently a composite made up from San Francisco police mug shots. *Author's collection.*

If you are maimed for life and incapacitated for work, $250 shall be paid to you and a subscription taken to defray costs of your journey home to China.

...Furthermore, whenever you exert your strength to kill and wound enemies of Pong, and in so doing you are arrested and imprisoned, $100 per year shall be paid to your friends during your imprisonment.

Signed and dated at the tong headquarters in San Francisco's Chinatown, it was a surprising document that clearly indicated the strength and determination of the tongs.

The killings and vice of the Chinese Quarter had forced the police to initiate a "Chinatown Squad" in the late 1880s. Several plain-clothes officers under Sergeant William Price were first used in the Quarter, but very little changed. Price then sought and obtained permission to break up all the highbinder meeting places. Augmenting his squad and arming them with sledges and axes, Price embarked on a systematic campaign of destroying the meeting places. He caused some twenty or thirty thousand dollars worth of damage, but in the end the meetings went on and little changed. The tong wars continued.

The consummate villain of the tong days in San Francisco was one Fong Ching, called "Little Pete." If he had not been such a scoundrel, his life might have been an extraordinary success story. Born in Kow Gong, near Canton, China, in 1864, he reportedly came to California with his father ten years later. The boy attended the Methodist Mission Sunday School, as well as a grammar school where he became proficient in the English language. He was sixteen when his father died, but he was already working as an errand boy for a Sacramento Street shoe factory. Although his pay was small, Fong Ching dutifully sent a portion of his meager earnings home to his family in China. He seemed to have ambition and a game plan at a very early age.

After joining the Sam-Yup Company, young Fong Ching became an interpreter and acquired knowledge of all the tong's business dealings. In his spare time, he liked to hang out in his uncle's Chinatown shop, where he met many Americans and police officers. He learned that some policemen could be bought. White people liked jokes and Fong Ching always had a good story to tell. A favorite tale concerned a miner who ordered a meal in a Chinese restaurant. When he asked what the first course was, the waiter (who could speak little English) replied "Quack, quack." Well

Smart and wealthy, with a great many friends, Little Pete had it all, but wanted more and would not take his family back to China. *Author's collection.*

pleased, the smiling miner ate his first course then began on the second. Finishing that, he asked what it was and the waiter replied, "Bow wow."

A quick study, the boy merged his Chinese acumen with the white man's business methods to map out his own future. With his inside knowledge of Chinese affairs, he began brokering the importing of both people and goods, including prostitutes and smuggled goods.

Pete was well-liked in Chinatown, and Caucasians with whom he dealt admired his polite manners and perfect English. His growing presence in Chinatown required Fong Ching to dress the part, and he began wearing expensive Chinese clothes. Applying American business tactics to his sinister Oriental operations, he was soon being admired by Chinese and Caucasians alike.

And, he saved his money. When he had acquired the experience he sought, he borrowed the needed extra funds and bought his own shoe factory. Now, Fong Ching was really on his way. Hiring an uncle, his brother, and some forty other employees, he called his enterprise F. C. Peters & Company. He knew many white businessmen would not buy from a Chinese wholesaler, so he used the brand

name F. (Fong) C. (Ching) Peters, although many San Franciscans were aware of his scheme. He hired a white bookkeeper and salesmen at high salaries, the F. C. Peters shoes were sold throughout California, and the young entrepreneur was soon independently wealthy. Because of his stature, Fong Ching became known far and wide as "Little Pete."

Pete married a young woman named Chun Li, and he and his bride settled in a suite of rooms above his shoe factory. Eventually, the couple

Highbinders of old San Francisco.
Sutro Library.

had three children and all the social standing and wealth that eluded most of their race in the new land. But there was a sinister restlessness in the young Oriental. Ownership of several lucrative gambling dens did not satisfy Pete, either, and he founded a new tong, the Gee Sin Seer. According to one early source, Pete recruited a coterie of hatchet men, or highbinders, for his new tong. These were the boo how doy, the fighting men of the tongs, the killers and thugs who plagued Chinatown with protection rackets and kept the gambling dens, lotteries, and prostitutes in line. Although Pete was highly successful and admired in his legitimate enterprises, he found that only in his illicit enterprises did he find true satisfaction. His new tong was very successful and tribute from his victims mounted every day. Others were envious of this success and the Bo Sin Seer tong was established to counter Pete's rising influence.

By the mid-1880s the tong rivalries in San Francisco were becoming fierce. Although Chinatown had long been a closed society and inscrutable to local government, regular police patrols were in force now, as the authorities tried to maintain some kind of control over the foreign presence in the city's midst.

When a rival tong member tried to stir up trouble in one of his gambling dens, Pete had one of his highbinders kill him, or "wash his body" in tong language. As a result, it was not long before Pete had a price on his head, and he hired Lee Chuck, China-town's top boo how

Attorney Hall McAllister.
California State Library.

doy, as a bodyguard. He also purchased an arsenal of pistols, as well as two steel-chain vests for Lee Chuck and himself.

In late July 1886, a police detective told Lee Chuck to be on his guard as there was a plot to kill him. For the next few months Chuck was on his guard wherever he went. One day, while walking warily down Spofford Alley, Chuck suddenly confronted his purported assassin, Yen Yuen. After a brief snarling match, Lee Chuck pumped five bullets into his opponent, then fled at the approach of several police officers. A confederate of the dying Yuen probably snatched his weapon, then disappeared into the gathering crowd. Policeman John Martin captured Lee Chuck, but only after the highbinder had tried to shoot him, also.

Feeling that Lee Chuck had risked his life on his behalf, Little Pete followed his natural instincts now and sought out officer John Martin and offered him a $400 bribe if he would testify that Yen Yuen had been killed in self-defense. He offered several other bribes, also, and was promptly hauled down to headquarters and charged with sundry attempts to bribe officers, but the popular Chinese businessman was quickly out on bail.

In late January 1887, the Lee Chuck trial began in the Superior Court. Pete secured the best lawyers for his beleaguered bodyguard and now instigated a campaign to bribe the jury. Not content with that, Pete attended court every day and was even thrown out once when caught trying to prompt witnesses. Lee Chuck was convicted and sentenced to hang, but was later granted a new trial. He was tried two more times on appeals and was finally sentenced to fifty years in San Quentin.

Pete, meanwhile, went to trial on the bribery charge a few weeks before Lee Chuck's first trial commenced. Again, Pete obtained the city's best legal talent, including Hall McAllister, one of the more noted barristers on the Coast. Pete next astounded his counsel by insisting that he was going to admit the attempt to bribe the officers. His lawyers let out a yelp and refused to entertain such an idea.

"Gentlemen," Pete insisted, "I am merely a Chinaman and a jury will never believe me against white police officers. We all know that. I will say I did indeed offer them a bribe and that they took it, but it was only offered to insure that they tell the truth. The police have been taking money in Chinatown for years and these officers only arrested me when I would not give them more."

After futile attempts at reasoning with their client, the attorneys finally gave in. And to their great surprise, eleven days later a hung jury was the result. On May 16, 1887, a second trial began, but it too resulted in a hung jury.

In late summer of 1887, a third trial began. Both of the last two trials resulted in more bribery attempts and various documents showing Pete had bribed various municipal officials. He had also paid Chris Buckley, the Democratic political boss, a large sum to work for his release. On August 24, Pete was convicted after the jury had deliberated only thirty minutes. After a severe dressing-down from Judge Dennis J. Toohy on September 7, 1887, Pete was finally sentenced to five years at Folsom State Prison.

Little Pete's Folsom mug shot.
California State Archives.

Pete was admitted to Folsom on September 7, 1887. His power was intact, even in prison. Of all the Chinese convicts, only he was allowed to retain his Chinese queue—the long pigtail of tradition. Released at the end of his term, Pete returned to San Francisco and picked up his life where he had left off. Prison had taught him nothing, however, except that in his dealings with the "white devils," he must utilize much more caution.

San Francisco planned a large midwinter exposition during 1894 in Golden Gate Park. When the steamship *Gaelic* arrived in port with a large contingent of Oriental women for the Chinese pavilion, their chaperone was revealed to be Chung Ying, a cousin of Little Pete. The local press raised the warning that these women would be admitted into the country only for the term of the exposition, but would disappear one by one as the fair progressed. Sure enough, when a treasury agent later investigated, only thirty-seven of the 257 original Chinese women admitted were still at the pavilion. The press estimated that Pete had already netted some $50,000 selling the girls as prostitutes.

Even as he was hip deep in his nefarious activities, Pete was always launching new schemes. He loved to play the ponies at the Bay District track and he did not like to lose. By paying relatively small amounts to trainers, stable boys, bookmakers and others, Pete was able to consistently make the races pay. When this palled on him, he schemed with the jockeys riding the horses most likely to win in the various races. The jockeys would be bribed to do as Pete said—one being designated as the winner, and the others losers.

A typical race consisted of the handicappers all picking a nag named Wheel of Fortune as the most likely winner. Pete paid Wheel's jockey to lose, while arranging that a long shot named Rosebud would be the winner. Pete's winnings were really piling up when Art Hinrichs, one of his jockeys who was supposed to lose, bet his bundle on his own horse winning, instead. While the jockey made a nice chunk of change at 10-to-1 odds, the other jockeys were so furious at the betrayal that Hinrichs had to hire a bodyguard.

When Hinrichs finally ratted to track officials, Pete temporarily made himself scarce at the track. Pete's favorite jockeys—Hinrichs, Jerry Chorn, and Hippolyte Chevalier—were banned from racing, but it did not matter. Pete just paid others to stand in for him, bought a new set of jockeys and made more money than ever.

Although Pete did not realize it, his own race had been run. Despite his charm and personality, he had made enemies over the years.

Some thought he was behind the murder of Chew Ging, a Suey Sing tong member. Ging was also reported to be a See Yup, while Pete belonged to the Sam-Yups and the murder had generated a deadly feud between the two rival tongs. Pete was still at loggerheads with the Bo Sin Seer tong, while his success in the slave girl trade resulted in more envy. Also, Big Jim, the local Chinese lottery king, was considered an arch rival. Big Jim was even thought to be richer than Little Pete. And there were others.

Pete still retained several Chinese bodyguards for his protection, but he hired a tough named Ed Murray also, since he knew any highbinder would hesitate at killing a white man. Murray was a big man and fast on the draw, but when there were no attempts on his life, Pete became less cautious. He finally discharged Murray, but friends insisted he obtain another white bodyguard, and C. H. Hunter took over the position.

Pete's wife obviously knew of her husband's seamy side. The trials and gossip with her friends and neighbors led her to know instinctively how his life would end. Reportedly, she begged Pete to sell out. They could return to China, she coaxed, and lead a wealthy and safe life with their children. He laughed at her first

A Chinese barber shop in Little Pete's time. *Author's collection.*

request, but became nasty at the second. This was his life, he said. He would never leave. As for the children, they were Americans. This was their home.

On the eve of the Chinese New Year, January 23, 1897, Pete decided to join some friends for drinks. There was a barbershop on the ground floor of the building where he lived, and around nine o'clock in the evening he entered through a back door and sat down for a shave. Finding no suitable reading matter, Pete sent Hunter down the street for a sporting publication. When the bodyguard objected, Pete raised his hand with a smile. "Go, go—I'll be all right."

When Hunter left, Pete settled in his chair and leaned back. A few moments later, as barber Ah Jung engaged in some small talk with his customer, he didn't notice a man slip into the shop and swiftly move up to Pete's chair. The pistol, already in the assassin's hand, exploded in a burst of powder smoke. The first shot hit

Little Pete. dead on the floor of his barber shop, as sketched by a newspaper artist. *Author's collection.*

Pete in the right eye, and a second bullet hole appeared just above it a moment later. After a third bullet ploughed into Pete's chest, the killer spun about and ran from the scene. Pete fell to the floor, as the shop's occupants quickly emptied into the street. Sprawled in a spreading pool of blood, his eyes glazing, Pete could not see the huddled crowds of people gathering to look through the shop's front windows.

Little Pete was dead! Even as police officers chased two suspects, word spread throughout Chinatown. There were those who cheered at the news—See Yups and others of Pete's enemies. They knew another would take his place, but for now it was enough to wallow in the joy of the moment.

Chun Li, Pete's wife, was devastated. Her worst nightmare had come true. She immediately advertised a $2,000 reward notice in the press, and she posted it throughout Chinatown. "I shall follow the murderers to the end," she said. "If this $2,000 is not enough, then I will offer more."

LITTLE PETE'S WIDOW ——
SEEKS VENGEANCE.
NOTICE!
A REWARD OF $2,000
Is hereby offered for the conviction of the murderers of FONG CHING, otherwise known as LITTLE PETE, who was murdered in this City on January 23d, 1897.
CHUN LI,
WIDOW OF FONG CHING.
San Francisco, January 27th, 1897.

Reward notice for Little Pete's killers. *Author's collection.*

Although the police promptly rounded up several suspects, they were soon released for lack of evidence. One suspect was tried, but he was released when the jury could not agree on a conviction. Despite the reward, the killers were never caught.

Pete's funeral attracted some 30,000 Chinese, as well as many tourists from around the area.

The tong wars raged intermittently throughout California and the nation during the first decades of the twentieth century. In December 1899, the San Francisco *Examiner* ran a headline reading "Murder Opens Fierce War in Chinatown." In March 1917, the front page of the *Fresno Republican* reported, "Gunmen in Five Coast Cities Renew War," with a subhead reporting "Six Men Dead as a Result of Outbreak of Chinese." On July 12, 1921, the *Madera Daily Mercury* announced "Two Arrested for Tong Killing."

Chun Li, Little Pete's wife and mother of their children. *Author's collection.*

Gradually, however, the murderous elements of the tongs died out. Succeeding generations sought new methods of controlling the Chinese community. Law-abiding Chinese had suffered terribly during these troubles and many of them quietly began cooperating with the legal authorities and the police in trying to stem the tong stranglehold on their society.

And in the end, they won.

In a curious postscript to the nineteenth-century custom of shipping the bodies of relatives and friends home to China for burial, a recent dispatch in the *New York Times* announced a reversal of the procedure. When a Chinese-American learned his family plot in China was about to be disturbed by the government, he hastily flew to his homeland and returned with his ancestors' bones. Other Chinese-Americans have done the same. Times, traditions, and circumstances have changed. At last, it seems, our Chinese-American friends and neighbors are here to stay.

BOOKS

Boessenecker, John. *Gold Dust & Gunsmoke*. New York: John Wiley & Sons, 1999.

Buck, Franklin. *A Yankee Trader in the Gold Rush*. Boston and New York: Houghton Mifflin Company, 1930.

Carr, John. *Pioneer Days in California*. Eureka: Times Publishing Company, 1891.

Cox, Isaac. *The Annals of Trinity County*. Eugene, Oregon: Harold C. Holmes, 1940.

Dicker, Laverne Mau. *The Chinese in San Francisco*. New York: Dover Publications, Inc, 1979.

Dillon, Richard H. *The Hatchet Men*. New York: Coward-McCann, Inc., 1962.

_____. *Humbugs and Heroes*. New York: Doubleday & Company, 1970.

Duke, Thomas S. *Celebrated Criminal Cases of America*. San Francisco: The James H. Barry Company, 1910.

Farkas, Lani Ah Tye. *Bury My Bones in America*. Nevada City: Carl Mautz Publishing, 1998.

Hoexter, Corrine K. *From Canton To California*. New York: Four Winds Press, 1976.

Lee, C. Y. *Days of the Tong Wars*. New York: Ballantine Books, Inc., 1974.

McLeod, Alexander. *Pigtails and Gold Dust*. Caldwell, Idaho: Caxton Printers, 1947.

NEWSPAPERS

Columbia Weekly, September 1856

Madera *Daily Mercury*, July 12, 28, 1921

Mariposa Gazette, November 19, 1856

Fresno Republican, March 6, 1917

Sacramento *Daily Union*, September 9, 11, 13, 1854

Sacramento State Journal, September 1854

San Francisco *Daily Alta California*, July 24, 25; October 28, 31, 1856; September 17, 18, 1862

San Francisco *Bulletin*, February 2, 3, March 4, 1891; April 1, 1899

San Francisco Call, June 18, 1887; January 24, 25, 1897

San Francisco *Chronicle*, March 28, 1896; January 24, 25, 26, 27,1897

San Francisco *Daily Herald*, January 4, 5, 7, 8, 12, 1854; September 17, 1862

San Francisco *Examiner*, November 14, 1894; January 25, 29, 1897; February 26, April 2, 1899

Sonora Union Democrat, September 1856

Stockton, *San Joaquin Republican*, October 28, November 9, 1856

OTHER SOURCES

Barth, Gunther, "Chinese Sojourners in the West: The Coming," *Southern California Quarterly*, Historical Society of Southern California, March 1964

Chacon, Ramon D., "The Beginning of Racial Segregation: The Chinese in West Fresno and Chinatown's Role as Red Light District, 1870s–1920s," *Southern California Quarterly*, Historical Society of Southern California, Winter 1988.

DuFault, David, "Chinese in the Mining Camps of California," *Southern California Quarterly*, Historical Society of Southern California, June 1959.

Masters, Frederick J. "Among the Highbinders," *The Californian Illustrated Magazine*, October 1891–May 1892.

North, Hart H., "Chinese Highbinder Societies in California," *California Historical Society Quarterly*, March 1948.

Tsai, Shih-Shan Henry, "The Chinese and 'Gold Mountain,'" *The Californians*, March–April 1988.

Wilson, LL., D., and Thomas B., "Old Chinatown," *Overland Monthly*, September 1911.

Chapter 9

The Way of a Man with a Maid

Jim Bethel's Indian Feud

The plains of California's great San Joaquin Valley were an Eden in the early nineteenth century. Herds of wild horses, antelope, and elk roamed the shores of the vast Tulare Lake, which was home to birdlife that could blacken the skies in flight. Giant grizzly bears feasted on a beached whale to the west near the shores of Monterey, while their cousins caught salmon in rivers originating in the mighty Sierra to the east.

Crossing the grassy plains from Stockton or San Francisco, the forty-niners entered the Gold Rush country via a series of rocky, small knolls which quickly evolved into oakstudded foothills. In the spring and fall these plains and hills were covered with grasses that looked like a bright green carpet from a distance. In the baking heat of summer, the carpet assumed the gold and ochre hues of dead grasses waiting for Nature's nurturing rains to make them green again. Among rocky outcroppings were scattered the gnarled and rough evergreen oak trees, their fingered branches reaching to the skies. The oaks never changed. A little higher, the terrain evolved into oak trees interspersed with scrub pine and scattered manzanita and chapparal. The mining country was located along the rocky streams and rivers tumbling out of the higher, redwood and pine forests. This was where fortunes in gold were made, but also where disappointment frequently prevailed.

The area surrounding the mining towns of Mariposa and Millerton was also the home of the Yokuts and Monache Indians. Yokuts groups, the Chukchansi, Pitkache, Dumna, and others, were neighbors of the Monache, or Western Mono, who generally lived at elevations above 3,000 feet. The Mono were close culturally to both the eastern California Paiutes and the Yokuts, except in language. All three groups had escaped serious contact with the early Spanish, who were seeking converts to Christianity. With the coming of the gold rushers in 1849, however, the Yokuts and Mono world changed quickly and irrevocably.

Even the early arrivals during the California Gold Rush quickly found that many of the richest mines had already been claimed. While there were no particularly large towns in the new territory in 1848, Los Angeles, San Francisco, Monterey, and other villages had all but emptied of residents, gone in search of gold.

Mexicans were early arrivals, also. Traveling the blistering desert up from the state of Sonora, they staked their claims in the area that would later become Tuolumne County and the towns of Sonora and Columbia. Thousands arrived from South America, also. The harbor master at San Francisco estimated that some 62,000 immigrants had arrived from around the world in the six months preceding April 1850. By the following June, some 635 abandoned ships clogged San Francisco Bay, the crews and even the captains fleeing inland hoping to make their fortune. Discharged American soldiers, gold rushers from the Sandwich Islands (Hawaii), Australia, and the South Seas also helped glut the popular central and northern mining areas, causing miners to spread out looking for less crowded and better paying claims. By late 1851, miners were washing gravel in gullies and ravines from Weaverville and Shasta in the north, to Mariposa and Agua Fria and along the San Joaquin River far to the south.

Young Jim Bethel arrived in the early Gold Rush days, sometime in 1849. He first shows up in the 1850 census as a resident of the burgeoning village of Stockton. Like most new arrivals, he quickly headed for the mines. Bethel's first view of the great San Joaquin Valley was probably the same as that recorded by pioneer Jeff Mayfield, who described his family's arrival in 1850. The Valley provided a startling and beautiful sight:

There was a strong west wind blowing, and it was waving the tall, grasses in the valley and changing its floor into shifting splotches of green and yellowish green... The entire plain, as far as we could see, was covered with wild flowers. Almost all the flowers were new to us ...As we passed below the hills the whole plain was covered with great patches of rose, yellow, scarlet, orange and blue. The colors did not seem to mix to any great extent. Each kind of flower liked a certain kind of soil best and some of the patches of one color were a mile or more across.

Young Bethel probably worked some of the more crowded mining areas, then began moving south. Sonorans, from Mexico, had been mining in the area of Agua Fria since the summer of 1849. The Special 1852 Mariposa County census lists him as James H. Bethel, a twenty-year-old miner from Missouri.

Mariposa County was one of the original California counties, stretching from present day Merced to as far south as Los Angeles. It was the largest county in the world at that time, and by the winter and spring of 1850 some 3,000 miners were working in the area. As the Stockton newspapers reported, large nuggets were being discovered daily, and more and more miners began arriving at Agua Fria and the new town of Mariposa.

Agua Fria, one of the earliest of the Mariposa mining camps. *California State Libary.*

When the local Indians realized they were losing their land and villages to these hordes of miners, there was trouble. Miners formed volunteer groups and casualties were suffered by both sides. Some seventy miles to the south, a military post was established on the San Joaquin River a few miles above the mining camp called Rootville. Fort Miller had a calming effect on the area. Indian agents and commissioners managed to establish various reservations and secure an uneasy peace, but the local Yokuts Indians would never fully recover from the clash of cultures that now enveloped them. An army captain, Erasmus D. Keyes, who had escorted the Indian agents to the area, wrote of those tragic days some years later:

> It was on the very site of Fort Miller, in the same month of May seven years before (1851), that I saw assembled above 1,200 aborigines, natives of adjacent plains and mountains, many of whom had never seen a white man till they came to treat with us. I was then impressed with the appearance of several chiefs, and remembered the general aspect of all. Especially was I struck with the activity of the young Indians of both sexes while they amused themselves with football and other rough sports. As all those Indians had been assigned to a reservation of which Fort Miller was a central point, I inquired for several individuals whom I remembered. I was told that they were nearly all dead, victims to drunkenness, and that of the whole number I then saw in such full activity, not above fifty remained...

Liquor, for the Indians, was to become a vicious and overwhelming problem for many years.

During this period, Jim Bethel drifted south from the crowded Mariposa mines to Coarse Gold Gulch and other areas adjacent to the San Joaquin River. He was six feet tall, good looking, and neat in his habits. Like so many others, he probably never made a big gold strike, but kept moving about hoping to locate a good-paying claim. When they ran out of food money, these unlucky prospectors went to work at a mine or some other job for wages. They were off prospecting again, however, just as soon as they saved up a few dollars.

Unlike so many of these rootless wanderers, Bethel seems to have stayed in the area. In 1851, he was mining in the area of Texas Flat, on Coarsegold Creek. That summer he is recorded as voting at the county election, along with Joe Kinsman, William Faymonville, Theodore Strombeck, R. T. Burford, and others. He later mined for a time on the San Joaquin River around Rootville, after that village had changed its name to Millerton in honor of the fort upriver.

Although listed as a teamster living with a local Millerton merchant named James Blackburn and his wife in the 1860 census, Bethel still probably prospected along various nearby creeks between jobs. He was wearing a mustache and goatee now and hauled supplies to Texas Flat and other mining camps and trading posts in the hills and mountains. In the early 1860s, Bethel is said to have moved into a cabin on what was called the Ramsey Place on the road to Crane Valley. Here he ran a few cattle and hogs, grew some crops and panned for gold when the urge struck him.

During his prospecting and wagon trips through the hills above Coarsegold and Millerton, Bethel frequently came into contact with the local Indians. The Dumna Yokuts still lingered in the area along the San Joaquin River across from Millerton. Downriver were the Hoyumne and the Pitkache. The Chukchansi and Mono had rancherias, or villages, in the area of his ranch, and he frequently visited them and showed an interest in learning their languages. Exactly how this took place is not clear, but we can assume that Jim became friendly with a Chukchansi chief who was perhaps flattered that a white man was interested in his culture.

When Bethel asked for an Indian woman who could keep house for him and also assist with his language lessons, the chief selected Neh ku wee. Jim was illiterate, but the Indians had no written language and soon he was conversing in a rudimentary manner with his housekeeper and other Indians. The words were pleasant in their sound, as noted by an early pioneer. There was none of the grunting effect that is usually thought to be characteristic of the speech of all the American Indians. On the contrary, the sounds are formed well within the mouth and the result is a peculiarly soft, distinct and pleasant enunciation.

An Indian camp in the hills above Fresno, ca.1890s. *Fresno City and County Historical Society.*

During the course of the lessons, Neh ku wee was undoubtedly picking up English words, also. It was not surprising that a romance soon blossomed between the lonesome white man and his tutor. When Jim asked the woman to live with him, he was told that an Indian of the village had a prior claim, and an awkward situation developed. There are no details as to what happened next, but court testimony years later indicated there was a confrontation and Bethel killed the Indian suitor with three well-placed shots. There were those who said a bitterness was engendered that day, a feud that would last some forty years. Jim and his chosen bride were married after the Indian fashion and they were pleased when a son, Robert, was born in 1864.

There were many other white miners throughout California who either married, or merely consorted with, Indian women. "Squaw men" they were called at the time, and their progeny were "half-breeds." These terms were as contemptuous as they were racist, yet these mixed unions were sometimes accepted to a limited extent by local white society, so long as the couple was personable and hard-working.

Such unions resulted in few objections in the Indian rancherias. Hunger often stalked the native villages in winter. Marriage to a white man meant flour, bacon, and blankets, not just for the woman, but for her family and rancheria, also. And why not, reasoned the native inhabitants? Were not these white people living on land taken from the Indians?

The 1860 and 1870 censuses for the Fresno County area report emigrants from Scotland, Mexico, Italy, Canada, Denmark, and Chile, as well as from nearly every state in the union. The majority were single men, far away from home and lonesome for female companionship in a land where white men still greatly outnumbered white women.

Bethel saw these mixed unions all around him. Joe Medley, who fiddled at all the dances along the San Joaquin, was happily living with Suse, a Chukchansi woman. Joe was a great fiddler, but liked his whiskey. Suse was a good housekeeper and wife and at least one observer thought Joe got much the best of that arrangement.

Joe liked to brag that no white woman was cleaner or a better cook than his Suse, and his being a man of conviction, eventually they were married. Aunt Suse was much loved by her neighbors, Indian and white alike.

Theodore Strombeck was another who took an Indian wife in the early days. His marriage in 1858 to eighteen-year-old Memerite, another Chukchansi girl, was a strong one, producing nine children. He had come to California from Sweden in 1847, and after gold was discovered the following year, operated boats and pack trains to carry

supplies to the mining camps. In time he acquired a ranch at Texas Flat, the mining camp which had been renamed Coarsegold Gulch. Strombeck recognized the many sterling qualities in his mate and remained with her all his life.

Although many white men fully appreciated their native American spouses, others shamelessly abandoned these Indian unions whenever it suited their purposes. Sam Bishop was a young man who worked as a blacksmith on the nearby Fresno River Reservation in 1852. He was a farmer and blacksmith by trade and was hired to teach the Indians how to raise crops. He lived with an Indian girl, daughter of a chief, and had much influence with the tribe. Still, when he acquired land in the Tejon area, he did not hesitate to abandon his Indian paramour. He acquired large ranching interests, the town of Bishop in Inyo County being named for him. When he moved to San Jose and became quite wealthy, he married a white woman and his family probably never knew of his earlier liaison on the plains of the San Joaquin.

Theodore "Swede" Strombeck. *Author's collection.*

Jim Bethel is listed in the July 1870 census as being thirty-seven years old and living with his six-year-old son, Robert. His wife was not listed with him, which perhaps meant they had an intermittent relationship. Indian families were very strong and native women living with white

Memerite Strombeck. *Author's collection.*

Pine Ridge, one of the mountain communities vulnerable to Indian attacks. *Fresno County Library Collection.*

men often customarily spent much time visiting relatives. Or, Bethel's wife may have died at some point since there are few indications of her presence in records.

But there could have been another reason Bethel's wife was not listed with him on the census that summer of 1870. There had been vague rumors that Paiute Indians from Inyo County had crossed the Sierra and were agitating the Monos, Chukchansi and other Indians in the foothills above Millerton and Coarsegold Gulch.

One morning, all the Indians around Millerton and Coarsegold Gulch were reported missing. Scott Ashman's farm on the San Joaquin was typical of what occurred in various localities. A large number of Indians were helping with his harvesting and had promised to finish the job the next day. When they did not return the following morning, he went to their village, only to find it evacuated. All the local whites knew that the first actions of the Indians when preparing for war was to take their women and children to the mountains and out of

J. Scott Ashman was later sheriff of Fresno County. *Author's collection.*

210

harm's way. To the whites, the principal concerns were the mountain settlements at Humphrey and Mock's sawmill, Crane's Valley, Toll House, and other isolated areas that were vulnerable to an attack. The first rumors were published in the Fresno *Expositor* on August 24, 1870:

> We learn that the Indian uprising... was instigated by an old witch... who being made acquainted with the grievances of the red man, went out alone into the mountain fastnesses and returned after a time and reported to the rest of the Indians who were at a fandango, that he had discovered the Great Spirit and that being had informed him that at the appearance of the new moon, the whites were all to die, together with their cattle, sheep and hogs, and all the Indians in the service of whites, also... It is said that the witches, or medicine men of the tribes are urging them to make war on the whites...

It was not difficult for the whites to believe this. It was well known that the Indians, as usual, had much cause to be disturbed and they might very well have reached the point where they had nothing more to lose. The *Expositor* underscored the local Indian complaints:

> The Indians have many grievances to complain of and that they should be incited to seek revenge does not seem improbable. They depend in a great measure, for their sustenance upon the grass seeds and acorns that they gather in the mountains. This season cattle and hogs have been driven thither in great numbers and as a consequence they have been robbed of their grasses and acorns. In some instances, we have been told, white men have forbidden them, under any circumstances, to gather acorns at different points in the mountains as they wished to pick them up to feed their hogs upon. Some Indians had small gardens of corn and melons that were broken into by cattle and hogs and completely destroyed, so naturally enough the poor lo, seeing starvation staring them in the face, have undoubtedly made some harsh threats... While we do not apprehend any danger, we think it would not be amiss to warn the settlers that the Indians have some rights which should be respected.

Jim Bethel's wife had undoubtedly been told she must return to her people who were leaving for the

Yokuts medicine man. *Author's collection.*

mountains. Most of the Indian women living with white men did the same thing, although it is recorded that Joe Medley's wife, Suse, stayed with him even though her loyalty might prove to be fatal.

Clearly something had to be done. A meeting of settlers was held at Toll House in late August, where it was determined that an armed party would go into the mountains and try to find out just what was meant by the disappearance of the Indians. Another meeting was held at Beasor's store, near Crane Valley. Some fifty local whites and a large group of Indians gathered to discuss the many rumors and events. The principal Indian chiefs were questioned as reported by interpreter J. M. Ault to the *Expositor*:

> ...They stated that they had never contemplated any difficulty with the whites; that while their gardens had been destroyed by livestock, and other wrongs had been inflicted upon them, they preferred to suffer rather than raise a difficulty, and that they wanted peace, but should other Indians see fit to raise a fight, they would stand by the whites... It is the opinion of Mr. Ault that there is not a particle of danger of any trouble, and that the reports were gotten up by parties who had stock in the mountains, with a view to frighten away others, so that they might have more pasture room.

At Humphrey and Mock's mill another group of some twenty-five men was formed. George Crammer was one of the party and later wrote about the excursion to look for the Indians. The group camped at Stephenson's Meadow and sent John Lewis and three other men out to locate their quarry. About twenty miles into the mountains, they caught an Indian and forced him to lead them to the Indian encampment. They rode into a camp where some fifty or sixty Indian fighting men tried to flee with their families before the whites convinced them they meant no harm. The Indians finally agreed to return with them to Stephenson's Meadow the next day.

When the four white men woke the following morning, however, the Indian men had again vanished, leaving only some old people and children. It was later learned that the Paiutes had threatened to kill them all if they went back to the whites. When the old Indians and children were returned to Stephenson's Meadow, John Lewis, Johnson, and several others returned to again seek out the Indian camp. They located the Indians, then decided to wait until morning to make contact again. After building a small fire and eating, they decided to move away from the fire to make their beds for the night. Later, shots were fired into their camp and they quickly saddled their horses and rode for Stephenson's Meadow. All then returned to Humphey and Mock's mill.

At this time a large camp meeting was being held at Jasper Musick's Dry Creek ranch. Vince Moore made the ride from Humphrey's mill to give the warning. The *Expositor* eagerly looked forward to the breaking news, but the editor became concerned at this point, as noted in the August 31st edition:

> ...At all events it stands all settlers in exposed parts to be prepared in case of an emergency. The Indians are sufficiently numerous to cause considerable trouble before they could be put down, as people are illy prepared for any such a turn of affairs.

The settlers could not afford to ignore the situation and everyone was fortunate that no bloodshed had occurred. And all parties heaved a collective sigh of relief when the uprising proved to be a tempest in a teapot. Still, in such a climate of fear and misunderstanding, how long would it be before there was a serious Indian outbreak.

Jim Bethel's part in these troubles is not known. Although his wife had apparently gone to the mountains with her people, Jim himself probably felt safer avoiding the situation. He did not want to remind the Monos that he had killed one of them at a previous time. In any case, the war was officially put to bed when a local Indian chief nicknamed Cow-whopper was interviewed.

"What for white man want to fight Injun," he asked? "Injun no want to fight. You think Injun damn fool?"

Alcohol was the constant solace of a native people buffeted repeatedly by the

Indian woman in the mountains with her acorn-gathering basket. *Jeff Edwards collection.*

winds of change that forced them into a place somewhere between their old life and the new—people frustrated by years of injustice, the loss of their lands, and a hundred other grievances. The Indians' old world was gone, and few of them would be accepted into the new.

In neighboring Tulare County the liquor problem was underscored by a horrible crime. After a prolonged drinking spree, several Indians accosted a white woman and her two children near Porterville and killed all three. The incident could have resulted in a bloodbath, but cooler heads prevailed. No one knew what might happen the next time, however.

Although selling liquor to Indians was against the law, their acquisition of whiskey was a constant complaint in the press at the time. The Millerton Chinese grog shops were frequently blamed for this liquor traffic, but everyone knew whites were just as culpable. No matter how law-abiding a saloon keeper was, the rotgut would reach the Indians, reported a pioneer of the time.

On one page of the Register of Fresno County Licenses, there are twenty-three names with nineteen of them listed as traders, billiard hall owners, and liquor dealers in the hills. All three of these types of businesses sold liquor over a bar, and there were many more pages of such dealers in the register. The bottom line was that if an Indian wanted liquor, he would get it one way or another. Drinking too often resulted in needless tragedies and with so much liquor being sold in the mountains, it is a wonder there was not much more trouble. But there was enough.

A typical melee took place in late October 1870, as reported in the Millerton press. Two drunken Indians had an altercation just below town and Joe, a Dry Creek Indian, began beating his opponent with a club. When Judge W. T. Rumble saw the scrap, he rushed over to stop it and Joe fled, along with a pal named Tom. Judge Rumble directed two other Indians to chase the fleeing figures, but Joe suddenly turned and shot and killed a pursuer named Cholo. Tom was soon picked up by Sheriff Walker, but Joe remained a fugitive. Occurrences of this kind were constant and tragic and, of course, destroyed not one person, but two. These incidents were bad enough, but the whites were constantly adding to the problem, also.

On May 31, 1871, under the heading "Indian Killed," the *Expositor* recorded the following incident in a terse and brutal manner:

A few days since an Indian stole a horse from Mr. John Hughes of Upper Kings River. The owner, discovering his loss, went in quest of his property. He discovered it in the possession of the Indian who,

Fresno Flats as it looked in 1910 during its declining years. *Author's collection.*

finding that he was caught, showed fight. The Indians took charge of the body and buried it with the usual ceremonies of his race.

Meanwhile, sometime in 1872 Jim Bethel had filed, or bought, a possessory claim of 160 acres at Big Springs. He paid his assessment and listed his property as a house, barn and fencing, two farm wagons, two horses and one mule, fourteen work oxen, twenty-two hogs, some poultry and thirty dollars worth of firearms. He was active enough in local politics to be appointed roadmaster for District 2 in 1873. He also conducted political meetings and during elections his place served as a forum for local Democrats, as well as a polling place. Jim drew Grand Jury duty in November 1878, and later in the month the county awarded him a two-year road building contract for $950.

Jim gained another son in 1878. He named him Beige, perhaps a Bethel family name. Neh ku wee was apparently living with Jim much of the time, although she is not listed with him in the 1880 census. She may have taken the baby home to raise him in her village.

In late September 1879, there was more whiskey trouble in the mountains. The village of Fresno Flats lay deep in Indian country, near where Oakhurst is located today. Bethel's ranch was some ten or twelve miles to the southwest.

The incident was reported in the *Expositor*, October 1, 1879:

An Indian by the name of Will, having procured whiskey, got ingloriously drunk. It seems that a man by the name of Mike Baker had bought a bottle of whiskey at the saloon and had left it on the table for awhile, and when he looked for it, it was gone. Someone had seen the Indian take it. Mr. Baker asked the Indian to bring it back, but the Indian drew a knife, and, I believe, made a pass at Mr. Baker with it. Mr. Baker stepped back a few paces, drew a six shooter and fired, shooting the Indian through the head, and fired another shot through his head after he was down. ...It is a disgrace to the citizens of Fresno Flats that Indians get whiskey whenever they wish it and have money...

There was a grand Leap Year Masquerade Ball on New Year's Eve, the last night of 1879. It was to be held at Fresno's Metropolitan Hall, in the valley town established on the railroad in 1872. From Mariposa to Visalia and all through the mountains, invitation committees were established and preparations were made. Jim Bethel was on the Fine Gold Committee and perhaps joined the celebration himself. One hundred and twenty attended the affair and the *Fresno Republican* reported the evening was a great success, both

The Spring Valley mountain stage stop, on the road to Bethel's, was typical of such road stops in the mountain areas. *Collection of Mrs. John O'Neal.*

financially and socially:

> ...At 12 o'clock the managers called the assemblage to order and announced that two prizes were to be awarded... The Committee awarded the ladies prize to Miss Lizzie Litten, who sustained the character of a lively old lady in dress and action to perfection. The gentleman's prize was awarded to Sam Mayer, who personated a Hod carrier so perfectly as to mistify [sic] his most intimate associates... Many other characters were excellently well portrayed... Afterwards the crowd adjourned to the French Hotel where a sumptuous repast was served up after which dancing was resumed until 5 o'clock the next morning.

La-Ache, or Jack, a young Indian of Fresno County frontier days. *Fresno City and County Historical Society* .

Young Bob Bethel was growing up into a fine looking boy, as handsome as his father. The 1880 census reports him as being sixteen years old and living next to the Walker family. Mary Walker was a Chukchansi Indian woman whose white husband, Charles Franklin Walker, had died in 1877. Mary had six boys and Polly, the only girl, to look after. The two older boys worked the family farm to support the family. Bob went to the school on the Walker ranch with three of the Walker boys and was particularly close to young Charles Walker. A family friend reported he cut school as much as possible and his [Bob's] behavior was about what he wished it to be.

There was trouble in the Bethel family at this time, however. The 1880 census listed Jim as single and living alone. His wife was probably very independent and it can be surmised that the two merely went their separate ways, Neh ku wee living with her family much of the time.

Jim Bethel loved and spoiled his son. This, coupled with the natural rebelliousness of a teenager, probably caused Jim to eventually place Bob in Mary Walker's care.

Bethel had established a roadhouse at his ranch by now, and he paid his three-month fifteen-dollar liquor license fee in August

1880. His residence was listed as North Fork, San Joaquin (river). Even a rough frontiersman knew it was not good to raise a young boy around a saloon. A note in Joe Kinsman's diary is a good indication of the environment:

> Nov. 15, 1880 - Went down to P Harris store got some sugar then back home. On the way to Harris meet an Indian packing one of his tribe that had got killed near Bethel's Whiskey Hell. Weather clear and cold.

But Bob was growing up fast. When he felt like it, he visited his father and when he had his fill of school he moved back with him. A report in the *Weekly Expositor* indicated a small, but busy and lively settlement at Jim's place:

> Bethel's store is on the Crane Valley road, about forty miles from Madera and not much further from Fresno City, and although not incorporated still it is no slouch as a town. The buildings constituting the town are a dwelling, a store, a barn and a blacksmith shop. The surrounding country is inhabited by some Indians and some Anglo Saxons. The latter are engaged in stock raising, and the principal stock is the festive swine, but some of the ranchers raise chickens.

When Bob was nineteen, he selected a full-blooded Mono girl, Annie, as his bride. The girl was the daughter of Chief Charles Pomona and Jim thought his troubles with the boy were over. He bought another ranch on the Fine Gold Road, paying $1,400 for the improvements, cattle, and homestead. The property adjoined Jim's place. When Bob married Annie after the Indian fashion, Jim let them move into his house and he slept in the saloon. He later gave the Fine Gold property to Bob, after selling the cattle and getting his money back. It was said that Jim got the property and cattle, while the erstwhile owner just got the experience.

Bob's son, born in October 1882, was named Charles Henry. He could have been named after Bob's friend Charley Walker, or after his father-in-law. Still, Bob had a wild streak in him that was not to be calmed by marriage and family. E. L. Penry, a family acquaintance, once discoursed on Bob Bethel as follows:

> As I have said, Bob was fairly thoughtful and considerate of his father when sober. In Appearance he was a son to be proud of, for he was handsome in a devilish way. He always dressed well, and rode a fine horse with excellently mounted saddle and bridle. He wore his

derby down over one eye in an oh-go-to-hell manner. There was never a more swaggering, swashbuckling young rascal than Bob Bethel. Yet, he was a fairly decent fellow when sober. He made most of his living on the ranch Jim had given him.

He was as industrious as the average half-blood. Every so often, however, an overwhelming craving for liquor would come upon him and his wife would not see him for several days, for which she was no doubt thankful. During such periods he was a dangerous man, and engaged in numerous fights and shootings, though I never heard of him killing anyone.

Apparently, one of the conditions of Bob's marriage was the transferral of a piece of Bethel land on which old Chief Pomona and his fellow tribe members could settle. This was undoubtedly the chief's price for Bob's marrying his daughter. Jim had agreed because he thought it would be good for Bob's marriage. In his heart he knew just how unpredictable his son was. When he was drinking, which was becoming all too often, he was capable of anything. Recalling an evening at Jim's saloon, E. L. Penry described how Bob used to lash out at his father:

I remember well one night when a crowd of Indians and half breeds were drinking in and about Jim's saloon. Bob was treating freely at his father's expense. Jim finally grew weary of receiving nothing from most of the crowd. Drawing Bob aside, he remonstrated gently with him. Bob was well keyed. Jim should have known better than to find the least fault at such a time. Bob instantly flew into a savage rage and raked his father with such a fire of curses that I involuntarily glanced to see that no one was between me and the door. Jim actually writhed as a man does when about to be struck with a blacksnake [whip]. This is no time for you to interfere with what I do! the boy told his father, though I do not quote him verbatim. You're to blame for what I am and the position I'm in! Here I am, nothing more than a halfbreed! That's something to be proud of, isn't it, old man? I'm neither an Indian nor a white man! The decent whites won't have anything to do with me and I don't blame them, considering what a _____ of a father I've got. And, if I don't treat the Indians and half-breeds right, they'll throw me down. Then, what'll I do?

Thereupon he went back to his drinking and his friends, to presently get into a drunken fight with another half-breed.

This same E. L. Penry rode into Harry Blanchard's ranch one day and witnessed another of Bob's brawls. Bob and an Indian were wrestling amid a cloud of dust in the middle of the road:

> Both were pretty mellow. Bob had the Indian down and was endeavoring to open his pocket knife in order to cut the Indian's throat. The latter struggled to such an extent that Bethel could use only one hand and his teeth with which to open the knife. He was in such a fuddled state, however, that, after many attempts, he gave it up. Then, using the back of the blade, he scraped the skin off the Indian's face. Did Blanchard or I interfere? No, we did not. Why? Because we were like the average citizen of yesterday and today, but I hope not tomorrow. It was none of our business.

In late July 1885, the *Expositor* reported Constable Moore, from Fresno Flats, arrived in Fresno with "Indian Frank" who was charged with assault to commit murder on the person of Bob Bethel. This may have had to do with the above fight in the road.

Jim still hoped the birth of a second grandson, Pinky, on July 4, 1886, would have a steadying influence on his son, but this did not happen, either. When Bob caught the eye of another comely young Mono girl, he deserted Annie and took up with his new love. Knowing there would probably be trouble, Jim ordered Pomona and his people from his property. When Pomona showed up in the door of the Bethel saloon one day, Jim could see the old chief was still furious at the treatment given his daughter.

Some hard words were used by both men, with Pomona reportedly threatening the saloon keeper with a weapon of some kind. Jim grabbed his Winchester and dropped the Indian with a shot to the head. It was over in a moment. After sending word to the rancheria to come claim the body, Jim probably decided not to make any more demands about the Indian village being moved. Since no trial records for the shooting are listed in the Fresno superior court archives, it is supposed Jim was exonerated at a justice court hearing. Now, however, he must always be on his guard. George Washington Smiley, a neighbor, had come to California from Missouri with Jim in 1849 and later recalled those dangerous days:

> I know that James H. Bethel had his gun at hand for years after he killed the old man Pomona. He never went off his place without his gun, and he wouldn't go to North Fork without his gun. He told me he wouldn't come home at night; he told me he expected to be killed by the Indians, he was always watching for that.

Bob also kept a low profile for a while. He had shot an Indian in the leg during one fracas and had enumerable scraps with others. Deserting his wife was just the latest of his transgressions. He was afraid of no one, however, and when a call went out for posse members to help capture a local horse thief, Bob did not hesitate to sign on.

Frank "Tex" Kellett had a reputation as a horse and cattle rustler who terrorized mountain settlements and Indian villages in his spare time. In 1881, Tex and his partner, one Bender, were stealing stock in California and driving it over the mountains to Nevada for sale. The outlaws made several raids before Bender

After his release from prison for the horse theft, Frank Kellett took to robbing stages. *Author's collection.*

was killed in Nevada and things got too hot there for Tex. When he stole a horse from the large Daulton ranch near Madera, officers were again on his trail.

Tex was spotted by Constable John M. Hensley in August 1887, but before he could identify him the outlaw had disappeared again. Assuming the fugitive would be heading for the "horsethief trail" near Mammoth Pass in the high Sierra, Hensley picked up his posse along the way. Tom Beasore and Bill Taylor were herding cattle and agreed to join the lawman and several other ranchers he had recruited. Bob Bethel and Frank Schulte were also solicited to go along as trackers.

At Beasore Meadow, Bob Bethel spotted Kellett bathing in a small lake near his staked-out horse. The outlaw apparently saw the posse about the same time. "...As he broke for his gun he was fired upon," noted an account in the *Expositor*, "and was hit twice in the leg and fell. He had his pistol on, and being assured that the constable did not mean to kill him, put up his hands and surrendered. Tex was badly frightened, fearing that the people there would lynch him, but Hensley quieted them." Bill Taylor later said that it was Frank Schulte who shot Kellett. The outlaw received a ten-year sentence after pleading guilty in the Fresno County Superior Court.

But Bob could not stay out of mischief for long. Soon he was again hanging out around the Bethel store and in the late Pomona's nearby village. Bob's arrogant attitude, fueled by bad whiskey, predictably resulted in more tragedy. E. L. Penry, who lived in the area, is again a source for the following events:

On a night in about June [February], 1888, the Indians were holding a big fandango at Pomona's Rancheria, just below Jim Bethel's place. Bob Bethel and Charlie Walker, another half-breed, were riding back and forth between the saloon and the rancheria. They would drink awhile at the former, then go down and shoot into the crowd of bucks and papooses to see them scuttle into the sheltering brush and darkness like so many quail. The sodden fools no doubt thought that it was extraordinary sport. It was a little less than an act of providence that no one was hit. It will never be known conclusively, but it is very likely that the young bucks' smoldering hate and rage finally burst into flame, and that they arranged to effectively terminate the terrorism. To get the Indians' viewpoint, think how you would feel if you and a crowd of men, women and children were having a dance, and two drunken Indians came among you and began shooting promiscuously. I doubt if you would permit them to live half an hour longer.

Once again the half-breeds galloped madly down to the rancheria, leaped from their horses, who were foaming at the mouth from their Spanish bits, and once more emptied their revolvers where the Indians were thickest. Squaws, bucks, and papooses again fled from the firelight into the encircling darkness; Bob and Charlie reeled up to the fire, reloading their guns. Suddenly from out in the brush there came the short, spiteful bark of a pistol, and Bob Bethel, with the leaping firelight playing on his drink discolored face, crumpled to the ground dead.

Under the heading, "An Indian Fight in the Mountains," the *Expositor* of February 9, 1888, gave other details of the tragedy, including at least one casualty of the indiscriminate shooting:

The "Pow-wow" of the Indians near Bethel's store in this county ended last week with the usual results. Chas. Walker and Bob Bethel, both half-breed Indians, were in attendance and becoming full of fire water, a row took place which after several shots were fired it was found that John Bugg, a Digger, was shot and mortally wounded.

This for a time put a stop to the festivities, and all seemed quiet. The Indians dispersed, leaving Walker and Bethel masters of the situation. Night coming on they built a camp fire preparing to remain where they were. Bethel and Walker began drinking among themselves and yelling their respective war whoops until the welkin rang. The Indians who had dispersed, brooding over the shooting of Bugg and having no love for the father of Bethel who some time ago shot and killed Pea Meno [Pomona], an Indian chief, returned to the scene, but not openly. The country being very woody they crept behind the bushes until within a short distance of the unsuspecting Walker and Bethel who were standing with their backs to the fire and were an easy mark. ...At a given signal the Indians fired and Bob Bethel fell dead, pierced by five bullets. The Indians then retreated and Walker being so frightened was unable to ascertain who the murderers were...

Jim Bethel, an undated portrait, but he looks to be about fifty years old. *Courtesy William L. Klette.*

The half-blood Indian John Bugg, mentioned above, was a hard-working miner in the North Fork area when he was sober, but a holy terror when drinking. The son of a local white rancher, Bugg had one eye gouged out and bullet and knife scars covering his head and body. He apparently recovered from any wounds he received at the hands of Bethel and Walker and was reported still brawling in 1893.

Bob Bethel's body still lay in the woods, some distance from his father's house. When Charlie Walker brought Jim the news, the old man was afraid to go after the body. Pomona's death was still fresh in the minds of many Monos who also might take the opportunity to kill Jim. Jim's neighbor and friend, Judge George Smiley, vol-unteered to bring back the body. On the way to the Indian rancheria Smiley met an armed Indian, but otherwise had no trouble. The body was recovered and laid out in Jim's home.

They buried Bob across the road from the Bethel saloon. "The old man," recalled Penry, "was as griefstricken as if his son had died an honorable death."

It was a week later that a Dr. Cline arrived to conduct an autopsy. Jim was outraged and, according to Penry, argued against the procedure:

"By God! They shouldn't do it!" Jim declared, pacing frantically up and down. "It isn't right! To me it's like killing him over again!

They won't learn more than they know already; not a bit! I feel like going up there with my shotgun and telling them they can't dig him up, but it wouldn't do any good. They'd just arrest me and put the handcuffs on me. By God, I tell you it isn't right!"

A light rain was falling and Jim had a tarp held over his son's body as the autopsy was performed. As Jim had declared, nothing more was learned; except that it was a .44 pistol bullet that, entering at the front, had traveled slightly upward and lodged near the middle of the spine. However, nearly every man in the mountains had such a weapon. I had one myself.

After the autopsy and interview of what witnesses could be found, it was declared that Bob had been killed by parties unknown. As Penry, Harry Blanchard and an Indian half-blood named Joe Burns were later walking down the road, Burns stepped in front and confronted his two friends. "What do you think of that shot," he asked?

"Why, what do you mean Joe?" asked Harry.

Document from the Indian Dick trial. *Fresno County Superior Court Archives.*

"Wasn't that a pretty good shot at fifty yards?" returned Joe.

"How do you know it was fifty yards?" demanded Blanchard.

"I was laying behind a log that far from the fire," Burns responded. Then, resuming his walk, he would say no more. Penry recalled later that this pretty well satisfied Blanchard's and his doubts as to who had actually fired the shot that had killed Bob Bethel.

Penry and Blanchard knew better than to get involved in the matter. They were well aware that Joe was an excellent shot and the case would be difficult to prove in any case. In the mountains it was safer to mind your own business.

Jim Bethel stayed close to his store and around the company of other people for the immediate future. Judge Smiley and other friends talked of the earlier killings and of a blood feud between Jim and the Monos. Jim had killed two of the tribe and his actions alone were enough to stir up a vendetta. A feud did not seem likely, but it was best to stay on your guard. The nights were long and every shadow might harbor an assassin.

In mid-March, one "Indian Dick" was jailed at Fresno Flats and later brought to Fresno and charged with the Bethel murder. "The officers are on the lookout for the rest of the gang with some hopes of corralling the whole lot," reported the *Republican*.

In late July "Indian Frank" was brought in, also. He had been involved in several scraps with Bob Bethel and seemed to be a likely suspect. Interestingly enough, the half-blood named Joe Burns, who was later named by Penry as the killer, was one of the twenty-seven witnesses called for "Indian Dick's" trial. Others were Jim Bethel, rancher John Bugg, John L. Hunt, John J. White, and Pat Monahan. Eight Indians were called as witnesses, also. There was little hard evidence, however, and "Indian Dick" was declared not guilty after a trial of several days. He was released on August 2, 1888. Frank, too, was soon released and Bob's killer was never officially identified.

The witness named John Bugg was a local rancher after whom the colorful Indian "John Bugg" was named.

Annie, Bob's wife, remarried in time and lived a long life. She died at the Madera County Hospital on February 18, 1932. Bob's son, Charles Henry, died at the Clovis Sanitarium on July 16, 1947.

In July 1892, Jim was in Selma, a small town just south of Fresno, when tragedy again struck. While Jim was engaged in conversation with Dr. H. H. Majors, a local veterinarian and stable owner, the two men began arguing violently.

"I was an onlooker," claimed Clarence J. Berry later, "but did not interfere until Bethel drew a knife on Dr. Majors. I then stepped up and demanded that Bethel give me the knife, saying at the same time that if he wanted to fight he should fight in a manly way. Bethel struck at me with the knife, and to this day I bear this scar between the thumb and forefinger of my left hand to show where the knife blade caught me." Berry then punched Bethel, knocking him down. Throwing out his hand to break the fall, Jim was unfortunately still holding his knife and his right eye was seriously damaged by the knife blade. With blood streaming down his face, the old man now gave up his weapon to Berry, who turned it over to an officer. Stating he had been attacked, Jim now demanded the officer arrest Berry and Majors for assault and the

Selma, in 1900, was still a frontier town in many ways. *Selma Public Library.*

three men were hustled off to a justice court. A physician was summoned, and Jim was given medical treatment and told the sight in his right eye had been destroyed.

There were plenty of witnesses to the brawl and charges against Majors and Berry were promptly dismissed when Judge W. B. Cullom learned the true circumstances from various spectators. The judge even commented that, if anything, Berry was entitled to credit for preventing a possible murder.

When Jim caught the stage at Fresno to return home, he must have been ruminating about the injustice of life. In later years he ruminated frequently every time he read about Clarence Berry's highly successful career in the local press.

Clarence Berry seemed to have everything going for him. He had been married to a Selma girl, Ethel Bush, in March 1896, and the happy couple had left immediately for the Yukon, where a gold rush was underway. They stopped for a few days at Juneau, then made the trek over Chilkoot Pass and down the Yukon River. He made his first big strike on December 6, 1896, then began buying up other claims in the area. Selma residents soon followed and word of Berry's great good fortune spread up and down California. And Jim Bethel was furious and still ruminating.

In the spring of 1897, Berry and his wife returned to San Francisco as millionaires. Hailed as the "Klondike King," Berry was mobbed at the wharf by people who wanted to show him how to invest his riches, but Berry was more than capable of managing his own affairs. Later he would expand his financial empire by investing in various oil discoveries around the Valley.

Aching to somehow garner a share of Berry's good fortune, Jim Bethel finally came up with a plan. He talked it over with lawyer W. D. Crichton and decided to sue for the loss of his eye. The statute of limitations did not apply because Berry had been out of the state for much of the time since the incident had occurred. It was decided that $20,000 would compensate Bethel for loss of his eye, while an additional $5,000 would help to ease his pain and suffering. At the time, Berry was in San Francisco preparing to leave for the North, and Jim and his lawyer gambled he might make a quick settlement in order to not be detained. Interviewed by a reporter from the San Francisco *Call*, Berry gave a detailed recitation of how Jim had lost his eye, then quickly dashed Bethel's hopes:

> I look upon the suit as an attempt to extort money from me, for it is entirely without merit... I have been in Fresno for months, yet Bethel made no attempt to bring suit or serve summons on me. The day I left he filed his complaint and had the summons served on me here today, probably expecting that in order to go to Alaska I would compromise. I intend leaving for the gold fields within the next few days and will not delay for a minute on account of the suit.

When Berry again sailed for the Yukon, Bethel's hopes left with him. Of course, nothing came of the suit.

In December 1904, Jim received news that his younger son,

Beige, was dead. It was another tragedy in a family that seemed destined to have more than its fair share of grief. Only twenty-five years old at this time, Beige had been married in July 1902 and his suicide was apparently totally unexpected. An article in the *Madera Mercury*, December 10, reported the details of the incident:

> Deputy Coroner T. M. Ryan returned this morning from North Fork, where he held an inquest over the remains of B. Bethel, a half-breed who committed suicide there last Monday night. The testimony showed that Bethel, who was despondent because his mother would not deed her homestead to him, placed the muzzle of a 38-55 calibre Winchester rifle to his forehead and pulled the trigger, blowing his head off... .

Beige's wife said her husband returned home from work about nine o'clock that night and was angry. He threatened to kill himself and said his mother and others would be glad. Then, before anyone could stop him, he killed himself. A sister-in-law, Minnie Merritt, told much the same story and the resulting coroner's jury brought in a verdict of suicide.

In later years, however, the coroner's verdict would be questioned. As early as 1908, it would be suggested that the death was not a suicide, but a murder. "It was impossible," noted a newspaper article, "for him to have shot himself from the nature of the rifle wound [and] the fact that there were no powder marks on his body."

The article further notes that it had never been known for a half-blood Indian to take his own life.

No contemporary evidence for this murder theory has been located and the idea that all the family member witnesses were lying and the coroner's jury was "fixed" in some way seems highly unlikely. Still, Beige's death was enough to once again raise the specter of the old feud stories.

Jim buried his son next to Bob on the hill across the road. Several others had been buried there over the years and the spot came to be known as a private cemetery, or more properly, a local "boot hill."

Jim Bethel was beginning to show some wear. He was in his seventies and although he had survived many dangerous situations, he could not dodge "father time." He was living alone at his old place now and had watched as the nearby village of North Fork grew. E. L. Penry recalled Bethel's mountain hospitality in the closing years of the nineteenth century:

> On drowsy summer days, when everything was flooded with bright sunlight, the crickets whirred monotonously, a buzzard wheeled aloft in the cloudless blue sky... I liked to sit on the porch before Jim's saloon and listen to him talk.
>
> Many a white woman nearly exhausted from having ridden seemingly countless hours in a buckboard under a cruel sun, and through endless clouds of choking, powder-like dust, has had Jim Bethel's hospitality extended to her.
>
> If a man and his white wife happened to halt before Bethel's place when there was not a crowd of drinkers about, Jim would not stop insisting till both climbed out to rest. He would conduct them into the front room of his dwelling house. The room was bare of furnishings. It was so clean that you thought that even the furniture had been scrubbed out. Bethel would then take a comfortable rocking chair down from the joists overhead, saying; "This is for use whenever a lady honors me with a chance to visit. The boys are inclined at times to become rough, and I find it best to keep my furniture out of harm's way... ." If it were about noontime, he would add, "Dinner will be served presently."
>
> If man or wife objected that it would be an imposition upon his generosity, Jim would thrust one hand into the waistband of his trousers, make a grand gesture with the other, and declare that if they did not take dinner with him, he would feel it more than if they had slapped him across the face... .
>
> Taken as a whole, those old-timers were generous if nothing else.

Jim's daughter-in-law, Maud Merritt, lived in North Fork, and her family and various grandchildren probably visited old man Bethel. Members of the Walker family were around, also, as were Judge George Smiley and other personal friends who could now drop by and reminisce about old times.

Sitting on his porch, Jim could muse about the many changes he had seen since the pioneer days. It seemed like only yesterday that Crane Valley had been a beautiful camping spot and sawmill site. Wild mountain streams had flowed through the vale, but were now flooded by a dam and lost forever. A group of Fresno investors had harnessed some falls on the North Fork in recent years and

An unexpected stop in the mountains. From an illustration by Charles M. Russell. *Wells Fargo Bank.*

built a power plant a few miles above Jim's place. Now electricity was carried down to power Fresno homes, mills and street lights. Who could tell what changes would take place in another fifty years.

But with all the progress, stagecoaches still plied the mountain trails. In 1901, the stage from the Sugar Pine Sawmill was nearing Coarsegold when the coach slipped over a narrow part of the trail at about eight o'clock in the evening. Rolling over, the stage landed upside down in a creek, killing one man and injuring several others. "We fell in among a lot of sharp rocks," recalled passenger Ed Rey, "and it is a miracle that all of us were not killed, but the top of the stage saved us."

In the valley towns, in Madera and Fresno, you could occasionally see one of the new automobiles on the streets. It was not too difficult to envision these unique vehicles soon replacing the wagons and stagecoaches. Telephone lines now connected North Fork with Madera. The new century had indeed brought many changes.

Sometime in the early years of the new century, Jim Bethel gave up his saloon business. He found it hard to make ends meet, however, and was continually in arrears for back taxes on his property. In late 1905, Theodore Muhly, a young rancher who lived nearby, paid off some of Jim's back taxes for a half-interest in the Bethel property. The men were friendly enough and Jim stayed in his same house, on the property he retained. Muhly's Indian wife was Polly, the half-blood daughter of Mary Walker, who had looked after Bob so many years before. In her early thirties at this time,

Polly was like family to Jim and she called him "Granpa." He took most of his meals with Polly and her family.

Late on the afternoon of February 28, 1908, Jim had his customary supper with the Muhlys, then left about half past seven to return home. It was bitter cold and snow covered the ground. A thunderstorm blew in and a steady rain began to come down.

The following morning, the Madera coroner's office received a telephone call from the Crane Valley Powerhouse a few miles above Bethel's place. Jim Bethel had been killed the previous night. Muhly had heard two shots shortly after Bethel had left, but claimed he did not go to see what had happened, since he was unarmed. He went to bed and the next morning walked over to the Bethel place and found the old man lying on the ground at the end of his porch.

The news resulted in much newspaper coverage, as Bethel was widely known in the area. "Pioneer is found mysteriously shot," blared the headline on an inside page in the *Fresno Morning Republican*. The subhead read, "Was James Bethel of Madera killed by Indian Feudist?" The *Madera Mercury* featured two long columns on the front page, both with more modest headlines: "Jim Bethel Killed" and "Shot and Clubbed." While both newspapers gave much coverage to the legendary Bethel-Indian feud, the March 7 *Mercury* reported details of the crime and investigation:

> District Attorney Goucher arrived today from North Fork bringing with him the details of the killing of Jim Bethel which happened near that place last Friday night. Bethel had been shot in the right side of the head with no. 8 shot and while prone on his porch another shot had been fired at closer range for the shot, which missed, tore a hole in the front of the saloon about fifteen inches above the porch. The right side of the head had been battered in, the skull from the back of the ear to the corner of the eye and extending in a triangular shape to a point on top of the head was smashed. There were six incisions in the scalp where some blunt instrument had cut it.

The coroner's report and testimony of witnesses was included in the account, and the jury decided the murder had been committed by "unknown parties." Despite an extensive search, the murder weapon had not been found. Jim was buried next to his two sons in a casket made by neighbor Theodore Muhly.

Ernest Klette was one of Muhly's defense attorneys. *Author's collection.*

Several people noticed Muhly's odd behavior during and after the tragedy. The *Mercury* of March 14 noted:

> The feeling against Muhly in the mountains has been very strong, and at one time it was feared that Muhly would be lynched, but Undersheriff Hensley forestalled any attempt by having the suspect guarded.... When arrested Muhly said nothing, and if surprised at it, did not evince any emotion.

Various witness testimony at the coroner's hearing indicated him as a suspect, and in early autumn, Muhly was indicted to stand trial. Jury selection then began.

District Attorney George G. Goucher was an ex-state senator with a long legal background in Mariposa, Fresno and Madera counties. After an opening statement on September 11, outlining what he expected to prove, Goucher displayed and explained drawings and

At left is the old Bethel home where Muhly lived. Jim's saloon is to the right, with the road in the foreground. *Courtesy William L. Klette.*

photographs of the murder scene. Various witnesses were examined, including Bethel's twenty-six-year-old grandson Charlie, who diagrammed the inside of Muhly's house, where he had once lived. In the following days witnesses and evidence established that the missing shotgun had been used by both Bethel and Muhly for quail hunting. Pieces of coveralls and an old pair of shoes had been hidden and found to contain some kind of bloodstains. Muhly, unduly eager to bury his neighbor's body, had been seen making a coffin for Bethel during the coroner's inquest.

There were indications also that Bethel and Muhly were not on good terms. On the stand John Hensley stated that when he asked why Muhly did not go to the aid of his neighbor when he saw the flash of the shotgun that night, Muhly's response was evasive:

> "I didn't have any gun," was the reason the defendant gave, and at another time he told the witness that it was because he had taken Bethel out of many Indian rows, and was not going to take him out of any more. [Hensley] had asked the defendant to assist him in the search for the gun, and Muhly refused, saying that he didn't want to find any gun as he was suspicioned anyway... .

> J. H. Peabody testified that he saw Muhly at work plowing a field at the Muhly place, and told witness that Bethel "would plant no more melons there, damn him."

Theodore Muhly at San Quentin. *California State Archives.*

Both Muhly and his wife testified as to events of the murder night. Polly was cleaning up the dishes when a shot was heard about a half hour after the meal. Muhly was in the kitchen also, and related he heard Bethel call out, "Don't do it, boys!" Rushing outside, he heard a second shot and saw the flash over at the Bethel place. Instead of investigating, however, Muhly returned home and retired.

While Muhly testified that he had left the shotgun fully loaded at Bethel's place, Polly contradicted this by stating that the shotgun was unloaded and that there were no shells for it in her house. The murder weapon was never found. Another witness testified that Muhly was wearing freshly laundered coveralls the day after the murder.

Goucher spent five days detailing a great deal of circumstantial evidence pointing to Muhly's guilt. Defense team Frank Kauke and Ernest Klette were able to derail some of the prosecution's information, but they probably knew a hung jury was their best hope. They did know that a weak link in the case was the lack of a substantive motive for the murder, and the defense strategy now called for

Madera County district attorney George Goucher. *Author's collection.*

George W. Smiley to take the stand. An early pioneer who had known Jim Bethel since pioneer days, Judge Smiley was now instructed to tell what he knew of a feud between the Bethel family and the Mono Indians.

Judge Smiley's narrative was interrupted at various points as being hearsay, but he told an impressive tale that was meant to suggest to the jury that the murder was done by Indians as a result of the feud. Beige Bethel's death was brought into the story as another part of the chain of feud victims. Despite the tales, there was apparently no investigation into these suppositions. The *Fresno Republican* reported:

> There was evidence also that [Jim] Bethel, the dead man, had ordered an Indian from the premises some weeks or months before the homicide, also that an Indian was on the morning following the Bethel murder at the store at North Fork; that he had been drunk and aroused suspicion. From all this recital the jury was given to believe or conclude that in the absence of any motive on the part of Muhly, the Bethel murder was done by an Indian to avenge a long series of outrages upon the tribe at the hands of the Bethels.

The defense concluded its case in less than two days. The jury deliberations resulted in seven ballots and a dramatic swing in votes. The first ballot was five guilty and seven not guilty. The seventh ballot was ten guilty and one not guilty. When the verdict was announced, it was manslaughter with a recommendation for mercy. Clearly, the jury was unconvinced by the very weak circumstantial evidence, yet for some reason felt compelled to convict anyway. Judge Conley was as puzzled as he was outraged:

> The jury found you guilty of manslaughter. My judgement is that you should have been found guilty of murder. They recommended you to the mercy of the court. I have been unable to see why mercy was recommended. It was murder or nothing... . I believe that you killed him. Every circumstance points to the fact that you are the guilty person.

Judge Conley then sentenced Muhly to ten years in San Quentin. On appeal, the case was retried two times, but with the same result. On April 16, 1910, Judge Conley again sentenced Muhly to a ten-year term at San Quentin.

After serving a few years, Muhly appealed to Judge Conley to aid him in obtaining a pardon. The judge refused to help him unless he admitted killing Bethel. Muhly finally did confess, but claimed the killing was in self defense.

He was released on October 18, 1916, and returned to pick up the shattered pieces of his life with his family at his cabin in the hills. When he began behaving strangely in later years, Polly left him, refusing also to let the children visit him. He was found dead in his old home on December 23, 1945.

Attorneys Klette and Kauke had taken out a $1,100 mortgage on the Muhly property as a guarantee of payment on their legal work, but they were never paid. Eventually Klette acquired the property and used it as a second home.

Some years earlier, an article in the *Fresno Morning Republican* of September 28, 1908, closed the story on the tragic lives of the Bethel family:

> On the hillside near the Bethel road house is a collection of graves, most of them unnamed, forgotten and dilapidated. Four of them are the resting places of known dead and all the victims of death by violence.

The suppositions, the ancient stories, and family disruptions all belong to a time and place beyond the memory of living people. Was there in fact a feud between the Monos and the Bethel family? Certainly, the deaths were very real, but, in this modern age, so many years away from the distant past, only the cold winds, murmuring through the branches of ancient pine trees know the complete truth of this tragic tale.

UNPUBLISHED SOURCES

Assessment Book of the Property of Fresno County for the year 1872, Fresno County Library Collection

Cramner, George J., manuscript describing 1870 Fresno County Indian troubles, L. A. Winchell Papers, Fresno City and County Historical Society

Federal Census, Fresno County, 1860, 1870, 1880, 1900. 1910, 1920

Chapter 9
NOTES

Federal Census, Indian Population Schedule, Madera County, 1900

Great Register of Fresno County, 1867, 1890, Fresno County Library Collection

Kinsman, Joseph, Diary, June English Collection, Special Collections, University of California at Fresno Library

Klette, Honorable Ernest, unpublished autobiography, collection of author courtesy William L. Klette /C. Russell Georgeson

Klette, William L., correspondence with author, 2003-2004

The People of the State of California vs T. H. Muhly, Madera County Superior Court, Madera County Clerk's Office, courtesy Corrinne Buttram

Madera County Funeral Records, R. C. Jay & Son, 1932, 1947, courtesy Corrinne Buttram

Penry, E. L., "Since Liquor Went Out," typescript in collections of the Fresno City and County Historical Society

People vs. "Indian Dick," James Frost, Case No. 345, Fresno County Superior Court, Fresno County Superior County Court Archives

United States Department of the Interior, Office of Indian Affairs, Application for enrollment with the Indians of the State of California under the Act of May 18, 1929

BOOKS

Clough, Charles and Secrest, William B., Jr. *Fresno County, The Pioneer Years*. Fresno: Panorama West, 1984.

Hayne, Coe. *By-Paths to Forgotten Folks; Stories of Real Life in Baptist Home Mission Fields*. Philadelphia: The Judson Press, 1921.

Keys, E. D. *Fifty Years Observation of Men and Events*. New York: Charles Scribner's Sons, 1884.

Latta, F. F. *Uncle Jeff's Story*. Tulare: Press of Tulare Times, 1929.

McFarland, J. Randall. *Centennial Selma*. Privately printed. Selma, 1980.

Stenzel, Jane. *As We Were Told*. Coarsegold: Coarsegold Historical Society, 1990.

NEWSPAPERS

Fresno News, November 4, 1938

Fresno Expositor, August 24, 31, September 7, 14, 21, 28, November 2, 7, December 14, 1870; May 31, 1871; May 22, July 31, 1872; March 19, 1873; October 1, 1879; March 17, December 1, 1886; February 23, 1887; February 9, July 29, 30, August 5, 1888

Fresno Republican, November 9, 16, 1878; January 3, March 6, 1880; September 3, 1881; September 1, 1883; January 5, 1884; August 1, 1885; February 28, March 17, August 1, 2, 1888; April 10, 17, 1896; January 9, March 15, 17, 18, 1898; September 19, 1901; September 28, 1908; April 2, 1922

Madera Mercury, July 13, September 21, December 28, 1901; December 10, 1904; January 21, February 18, November 4, 18, December 16, 1905; March 2, 7, 14, September 12, 19, 26, October 24, 1908

Merced Argus, March 17, 1888

San Francisco *Daily Evening Bulletin*, August 29, 1870

San Francisco *Chronicle*, May 30, 1897

Tulare Times, December 10. 1870

Visalia Weekly Delta, February 16, March 22, 1888

Chapter 10

Addendum

It would be nice to record that the foregoing feuds were the sum total of such explosive transactions in early California, but such is not the case. Wherever land was in dispute, passions aroused, or injustice confronted, feuds might well be the result. Sometimes only one death was the consequence, but that death would surely affect many other lives.

Adding to and providing fuel for personal confrontations was the temper of the times. Even in the late nineteenth century, men went armed in isolated areas. The law was often a distant thing and time was precious. Add to this the perceived right of self-defense and you have the tinder for all the other little-noted feuds and vendettas that have colored California history. The personal aspect of much of this conflict was summed up in an early-day ballad:

> Wake up, wake up, darlin' Corie,
> And go get me my gun.
> I ain't no hand for trouble,
> But I'll die before I'll run.

This "stand-your-ground" mentality is nowhere better illustrated than in the Snelling-Edwards feud that bloodied Merced County in the late 1850s. Just as feuds might erupt over important issues of land, gold or personal honor, they were sometimes the result of the most banal trivialities.

The Snelling family had arrived from Missouri in 1851 and taken up land for a ranch in Mariposa County. When a small farming community grew up near their ranch, it was named after the family and was made county seat when Merced County was formed in April 1855.

The Snellings donated land for a courthouse, and William S. Snelling was appointed first postmaster. It was a large, prosperous, and highly respected family.

Sometime in mid-1857, William C. Edwards and a man named West were playing "crack-a-loo" for twenty-five cents in a Snelling saloon. West was a brother-in-law of William Snelling. The game was quite simple; men bet against each other to see who could pitch a coin closest to a designated crack in the floor. The *Mariposa Democrat* reported:

> A dispute arose, and a scuffle took place between the parties; during the scuffle, some of the bystanders interfered and were accused of foul play. Defiant and aggravating words passed, and the bitter feelings then engendered have been exhibited whenever the parties have met... weapons have been several times drawn and threats made...

Perhaps if William Snelling had not sympathized with his brother-in-law's dispute with Edwards, things could have been different. While leaving a Snelling hotel restaurant, Edwards noticed Snelling standing at the bar. Drawing his pistol, he snarled, "There's William Snelling, a son-of-a-bitch." His pistol exploded as he spoke and Snelling collapsed with a bullet in his side. As Edwards leaped over the bar, Snelling got off a quick shot with his derringer, which missed as his assassin escaped out the door.

Francis Bludworth.
Courtesy Jerry and Joyce Wilson.

After Edwards disappeared, Snelling's family and friends gathered around the dying postmaster. A hastily summoned physician shook his head, and three posses were quickly formed and galloped off in search of the fugitive.

One of the posse leaders was Charles F. Bludworth, who was married to Francis B. White, a granddaughter of the victim. Although not in office at this time, Bludworth had been appointed the first sheriff of Merced County, and he also had been one of the California Rangers who had tracked down the notorious bandit Joaquin Murrieta in the summer of 1853.

Charles F. Bludworth.
Courtesy Jerry and Joyce Wilson.

Edwards eluded his pursuers despite several reported leads. Although he had disappeared, several of his friends kept stirring the pot by making threats against Bludworth. Not willing to wait for the troublemakers to pick the time and place, Bludworth sought out James Wilcox, William Stevens, and one E. G. Barclay, the men who had been making the threats. When the three rode into Snelling one day and again began berating Bludworth, the ex-sheriff and two friends promptly headed for town.

It was early afternoon when Charlie Bludworth, his brother-in-law Benjamin White, and Dr. Jeffrey Goodin tied their horses at the Snelling courthouse. The three men stepped into the sheriff's office and confronted Stevens, Willcox and Barclay as reported in the *Stockton Daily Argus*, January 29, 1858:

> Bludworth entered suddenly and addressing Stevens, remarked with an oath that he, Stevens, was the first man who had threatened to kill him... at the same time drawing a single-barreled pistol and shooting him in the breast. After this Stevens rose and attempted to draw a revolver—Bludworth clinched him... shooting him again. Stevens finally fell dead.

The room was filled with powder smoke. Barclay then clubbed Bludworth with his pistol, which discharged. Dr. Goodin shot Barclay, who fell but returned the fire. Ben White now shot Barclay again, then clubbed him with his pistol. Young Jim Wilcox then shot and mortally wounded Dr. Goodin. It was a deadly, close combat, during which Stevens and Barclay quickly expired. Dr. Goodin died a few hours later with four bullets in him.

Wilcox rushed out the door in the confusion. Mounting his horse, he galloped off, making his way to San Francisco and a steamer to Mexico. Blud-

The old Snelling courthouse. The sheriff's office was on the lower floor, with the courtroom above. *Author's collection.*

worth and Ben White were still on their feet, unharmed. They surrendered to the astounded Sheriff George Turner, who had witnessed the tragedy.

The next day, William Snelling's widow, Clarrissa, had the difficult task of writing Dr. Goodin's widow in Missouri and apprising her of the terrible events. Bludworth and White were acquitted of any blame in the shooting. With a posse of picked men, Bludworth now tracked Edwards to Nevada where it was discovered he had been hanged for another murder a few days before their arrival. And all over a twenty-five-cent wager!

But all feuds were not slaughter, threats, and ambushes. Some came close to being hilarious and genuinely entertaining. If we can believe the Fresno *Daily Expositor*, two feuding families in the town of Sanger in Fresno County provided local entertainment for years:

Sanger was a lumber and supply center for the foothill communities of Fresno County. *Author's collection.*

That scriptural injunction, "Love thy neighbor as thyself," etc., is scrupulously violated by at least two families in this county. The Bradways and Kirches have been at "outs" for a long while. Their differences have repeatedly been ventilated in the courts at Sanger, and scarcely a week passes that each of the two families are not telling the justices of the second township how it has been much abused by the other.

The local merchants loved all this, as the neighbors of the two feuding families flooded into town to attend court and spend money in the saloons, hotels, and restaurants. "A circus," commented an 1889 issue of the *Expositor*, "could have no more attraction for the large audience of spectators who assemble on these occasions."

A typical performance, as reported in the *Expositor*, went as follows. The two families had four different cases to be tried on a particular day. The first was a hearing involving W. H. Bradway, who was bound over to keep the peace with Eliza Jane Kirch. The case was promptly thrown out for lack of evidence. The next hearing involved the people against A. L. and W. H. Bradway for assault with a deadly weapon. The evidence showed that Mat Kirch, the complaining witness, drew his pistol first, and the case was dismissed.

A. T. and W. H. Bradway then pleaded guilty to using vulgar language in the presence of women and children and paid a fine of twenty dollars each.

Eliza Jane Kirch was back on deck next. She was arrested on a complaint of Frank Brown, a member of the Bradway household who charged her with assault. Eliza demanded and got a jury trial and was questioned by one of the attorneys.

"Didn't you strike him with a piece of scantling?"

"Yes," replied Eliza.

"Didn't you threaten to brain him with a poker?"

"I never did; he has no brains."

When the reporter left, the jury was still out. "It is believed it will disagree," commented the *Expositor*.

To the west, along the windswept coast where the Roach-Belcher and Graham-Bennett troubles caused so much grief, another feud briefly ignited the countryside. It was a feud born in the passions of lawlessness, vigilante justice, and overbearing personalities. It was also the tale of a man who had to live, and die, by the extralegal laws he had helped to create.

Born in Ireland in 1826, Matt Tarpy and three of his brothers left their famine-plagued homeland when they heard of the great

California Gold Rush. They arrived in San Francisco in late 1851. It was said later that Matt had been particularly impressed with the San Francisco Vigilantes who had hanged four notorious criminals that summer of 1851. There were no Tarpys on the vigilante rolls, however, and indications are that the boys promptly headed for the northern mines, where they worked for a time. They no doubt read much about the Bay city vigilantes in the press, from which their impressions could have been formed.

The Pajaro Valley as it appeared a few years after Tarpy's vigilante exploits. *Author's collection.*

Disappointed in the mines, as were so many others, the brothers returned and found work in the Bay city. They saved enough money to move to Santa Cruz County in 1854, where they took up a land claim of 160 acres and established a lime quarry.

When his brothers returned to San Francisco, Matt remained and continued acquiring land near his property in the hills above the Pajaro Valley. In time he married Winifred Conway and they began a family, as the villages of Pajaro and Watsonville grew up in the valley below. As a property owner, Tarpy soon became an important member of the Democratic Party and was quite active in politics.

But there was trouble in the Tarpy paradise. In the 1860s and 1870s this was still frontier territory and horse thieves and rustlers preyed constantly on the isolated ranches of the area. Sheriffs and constables of the time were ill-equipped to deal with the fast-moving bandidos and few were captured and punished. As early as 1863, Matt Tarpy saw that it was necessary to show the outlaws that their

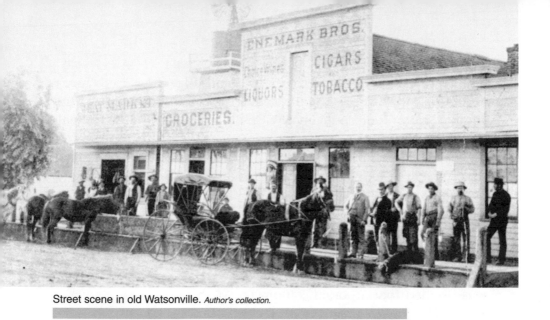

Street scene in old Watsonville. *Author's collection.*

continued depredations would not be tolerated. Acting on his own, Tarpy captured two Indians who had brutally murdered a Watsonville merchant. He and a friend next tracked a gang of horse thieves to Santa Clara, where they were captured and delivered to the sheriff. When Tarpy captured Francis Hedden, another horse thief, he refused the reward in order to call attention to the fact that the authorities were not doing their job.

For years Tarpy continued bringing the war to the outlaws, but it was a holding action and he was losing patience with the authorities. When he woke one morning in February 1870 to find several of his best horses missing, Matt was soon in the saddle and tracking his quarry. He found his horses at a small adobe on Panoche Creek, and in a gunfight, killed one of the thieves and captured another. Several of the rustlers made their escape.

At the town of Hollister, Matt told the story of his exploit to a gathering of people. Suddenly, he recognized one of the rustlers in the crowd. Seizing the fellow, Tarpy swore out a warrant and continued his journey back to the Pajaro Valley with his two prisoners.

Back in Pajaro, across the river from Watsonville, Tarpy turned his two live prisoners over to the constable. He was in Watsonville the next day when he heard the thief he arrested in Hollister had been turned loose for lack of evidence. Outraged that he should have to risk his life only to have captured outlaws released, Tarpy and his friend, Justice of the Peace Lucius Holbrook, retired to the Temple Saloon for a conference with saloon owner Charlie O'Neal. All three men were ranch owners and they were thoroughly disgusted at the failure of county law enforcement. They agreed that something had to be done and that the only solution was to organize a vigilante organization.

On the evening of February 26, 1870, a public meeting was held in Judge Holbrook's office. Nearly one hundred people attended and it was decided that an organization called The Pajaro Property and Protective Society would be organized. A constitution and bylaws were agreed upon and officers elected. Matt Tarpy and three lieutenants were appointed to go after criminals.

The area had a long history of vigilante hangings and the *Watsonville Pajaronian* gave the group a rousing send-off, declaring all residents should become involved in the new organization. Other news-papers in the area, as well as local merchants, were skeptical and decried the use of any extralegal actions. Tarpy and his group, however, plunged ahead.

Two Santa Cruz lynch victims in the days of the Tarpy raids. *Author's collection.*

For the next few years it was open season on the outlaws who infested the region. When Francisco Redondo stole a number of horses from local ranches, he was quickly caught and shot when he attempted to escape. The next horse thief was captured and locked up, but was gone from his cell the next morning. This happened some nine times in 1870, the outlaws apparently being taken from their cells at night, then executed and buried in unmarked graves.

When Antonio Guerrero was found murdered in his cabin, Tarpy and his men quickly traced the crime to Valentine Veraga, who implicated the two Gomez brothers. The brothers were found at the New Almaden mines and were turned over to Constable Barham at Watsonville. After a hearing in the local justice court, the three suspects were put in jail overnight, for transport to Santa Cruz the following day. Although two guards were placed outside the cell, some thirty or forty men broke into the jail around midnight and the next morning the three prisoners were found hanging from the bridge spanning the Pajaro River.

The lynchings and disappearances were soon laid at the door of Tarpy's vigilantes by his political enemies and the county press. John T. Porter, ex-sheriff, local farmer and Republican leader, had been feuding with Tarpy over politics for years, both men accusing the other of dishonest actions. In a long letter published in the *Pajaronian* on May 27, 1870, Tarpy defended himself and his vigilantes, stating that if they wanted to lynch any prisoners they would simply not have bothered returning them to the Watsonville officers. Despite the dangerous and difficult work of Tarpy and his men, some local citizens were turning against them now and there was an increasing call to disband the Protective Society.

The last lynching in the Pajaro Valley took place in late September 1870, when horse thief Sacramento Duarte was found hanging in his jail cell. During the next several years Tarpy and his men kept

An early day cattle roundup in the Pajaro Valley. *Author's collection.*

up their work and often aided local law enforcement in capturing various outlaws, including several of the Tiburcio Vasquez gang. However, despite the vigilante successes, there were many just waiting to pull Tarpy down when he made a false move. And when he did, it was a doozy... and it would be his last.

Tarpy had acquired over 1,500 acres of property over the years and in 1868 sold 400 acres to Murdock and Sarah Nicholson. Much property in the area was derived from the old Spanish land grants, which often had never been properly surveyed. Such was the case with the Nicholson parcel acquired from Tarpy. Things went along well enough for a few years, but a dispute developed over a portion of the property on which there was a grove of trees. The land ran along the road to San Juan and the dispute reached a point where the squabble wound up in court. Unfortunately, the case was postponed and a bitter feud was engendered.

Tarpy began cutting wood on the disputed property in late February 1873. When Nicholson rode out to assert his property rights, there was a shouting match and threats were freely exchanged. When Nicholson left to take a job in San Francisco, Tarpy took advantage of his absence to move a small house onto the property, then sent a hired man out to make some repairs.

When the hired man rode out to the place, he found Mrs. Nicholson, an employee named John O'Neil, and young John Smith already occupying the property. The occupants claimed they had taken possession on the advice of their lawyer. When Tarpy received the news, he was furious. He later claimed he attempted to obtain the aid of several officers, but because the property was in another county, they refused to go along.

Late on the afternoon of March 14, Tarpy rode out to the disputed land, armed with his Henry rifle, arriving sometime after dark. Lights were on in the house and inside the voices of Sarah Nicholson and the two men could be heard.

Firing several shots into the roof, Tarpy then shouted for the occupants to vacate his property. Startled and scared, the trio rushed out the back door and disappeared into the darkness. It was after midnight and apparently not sure what his next move should be,

Tarpy now took up a position in front of the house. At first light, Tarpy discerned Sarah Nicholson and O'Neil walking toward the house. Tarpy later gave his version of what followed:

> I was standing by a tree and stepped out in sight and commanded the man to retrace his steps and get off the premises. His manner and acts showed he wanted to fight and that he thought I would not fight. The woman kept pushing him off... and requesting me not to shoot. I repeatedly told her there would be no shooting if they would get off the premises and stay off. ...He partially tore himself from the grasp of the woman. At the same time drawing a pistol from his coat pocket, with an oath, said "the son of a bitch dared not shoot." Seeing my life in danger and thinking him so far from the woman that I could shoot him without hurting her, I fired, but the woman unfortunately thrust herself between us at the moment and received the shot...

John T. Porter, ex-sheriff and staunch Republican who disdained the extralegal methods of Democrat Matt Tarpy. *Author's collection.*

Sarah Nicholson, shot through the heart, collapsed and died. Although Tarpy turned himself in immediately, he had shot and killed a woman in a dispute, something that was anathema in those frontier days. Worse, she had been shot in the back.

Few believed Tarpy's tale. O'Neil's story, fostered by Matt's enemies, was generally believed. O'Neil claimed that after shouting, "I'll kill you, you God damned bitch," Tarpy had shot her in cold blood as she fled.

A coroner's jury added substance to the murder charges. At Mrs. Nicholson's funeral, an old man named Slankard stood up and characterized the feelings of many in the church:

"Gentlemen, if you permit this murderer to go unhanged twenty-four hours longer, you are all cowards."

Bound over to the Superior Court for trial, Tarpy was held in the Monterey jail while crowds began gathering in the Pajaro Valley. John Porter and other enemies held a mass meeting and resolutions were passed condemning the killing and demanding immediate action be taken. Angry mobs milled about the Watsonville streets through the night and next morning. Finally, a crowd of several hundred men began marching west, toward Monterey. Along the way, more men joined the procession and the mob flooded into Monterey on the morning of March 17, demanding Matt Tarpy.

Some four hundred men finally seized and tied up the sheriff and broke Tarpy out of the jail. As he was placed in a wagon and driven to a tree on the Salinas road the terrified prisoner begged for his life. There he was unceremoniously given the same treatment he had dished out to many others. The *Santa Cruz Sentinel* said it all in its issue of March 29:

> It is believed that had any of the party of lynchers committed the same deed, under similar circumstances, Matt Tarpy would have been the first to urge his hanging by lynch law, and been the most inexorable of executioners.

The property dispute that had initiated the feud was still pending. After three trips to the California State Supreme Court and some thirty years of litigation, the Nicholson-Tarpy land case was finally resolved in May 1916. The Nicholson descendants had won, but it was much too late for Murdock and Sarah.

Of course, feuding has always been an equal opportunity avocation. In the very earliest days of the California Gold Rush, transportation was a problem. Mexican California had only ox carts and a few carriages for utilization by officials. With the advent of the gold rushers, the first stagecoaches consisted of any type of wagon with boards nailed to the bed for seats. The first genuine coaches were shipped in from Mexico and South America, but by mid-1850 fine coaches were arriving from the East Coast. And by 1851 the beautiful, sturdily-constructed Concord stagecoaches began arriving from Concord, New Hampshire. Needless to say, by the mid-1850s, stagecoaches were traversing any section of California where people wanted to go. And, in time, sometimes the roads became crowded.

On a Sunday morning in mid-November 1857, a pair of stage-coaches raced neck and neck into Sacramento, scattering pedestrians and other vehicles along the way. As the coach horses galloped

madly through the heart of town, many citizens on their way to church jumped out of the way or gasped at the carelessness of the drivers. "We understand from eyewitnesses," noted the *Sacramento Daily Union*, "that the horses were driven in the full run so fast, indeed, as to attract general attention, astonishment and indignation at the recklessness displayed." Racing stagecoaches could occasionally be seen on the roads, but in town it was much too dangerous. The drivers of these two coaches, owned by the California Stage Company and the opposition line from Marys-ville, were promptly picked up at the depot by two policemen and deposited in the city jail.

As Sacramentans filed into the churches and slipped into their pews that morning, they could only mumble briefly about this most recent example of the rivalry between two of the local stage companies. It seemed obvious that the safety of their passengers, if not pedestrians, should be uppermost in their minds. If something were not done, someone would be killed one of these days.

Just a year later, in November 1858, the Fowler & Company stage line, carrying the mail between Sac-ramento and Tehama, decided to run on the east side of the Sacramento River.

Previously, the Fowler line's route had been on the west side of the river, bypassing

A Califoria Stage Company coach of the 1850s. *Author's collection.*

Marysville and going straight through to Sacramento from Tehama. Now, they were suddenly competing directly with the California

Stage Company. Even worse, the rate to travel to Marysville had been reduced to one dollar. As the *Sacramento Daily Bee* put it, "A feud naturally enough arose between the two lines." On the road, the two coach lines frequently came in contact with each other, and racing and hurling insults was the order of the day. Some drivers took it in their stride. Some did not.

Oscar Case, for example, was mad. He was a driver for the California Stage Company, out of Sacramento, and he was frequently reminded of the rivalry. He did not like the dispatchers constantly telling him to beat the opposition line to town. There were enough problems in stage riding as it was without risking a collision or wreck However, it was the Fowler line that had started the war, and Oscar became more furious the more he thought about it.

Oscar Case arrived for work in Marysville on Sunday morning, November 14, 1858, just in time to see his stage agent knock down the opposition stage driver, one J. Stinchfield. After the agent kicked the driver, Case told Stinchfield he was going to follow his coach and run into it. Stinchfield clambered to his feet and, mounting his stage, started his horses into an easy canter out of town. Looking back, Stinchfield saw a coach pulling out from the depot and he knew Case was following him.

Case whipped up his team and steadily closed the gap between his own and the coach ahead of him. Driving a heavy Troy coach, Case pulled up alongside the opposition coach and threw some firecrackers among Stinchfield's horses making them nearly unmanageable. Still galloping alongside the coach, Case now banged into it several times, once throwing one of the Fowler & Company horses to the ground.

An old California stage driver. *Author's collection.*

As they pulled into the Twelve Mile House relay station, Case threw more firecrackers at the horses, then cut in front of the opposition coach, crowding it into a fence. While the horses were being changed, Case and two friends at the station kept yelling at Stinchfield's passengers to "come ride with them or they would be killed before they reached Sacramento."

Sitting on the seat with Stinchfield was a rancher named Oscar Ames who had been terrified by Case's actions. During the stop he asked to borrow the shotgun of an inside passenger and he now cradled the weapon in his arm. He yelled to Case, "I'm no fighting man, but if you try to run into us again and threaten my life, I will defend myself."

The horses changed, the two coaches resumed their journey, and Case rumbled along close behind the opposition coach. Just outside of the village of Nicolaus, Case again banged into Stinchfield's coach, turning it around several times. Ames could not jump off since Case's coach was mashed up against his seat, and he began yelling for Case to pull away so he could jump off. When he refused to do so, Ames shoved the shotgun against Case and fired, tearing a hole through his shoulder and upper chest.

As Case screamed, the two coaches pulled apart and Ames jumped to the ground and sprinted toward Nicolaus. Wheeling his coach around, Case headed after Ames, but soon stopped and collapsed along the road, where he was found by two riders.

Ames turned himself in and on November 16 had a preliminary examination at Nicolaus. After all the testimony was heard, it was obvious that Ames' local reputation was good and that the shooting occurred only after great provocation. A postponement was allowed for Case's testimony to be taken and the hearing was resumed on November 26. It was reported in the *Union*:

> After the conclusion of the evidence, Justice Hart remarked that it was a plain case of self-defence, and directed that the defendant should at once be discharged. It is stated that Case, the wounded man, is still in a critical condition.

The incident put a chill on the feuding stage lines, particularly after Case's subsequent death. For a time, glares took the place of a string of obscenities when coaches of the two stage lines met on the road. Eventually, the competitors learned to get along. There would be other stagecoach feuds over the years, but few with such senseless and deadly results as occurred that chilly morning on the Marysville to Sacramento road.

DOCUMENTS

Federal Census, Sacramento County, 1860

Merrill, Charles, Collection; Clarrissa Snelling letter

Letters, Bertha Schroeder to the author, 1976 - 1981; genealogy and other information on the Snelling family

BOOKS

Boessenecker, John. *Gold Dust & Gunsmoke; Tales of Gold Rush Outlaws, Gunfighters, Lawmen & Vigilantes.* New York: John Wiley & Sons, New York, 1999.

Elliot and Moore (publishers). *History of Merced County.* Oakland, California: Pacific Press Publishing House, 1881.

_____. *History of Monterey County, California.* Oakland, California: Pacific Press Publishing House, 1881.

Fink, Augusta. *Monterey County; The Dramatic Story of Its Past.* Fresno: Valley Publishers, 1978.

Francis, Phil. *Santa Cruz County.* San Francisco: H. S. Crocker Company, 1896.

Harrison, E. S. *History of Santa Cruz County, California.* San Francisco: Pacific Press Publishing Company, 1892.

Lewis, Betty. *Watsonville: Memoies that Linger.* Fresno: Valley Publishers, 1976.

Outcalt, John. *History of Merced County, California.* Los Angeles: Historic Record Company, 1925.

Purdy, Tim I. *Honey Lake Justice; The Never Sweats of the 1860s.* Susanville: California, Lahontan Images, 1993.

Reader, Phil. *A Brief History of the Pajaro Property Protective Society: Vigilantism in the Pajaro Valley During the 19th Century.* Santa Cruz: Cliffside Publishing, 1995.

NEWSPAPERS

Fresno Daily Evening Expositor, April 18, 1889

Fresno Morning Republican, May 9, 1916

Madera Mercury, December 12, 1904

Mariposa Democrat, January 28, February 4, 1858

Sacramento Daily Bee, November 15, 17, 1858

Sacramento *Daily Union,* November 15, 16, 1857

San Andreas Independent, June 26, 1858

San Francisco *Daily Alta California,* January 27, June 24, July 4, 1858

Santa Cruz Sentinel, July 15, 1871; March 22, 29, 1873

Stockton Daily Argus, December 7, 1857; January 29, 1858

Stockton *San Joaquin Republican*, January 26, 1858; April 7, 1859

OTHER SOURCES

Chandler, Robert J., "Wells Fargo's Stagecoaching; An 1860's Turf War," *Journal of the West*, Spring 2003.

Wilson, Joyce and Jerry, genealogy, photographs and family reminiscences pertaining to the Snelling and Bludworth families

Index

Pacific Ocean House 40
Page, H. F. 105
Pajaro 244
Pajaro Property and Protective Society
    246, 247
Pajaro River 1, 247
Pajaro Times 23
Pajaro Valley 23, 244, 245, 247, 249
Pajaronian 247
Palance, Jack 47
Panoche Creek 245
Pascoe, Carl 161
Patterson, William 49, 51
Pearl Street (Monterey) 12
Pennsylvania 48, 122
People's Hotel 133, 134
Petaluma *Crescent* 129
Peterson, W. H. 19
Pickering, Loring 95
Pit River 130
Placer County 147, 149
Placerville 105
Platte Valley 28
Porter, John T. 247, 249
Porterville 154
Powell, W. S. 62, 63
Price, William 191
Pumpkin River, alias Kings River 52

Q
Quan, Ah 187

R
Rancho Llano del Tequisquite 1
Rancho Natividad 28
Rancho San Ysidro 1
Rattlesnake Creek 147
Read, Ed 112
Red Bluff 130, 143
Red Caps 179, 180
Redding 130
Redondo, Francisco 246
Republican County Committee 97
Republican Party 96
Reynolds, Bob 129, 130
Rice, Mrs. David (Matilda Graham) 38
Roach, Annie 22
Roach, William 7, 8, 11, 13, 15, 18, 22, 24

Roach-Belcher feud 243
Robertson, John 18, 19, 135
Robinson 151
Robinson, Mrs. 151, 152
Rock River Ranch 184
Rock Tree Valley 122
Rocktree Grade 139
Roland, Tex 168, 169, 170, 171
Rose, George 79

S
Sacramento 85, 181, 187, 250-253
Sacramento Daily Bee 252
Sacramento Daily Union 87, 183, 251,
    253
Sacramento River 130, 251
Sacramento State Journal 182
Sacramento Street (San Francisco) 191
Sacramento Union 75
Saint Louis 91
Salinas road 250
Salinas Valley 8, 15
Sam-Yap tong 184-186
Sam-Yup Company 191, 197
San Buenaventura 10, 14
San Diego 49
San Francisco 1, 4, 5, 6, 8, 35, 58, 69,
    73, 74, 76, 78, 80, 84, 86, 87, 92, 95,
    100, 106, 111, 114, 118, 150, 151, 175,
    176, 186, 187, 188, 189, 190, 192, 193,
    195, 241, 244, 248
San Francisco Chronicle 91, 105
San Francisco City Hall 99
San Francisco County 36
San Francisco *Daily Evening Bulletin*
    20
San Francisco *Daily Examiner* 84
San Francisco *Daily Herald* 176
San Francisco *Daily Morning Call* 73,
    74. *See also Call*
San Francisco *Daily Morning Examiner*
    83
San Francisco *Examiner* 199
San Francisco Golden Era 82
San Francisco *Herald* 5
San Francisco Presidio 149
San Francisco Vigilantes 75, 244
San Joaquin County 9

Whiskey Flat 147
Whiskey Hill road 22
Whitcomb, Alice (Frost) 135
Whitcomb, Owin 125
White, Benjamin 241, 242
White, Francis B. (Bludworth) 240
Whittington, Sarah (Church) 48
Wichita Herald 106
Wichita, Kansas 106
Wilcox, James 241
Williams, Ephraim 162
Williams, Isaac 31
Williamson, Thomas 15, 16, 17, 20
Willits 121, 131
Willits, Hiram 128
Willows 142
Wisconsin 122
Wong Ahong 181
Woods, William A. 154, 155
Woodward, Charley 170

Workingmen's Party 106, 108, 111, 113
Wright, William 71. *See also* Dan
  DeQuill
wui kun 176

Y
Yan-Wo 184, 185, 186
Yates, William 162
Yen Yuen 194
Ying, Chung 195
Yuba River 142
Yue-Ti 183
Yuen, Yen 194
Yuma Territorial Prison 154, 155
Yung, Charlie 177

Z
Zayante 33
Zayante Creek 29
Zayante Rancho 27, 30, 33

B orn in Fresno, California, in March of 1930, William B. Secrest grew up in the great San Joaquin Valley. After high school he joined the Marine Corps where he served in a guard detachment and in a rifle company in the early years of the Korean War. Returning to college, he obtained a BA in education, but for many years he served as an art director for a Fresno advertising firm.

Secrest has been interested in history since his youth and early began comparing Western films to what really happened in the West. A hobby at first, this avocation quickly developed into correspondence with noted writers and more serious research. Not satisfied in a collaboration with friend and Western writer Ray Thorp, Secrest began researching and writing his own articles in the early 1960s.

Although at first he wrote on many general Western subjects, some years ago Secrest realized how his home state has consistently been neglected in the Western genre and concentrated almost exclusively on early California subjects. He has produced hundreds of articles for such publications as *Westways*, *Montana*, *True West*, and the *American West*, while publishing seven monographs on early California themes. His book *I Buried Hickok* (Early West Publishing Co.) appeared in 1980, followed by *Lawmen & Desperadoes* (The Arthur H. Clark Co.) in 1994 and *Dangerous Trails* (Barbed Wire Press) in 1995. A biography of noted San Francisco police detective Isaiah Lees has been accepted for publication. A current project is a biography of Harry Love, the leader of the rangers who tracked down Joaquin Murrieta.